Highly topical! The question addressed in this book is: What is the source and meaning of non-Christian religions and how are these religious convictions related to the core message of the gospel? Dr. Philip Djung unfolds in a thematic way Hendrik Kraemer's thinking about these questions. In his contributions, which spanned several decades, Kraemer thought through aspects of the discussion from the perspectives of biblical theology and the science of religions and combined them in creative ways. Dr. Djung presents this vision afresh and brings it in a positive-critical way in interaction with later and different voices. In a convincing manner, he shows that the essence of Kraemer's approach is non-negotiable, at least when we want to do justice to the content of a number of crucial Christian convictions and to the content of the Scriptures.

Rev. Paul J. Visser, DS
Pastor, Protestant Church in the Netherlands
Chair, Foundation for the Promoting of Reformed Missiology and Ecumenics

This work gives us a better appreciation of renowned missiologist Hendrik Kraemer while also proposing nuanced but important adjustments to his theology of religions. Dr. Philip Djung praises Kraemer for vigorously defending the uniqueness of Christ and the necessity of Christian mission and evangelism as well as his holistic approach to non-Christian religions, but searches for a more organically unified vision. He finds this in a revised doctrine of revelation and grace derived from the Dutch neo-Calvinist tradition of Abraham Kuyper and Herman Bavinck, especially in its missiological application by Johan H. Bavinck. I consider Djung's project of bringing together two significant Dutch Reformed missiological traditions into a new synthesis to be largely successful and the result is new theological prolegomena to Christian missiology that promises to be a helpful guide in contemporary Christian engagement with the world's religions.

John Bolt, PhD
Director, Bavinck Institute, and Editor, Bavinck Review
Jean and Kenneth Baker Professor of Systematic Theology (emeritus),
Calvin Theological Seminary, Grand Rapids, Michigan, USA

In this timely and clearly argued doctoral dissertation, Dr. Philip K. H. Djung pointedly distinguishes Hendrik Kraemer's theological understanding of world religions. In doing so, Kraemer distances himself from J. N. Farquar's fulfillment position and William Hocking's cooperation position on the relation of Christianity to non-Christian religions. Kraemer maintains the radical distinction between Christianity and other religions and the need for Christian missions based on the uniqueness of Christian revelation, the gospel's distinctiveness, and the complexity of religion's relationship to culture.

Djung demonstrates where and how his opponents have responded with valid criticisms of Kraemer's position. The value of this dissertation is that it not only recognizes this validity, but that it demonstrates how meeting these criticisms with a clearer, stronger position on general revelation, the dialectical nature of religion generally, and a more holistic approach to religion would buttress Kraemer's basic assertion.

This study advances the Dutch neo-Calvinistic thinking on these matters in ways that are insightful and important in our era of globalization. It is a very important contribution that deserves widespread attention. It is highly commended.

James A. De Jong, ThD
President Emeritus,
Calvin Theological Seminary, Grand Rapids, Michigan, USA

Following Narendranath Datta's seminal speech on Hinduism at the World's Parliament of Religions in Chicago in 1893, Christian missiologists and theologians vigorously argued for the merits and strengths of Christianity at events such as the 1910 World Missionary Conference in Edinburgh, Scotland, and the subsequent 1938 Conference of International Missionary Council in Tambaram, India. In *Revelation and Grace: A Critical Appraisal of Hendrik Kraemer's Theology of Religions*, Dr Philip Djung expertly describes missiologist and theologian Hendrik Kraemer's treatment of the world religion debates that animated the globe from the late-nineteenth through the mid-twentieth century, and reveals how Kraemer's studies helped spur interreligious dialogues in the late 1960s. Djung has written a welcome reassessment of Kraemer's works and offers a thorough account of Kraemer's understanding of revelation, grace, salvation, the uniqueness of Christ, his appreciation of world religions and cultures, the necessity of Christian missions, and much more. This is a thought-provoking book for missiologists.

David Hartono, PhD
Former President, Asian Society of Missiology
Former Senior Pastor, GKKB, Pontianak, Indonesia
Former Senior Pastor,
St. Paul Evangelical Community Church, Cerritos, California, USA

This book sheds new light on the significance of Hendrik Kraemer and his theology of religions with its insistence on the centrality of the gospel, the necessity of Christian missions, and the uniqueness of Christian revelation. Djung carefully navigates Kraemer's main theological thoughts, and as a response to Kraemer's critics, he constructs a helpful amendment to read the missionary's theology in light of the doctrines of general revelation, common grace, and the work of the Holy Spirit as developed by other Dutch theologians such as Herman Bavinck, Abraham Kuyper, and Johan H. Bavinck.

Yudha Thianto, PhD
Professor of Theology,
Trinity Christian College, Palos Heights, Illinois, USA

Revelation and Grace

A Critical Appraisal of Hendrik Kraemer's Theology of Religions

Philip Djung

MONOGRAPHS

© 2021 Philip Djung

Published 2021 by Langham Monographs
An imprint of Langham Publishing
www.langhampublishing.org

Langham Publishing and its imprints are a ministry of Langham Partnership

Langham Partnership
PO Box 296, Carlisle, Cumbria, CA3 9WZ, UK
www.langham.org

ISBNs:
978-1-83973-219-5 Print
978-1-83973-470-0 ePub
978-1-83973-471-7 Mobi
978-1-83973-472-4 PDF

Philip Djung has asserted his right under the Copyright, Designs and Patents Act, 1988 to be identified as the Author of this work.

All rights reserved. No part of this publication may be reproduced, stored in a retrieval system or transmitted, in any form or by any means, electronic, mechanical, photocopying, recording or otherwise, without the prior written permission of the publisher or the Copyright Licensing Agency.

Requests to reuse content from Langham Publishing are processed through PLSclear. Please visit www.plsclear.com to complete your request.

Scriptures taken from the Holy Bible, New International Version®, NIV®. Copyright © 1973, 1978, 1984, 2011 by Biblica, Inc.™ Used by permission of Zondervan.

British Library Cataloguing-in-Publication Data
A catalogue record for this book is available from the British Library

ISBN: 978-1-83973-219-5

Cover & Book Design: projectluz.com

Langham Partnership actively supports theological dialogue and an author's right to publish but does not necessarily endorse the views and opinions set forth here or in works referenced within this publication, nor can we guarantee technical and grammatical correctness. Langham Partnership does not accept any responsibility or liability to persons or property as a consequence of the reading, use or interpretation of its published content.

Contents

Acknowledgments vii

Abstract ix

Chapter 1 1
Introduction
    1.1 Present State of the Question 4
    1.2 Thesis Statement 12
    1.3 Methodology 13

Chapter 2 15
Kraemer's Theological Framework
    2.1 Historical Context 16
        2.1.1 Fulfillment Theology 16
        2.1.2 Cooperation Theology 20
        2.1.3 Missional Emphasis 25
    2.2 Theological Approach 28
        2.2.1 Biblical Realism 30
        2.2.2 The Standpoint in the Christian Revelation 33
    2.3 Divine Revelation 36
        2.3.1 Christocentric Concept of Revelation 36
        2.3.2 General and Special Revelation 39
    Summary 44

Chapter 3 47
Kraemer's Understanding of the Nature of Religions
    3.1 Nature of Religions 48
        3.1.1 The Universality of Religious Consciousness 48
        3.1.2 Dialectical Character of Religions 53
        3.1.3 Holistic Approach of Religions 57
        3.1.4 The Intractability of Christianity 59
    3.2 Christian Attitude toward Non-Christian Religions 63
        3.2.1 Evangelism and Points of Contact 64
        3.2.2 Syncretism and Adaptation 68
        3.2.3 Tolerance and Interreligious Cooperation 75
    Summary 77

Chapter 4 79
    Critiques of Kraemer's Theology of Religions
        4.1 A. G. Hogg: "Faith and Faiths" 81
        4.2 Gavin D'Costa: "Karl Rahner's Anonymous Christians" 91
        4.3 M. M. Thomas: "New Humanity of Christ" 96
        Summary 104

Chapter 5 107
    Evaluations of Kraemer's Theology of Religions
        5.1 Analysis of the Critiques 107
        5.2 Examination of Thesis 1: *Sui Generis* Character of the Gospel 109
        5.3 Examination of Thesis 2: Radical Discontinuity 114
        5.4 Examination of Thesis 3: Holistic Approach of Religions 127
        5.5 Examination of Thesis 4: Warning of Syncretism 133
        5.6 Internal Tensions in Kraemer's Thought 150
        Summary 153

Chapter 6 155
    Revelation and Grace
        6.1 Revelation, Grace, and Salvation 156
        6.2 General and Special Revelation 172
        6.3 Particular and Common Grace 186
        Summary 196

Chapter 7 199
    An Amended Version of Kraemer's Theology of Religions
        7.1 The Uniqueness of Jesus Christ 200
        7.2 The Necessity of Christian Mission 206
        7.3 Divine-Driven Character of Religions 209
        7.4 Abortive Unity of Religions and Cultures 214
        Summary 218

Chapter 8 221
    Conclusion

Bibliography 225

Acknowledgments

Writing a dissertation is a very long journey. I am so grateful that God has sent me a company of "saints" along the way to assist, encourage, and accompany so that I could complete this journey. In the first place, I would like to express my deepest gratitude to my dissertation committee: Dr. John Bolt, my supervisor, for his guidance, valuable advice, and patience; Dr. James De Jong, for his helpful suggestions and insights; Dr. Ronald Feenstra, for his honest feedback and constructive critique; Dr. Paul Visser for his encouraging comments; and Dr. Lyle Bierma, Director of Doctoral Studies at Calvin Seminary, for his careful reading of this work.

I would also like to extend my deepest appreciation to Dr. Richard Mueller, Dr. John Cooper, Dr. Calvin Van Reken, Dr. Mary VandenBerg, Dr. Cornelius Plantinga, Jr., Dr. James K. A. Smith, Dr. Lee Hardy, and Dr. David Rylaarsdam, my professors at Calvin Theological Seminary. Their teachings and thoughts have greatly shaped my theological training. My special thanks to Dr. Cory Wilson for his valuable feedback to the proposal of this work and to James Bradley and Don McCrory for their valuable help in proofreading it. I would like to thank the faculty members of Singapore Bible College who have laid the foundations of my theological training. Special thanks also to Vivian Doub and the Langham Publishing team for their help in publishing this work.

I am very grateful for the community of believers in GKKB Pontianak, my home church in Indonesia; Woodlawn CRC and Church of the Servant CRC, my spiritual home in Grand Rapids; and IECLA/GII Hok Im Tong, the church I now belong to and serve. Their prayers and support have sustained me and my family during my years of study. Particularly I must mention Rich and Sandy Sytsma; Darshak and Nankal Toma; Paul and Priscilla Brink; and

Helen Bonzelaar. I am truly thankful for the love and friendship they have shared with my family for many years in Grand Rapids. I am also grateful to David and Grace Hartono, my spiritual mentors and dear friends, whose constant encouragement and prayers have given me the strength to carry on.

Last but not least, this journey would not have been possible without persistent support of my family. I would like to thank my mother, siblings, and all extended family members for their love, support, and prayers. I am extremely grateful to my wife, Sarinah, and my daughter, Sarah, for their presence, love, and care which has kept me moving forward to complete this daunting task. *Soli Deo Gloria!*

Abstract

This work examines Hendrik Kraemer's theology of religions. Kraemer opposes the theologies that marginalize the centrality of the gospel and the necessity of Christian mission. In response he proposes a theology of religions that maintains the *sui generis* of the Christian revelation, a radical discontinuity between the gospel and non-Christian religions, and the dialectical character of religions, and the holistic approach to religions. Kraemer aims to safeguard the uniqueness of Jesus Christ and to maintain the necessity of Christian mission in its traditional sense. Kraemer's critics agree with this emphasis, but they raise objections in regard to his view of non-Christian religions. They charge that Kraemer's theology is weak pertaining to the appreciation of non-Christian religions and cultures. This study shows that their charge cannot be substantiated. Kraemer is strong in both aspects. He maintains the uniqueness of Christ and appreciates non-Christian religions and cultures. However, his theological framework is weak. These shortcomings, however, can be addressed by navigating properly the doctrine of revelation and grace derived primarily from Herman Bavinck, Johan H. Bavinck, and Abraham Kuyper. Finally, this study proposes an amended version of Kraemer's theology of religions that maintains the strengths of Kraemer's theology of religions (i.e. the uniqueness of Christ and the necessity of Christian mission). However, it modifies its view of religions. This study accepts Kraemer's dialectical character of religions, but emphasizes the divine factor. Hence, religions are primarily divine. This study accepts Kraemer's holistic approach to non-Christian religions, but takes its unity as an imperfect one. Hence, it is not an organic, but abortive, unity.

CHAPTER 1

Introduction

This book examines Hendrik Kraemer's theology of religions. Theology of religions is a sub-discipline of Christian theology that studies the nature of religions and its related matters. It attempts to answer questions such as these: What are religions? Are they merely human products? Or, did they originate from God? What is the relationship between Christianity and other religions? Is Christianity unique? Or is it simply one of many religions? What are Christian attitudes towards adherents of other religions? How could Christians be both faithful to God's commission to do evangelism and tolerant of their non-Christian neighbors? This work deals with those questions and the answers as provided by Hendrik Kraemer.

Hendrik Kraemer (1888–1965) was a missionary, missiologist, Orientalist, and lay theologian of Dutch origin.[1] He was born on 17 May 1888 in Amsterdam, the Netherlands. He lost his father at the age of six and his mother at the age of twelve. Due to this circumstance, he spent his youth in an orphanage (1900–1905). Amid the hardship he endured, the young Kraemer found God's comfort through the readings of the Scriptures. At the age of sixteen, he decided to be a missionary to New Guinea and prepared himself by joining the Dutch Mission School in Rotterdam (1905–1911). Yet, his plan to go to New Guinea changed when he met Nicolaus Adriani, a Dutch missionary and linguist, who was in the Netherlands for vacation. Having noticed Kraemer's linguistic talent, Adriani successfully persuaded

---

1. For the time being, a full biography of Kraemer is available only in Dutch. See van Leeuwen, *Hendrik Kraemer*. For English-speaking readers, there are only some short biographies. See for example, Jongeneel, "Hendrik Kraemer," 374–375; Hoedemaker, "Hendrik Kraemer 1888–1965," 508–515; Verkuyl, *Contemporary Missiology*, 41–51.

him to come to the Dutch Indies Archipelago to work for Bible translation. For this purpose, Kraemer entered Leiden University to study the Indonesian language and literature (1911–1921). He wrote his dissertation on Javanese mysticism under the supervision of Christian Snouck Hurgronje, a renowned Islamic scholar in that era. Kraemer married Hyke van Gameren in 1919 and their marriage was blessed with three children – two daughters, and a son who died at the age of seven.

He began his career as a missionary in the same year he graduated from Leiden University. He was sent by the Dutch Bible Society to work in the Dutch East Indies (today Indonesia). After short stops to learn the religion of Islam – three weeks in Paris and four months in Cairo – Kraemer arrived in Java and served two full terms of his missionary tenure (1922–1937).[2] Even though Kraemer's official job was with the Dutch Bible Society, his work was not limited to Bible translation.[3] Instead, he was involved in various ministries, such as supporting theological schools,[4] analyzing various mission fields,[5] and advocating on behalf of churches in Indonesia.[6]

Kraemer returned to the Netherlands and became a professor of the history and phenomenology of religion at the University of Leiden (1937–1947). Finally, he ended his career as the first director of the World Council of

---

2. For Kraemer's description of his missionary work, see Kraemer, *Zes jaar padvinden* and *Mijn Tweede*.

3. Kraemer's official job title was the deputy for Bible translation. He was assigned to supervise revisions of Bible translation for several languages, such as Malay, Sundanese, Balinese, and Javanese. For Kraemer's work in Bible translation and literature, see Kraemer, *Mijn Tweede*, 4–6.

4. During his missionary years, Kraemer helped to establish two theological schools: Bale Wiyata and The Higher Theological School in Bogor. Bale Wiyata was founded by B. M. Schuurman in 1925 in Kediri. It was relocated to Malang in 1926 when Kraemer joined its teaching faculty. In 1934 Kraemer founded The Higher Theological School in Bogor. It was later relocated to Jakarta and renamed Jakarta Higher Theological School. Both schools are still operating in the present day. See van Leeuwen, *Hendrik Kraemer*, 42, 89–92.

5. With the liberty given by the Dutch Bible Society, Kraemer could travel to many mission fields in the Dutch Indies to evaluate, analyze their conditions and eventually give feedbacks for the improvements. The reports of these trips were later translated and published under the title *From missionfield to independent churches*. See Hendrik Kraemer, *From Missionfield to Independent*.

6. The case of the Protestant church in Bali is a good example of Kraemer's advocating activity. Bali, along with Banten and Aceh, was part of specific areas where missionary work was prohibited. Kraemer successfully argued with the Dutch colonial government that Christian missionary work was allowed in Bali. See Kraemer, *From Missionfield*, 161.

Churches' Ecumenical Institute in Switzerland (1948–1955). He returned to the Netherlands for his retirement and died on 11 November 1965.

Kraemer first received international recognition at the 1928 International Missionary Council at Jerusalem. His star, however, shone brightly ten years later at the 1938 International Missionary Council at Tambaram, India. After this conference, Kraemer emerged as a prominent figure in the Christian mission and the worldwide church. As part of the preparatory work of this conference, he was entrusted to write a book about evangelism to non-Christian faiths. The result was his magnum opus *The Christian Message in a Non-Christian World* (1938).[7] In this work, he proposed a theology of religions that maintained the *sui generis* character of the revelation in Christ. Jesus Christ is the way, the truth, and the life and in him alone salvation is found.

The significance of Kraemer's *The Christian Message* becomes apparent when we consider two trends of the theology of religions, namely, the "fulfillment theory" of J. N. Farquhar and the "cooperation theory" of William Hocking. Both theories have the same underlying belief, namely, the unity of all religions and continuity between other religions and Christianity. Other religions are believed to be not fundamentally different from Christianity for they too serve as paths to God. Christianity is superior to other religions only in the sense that it is the "fulfillment" or the "crown" of other religions, argues Farquhar in his *The Crown of Hinduism* (1913). In *Re-thinking Missions* (1932), Hocking proposes a redirection of Christian mission. Instead of searching for ways to convert other religions, the mission is to cooperate with all religions. Non-Christian religions are not enemies but allies of Christianity to fight against secularism. Kraemer rejected the positions of Farquhar and Hocking alike. Over against Farquhar's fulfillment theory, Kraemer maintained the *sui generis* character of the gospel, arguing that there is a radical discontinuity between the gospel and non-Christian religions.[8] Opposing Hocking's devaluation of Christian mission, Kraemer maintained the necessity of Christian mission as an inseparable part of the Christian church.[9]

Kraemer's *The Christian Message* was a bombshell. It created heated debates during and after the conference. In response to the critiques, soon

---

7. Kraemer, *Christian Message*.
8. Kraemer, 301–302.
9. Kraemer, 36, 45, 49, 435.

after the Tambaram Conference, in the first volume of the Madras Series *The Authority of the Faith* (1939),[10] Kraemer wrote an essay entitled "Continuity or Discontinuity."[11] In this essay, Kraemer attempted to clarify his position presented in *The Christian Message*. He resolutely sided with Karl Barth and affirmed a radical discontinuity between the Christian revelation and non-Christian religions.

In addition to *The Christian Message* and his follow-up essay "Continuity or Discontinuity," Kraemer also produced several works on the same subject, *Religion and the Christian Faith* (1956), *World Cultures and World Religions* (1960), and *Why Christianity of All Religions?* (1962).[12] He did so to communicate with different audiences and also to further clarify his position. He, however, did not change his fundamental position stated in *The Christian Message*.

1.1 Present State of the Question

The debate over Kraemer's theology of religions began even before the Tambaram Missionary Conference started.[13] The earliest response to Kraemer's position came from a group of Indian scholars who published their collective essays in a book entitled *Rethinking Christianity in India* (1938).[14] This book was published before the Tambaram Conference and purposely made available for participants of the conference. The responses were mostly critical of Kraemer's position. P. Chenchiah, for example, spoke

---

10. The Madras Series is the committee report on various issues discussed in the conference. The first volume of this series is comprised mostly of various essays in response to Kraemer's position in *The Christian Message*. See Paton, ed., *Authority of the Faith*.

11. Kraemer, "Continuity or Discontinuity," 1–21.

12. Kraemer, *Religion and the Christian Faith*; *World Cultures*; *Why Christianity*.

13. For those who are sympathetic with Kraemer's position, see, for example, Bishop Anastasios, "Emerging Perspective," 332–346; Hartenstein, "Biblical View of Religion," 117–136; Horton, "Between Hocking and Kraemer," 137–149; Moses, "Problem of Truth," 58–82; Newbigin, "Sermon Preached at the Thanksgiving," 325–331; Newbigin, "Christ and the World," 16–30; Perry, *Radical Difference*.

Also for those who oppose Kraemer's position, see, for example, Chao, "Revelation," 22–57; Chenchiah, "Christian Message," 143–196; D'Costa, *Theology and Religious Pluralism*, 52–79; Eck, "Religions and Tambaram," 375–389; Farmer, "Authority of Faith," 22–57; Hogg, "Christian Attitude," 94–116; Reichelt, "Johannine Approach," 83–93; Samartha, "Mission in a Religiously Plural World," 311–324; Smith, "Mission, Dialogue," 360–374.

14. The citations of this work are taken from the following edition: Devasahayam and Sudarisanam, eds., *Rethinking Christianity in India*.

against Kraemer's emphasis on the uniqueness of Christianity. For Chenchiah, Christianity stands on par with other religions. The only difference between Christianity and other religions is that in Christianity Jesus is the object of worship, but in other religions, he is not.[15] In addition, the critiques were given from a cultural and social perspective of Indian society. The solutions given are therefore not theological but practical. This is the drawback of this work.

There was no actual record of the debate over Kraemer's position in the Tambaram Conference. However, the report of the conference entitled *The Authority of the Faith*[16] captured diverse voices to Kraemer's position. As noted above, in this volume, Kraemer also contributed an essay entitled "Continuity or Discontinuity" to clarify his position and reaffirms his discontinuity position. The other contributors were divided in their views on Kraemer's position. D. G. Moses, K. Hartenstein, and Walter M. Horton supported Kraemer's position. They appreciate his effort to return to the gospel with the emphasis on the uniqueness and the finality of the revelation in Jesus Christ and attempt to supplement what they think is lacking in Kraemer's thought.[17] Except for a few reservations from Horton,[18] they, however, do not offer critical evaluations of Kraemer's theological framework. The opposition to Kraemer's thought came from T. C. Chao, Herbert H. Farmer, Alfred G. Hogg, and Karl L. Reichelt.[19] They focus their critiques on Kraemer's understanding of divine revelation. The question is whether there is only one form of the divine revelation, namely, God's revelation in Jesus Christ, or whether God also reveals himself in some way in non-Christian religions. Kraemer's opponents are confident that God also reveals himself "in nature, in history, and in the non-Christian religions."[20] The most penetrating critique in this volume comes from A. G. Hogg who contends that one should make a distinction between non-Christian "faith" and "faiths" or "beliefs." Hogg identifies

---

15. Chenchiah, "Jesus and Non-Christian Faiths," 58.

16. This book is the first volume of the The Madras Series, papers published by the International Missionary Council based on the Tambaram meeting. See Paton, ed., *Authority of the Faith*.

17. See Moses, "Problem of Truth," 58; Hartenstein, "Biblical View of Religion," 118; and Horton, "Between Hocking and Kraemer," 141–142.

18. Horton, "Between Hocking and Kraemer," 146.

19. See Chao, "Revelation," 22–57; Farmer, "Authority of Faith," 150–165; Hogg, "Christian Attitude," 94–117; Reichelt, "Johannine Approach," 83–93.

20. Chao, "Revelation," 32.

non-Christian faith with what Kraemer calls "the religious life present in non-Christian religions."[21] In Christianity, this religious life is "a life hid with Christ in God." In non-Christian religions, this religious life, although without Christ, is still "a life hid in God." Arguably, if this faith exists, then non-Christian religions cannot be seen as "a purely human phenomenon."[22] According to Hogg, Kraemer fails to make such distinction due to the Barthian influence in his theological framework. Hogg contends that one cannot say that Christians "are witnesses to a Divine revelation, while other religions are exclusively the product of a human 'religious consciousness.'"[23]

Still, despite the criticisms, Kraemer's view dominated the Tambaram meetings as seen in the "findings,"[24] the conclusion of the Tambaram Conference. The following quote of the findings reflects Kraemer's view on the nature of non-Christian religions.

> In the light of God's redemptive act in the Cross of Christ, we realize that all religious groping in the non-Christian world is a most earnest attempt of the human spirit to redeem itself from guilt and death. In spite of the fact that God has not left Himself without witness, we must state that at the same time the human spirit gropes to find God and comes under the influence of demonic powers in making its own gods and its own attempts at self-redemption. Therefore, turning to Christ does not mean an evolutionary fulfillment but a radical breaking with the bonds of one's religious past. Through His judgment Christ offers His Grace and meets the deepest longing of souls.[25]

Having said that, the Tambaram findings also acknowledged that on "whether the non-Christian religions as total systems of thought and life may be regarded in some sense or to some degree manifesting God's revelation, Christians are not agreed."[26]

---

21. Hogg's reference is found in Kraemer, *Christian Message*, 111.
22. Hogg, "Christian Attitude," 94–95.
23. Hogg, 96–97.
24. International Missionary Council, "Findings." (Hereafter IMC).
25. IMC, 170–171.
26. IMC, 184.

In spite of being the dominant voice for more than three decades after the Tambaram Conference, Kraemer's thought continued to be challenged. Asian theologians particularly expressed concern about his views on the nature of non-Christian religions and Christian attitude towards other religions and cultures. There are two names worthy of note, M. M. Thomas and S. J. Samartha. Both Thomas and Samartha were Indian scholars and had close personal relationships with Kraemer. So, even though they acknowledged Kraemer's influence on them, they respectfully disagreed with him in some aspects of his thought. Thomas shares Kraemer's conviction of the finality and decisiveness of Christ for human salvation. However, he is troubled with Kraemer's negative views of syncretism, which, in Thomas's opinion, creates obstacles for Christians to interact with other religions and their cultures. As Thomas sees it, this fear of syncretism has paralyzed Christians' interaction with other religions and cultures.[27]

In regard to Tambaram and post-Tambaram responses, however critical they might be of Kraemer's theology of religions, Kraemer's critics did not challenge its emphasis on the decisiveness and finality of the revelation in Jesus Christ. They shared Kraemer's conviction that Jesus Christ is the way, the truth, and the life, and that this gospel is to be proclaimed to all people in all nations. They might have disagreed with his view on what the Scriptures say about other religions, but they never questioned the Scriptures as the standard of judgment. This, however, began to change in the 1970s with the challenge from religious pluralists and inclusivists.

In 1968, three years after Kraemer's death, Samartha boldly claimed that "with the passing away of Kraemer an era in the history of theology of mission has ended." There will no longer be a division into "Christian" and "non-Christian" religions as Kraemer has proposed in *The Christian Message*; instead, "today one *talks* about Christian *faith* and other faiths."[28] Applying the term faith to other religions is a fundamental shift away from Kraemer, who applied the notion of "faith" exclusively to Christianity.[29] The generic use of faith implies that Christianity no longer has a monopoly on the truth;

---

27. Thomas, "Assessment of Tambaram's Contribution," 395.

28. Samartha, "Contact, Controversy and Communication," 25.

29. In *The Christian Message* Kraemer still used the term "faith" to refer non-Christian religions. Here, he still talked about Christian faith and non-Christian faiths. However, such usage changed in his *Religion and Christian Faith* where faith was exclusively attached to the

it is only one of many faiths available to all. From this time on, critiques of Kraemer's thoughts have been directed to his view on the decisiveness of the revelation in Christ and the authority of Scriptures as the standard of evaluation for other religions.

This shift was apparent when scholars returned to Tambaram for the fiftieth anniversary of the conference in 1988. Those who still held to Kraemer's position (e.g. Lesslie Newbigin and Bishop Anastasios) were now a minority voice. Instead, critiques from religious pluralists, such as S. J. Samartha, Wilfred C. Smith, and Diana Eck, were dominant. Samartha contended that after fifty years, the world had moved towards religious pluralism. The question was no longer about the relevance of the Christian message in a non-Christian world, but its credibility in the Christian world. So, Samartha called for a "drastic revision" of Kraemer's theology of religion.[30] In this pluralistic world, the authority of the Scriptures, the uniqueness of Jesus Christ, and the necessity of Christian mission have to be pushed aside or reinterpreted in order to accommodate the points of views of other religions. There is no one way to proclaim the gospel, but all religious adherents are expected to listen to the good news of other religions. In Smith's words, Christians, therefore, need "to listen . . . to the good news that Buddhists and the others manifestly have to share."[31] Again, the mission cannot be seen exclusively as that of Christianity, but it has to be understood as "one part of [God's] whole mission to mankind," because God works not only to Christians through Christianity, but also "to other people through their traditions."[32] Christianity can no longer claim to be the only channel of truth. Eck criticized Kraemer for his failure to recognize truth from other religions and speaks only from the perspective of Christian revelation. Eck says: "He [Kraemer] talks *about* Islam, as about other traditions, but the voices of Muslims do not enter in. In discussing this particular question, there is no dialogue with Muslims."[33] In conclusion, from the pluralists' point of view, Kraemer's theology of religions is therefore deemed irrelevant for today's pluralistic world.

---

term Christian. Hence, religions and Christian faith are in contrast one with another. See, Kraemer, *Christian Message*, v, 146; cf. *Religion and Christian Faith*, 27.

30. Samartha, "Mission in a Religiously Plural World," 316.

31. Smith, "Mission, Dialogue," 365.

32. Smith, 367.

33. Eck, "Religions and Tambaram," 380.

A more subtle, but serious, critique came from Gavin D'Costa, who holds an inclusivist position. In his book *Theology and Religious Pluralism*, D'Costa deals with three paradigms: exclusivist, pluralist, and inclusivist. He chooses Kraemer as a representative of an exclusivist position. Although D'Costa praises Kraemer as a "broadminded" exclusivist, he finds that Kraemer's exclusivism is internally incoherent. Kraemer's assertion that "salvation is only possible through confession and surrender to Christ" is not consistent with the idea of divine revelation. To deny the existence of divine revelation outside Christianity is in conflict with the biblical data. However, to acknowledge the existence of revelation in the world's religions diminishes the *sui generis* character of God's revelation in Jesus Christ. In addition, D'Costa also charges that Kraemer's exclusivist position cannot explain how Old Testament Israel was saved and the fate of millions of people who never hear the gospel.[34]

The survey of the literature shows that criticisms of Kraemer's theology of religions are concentrated into two groups. The first group of critics (Samartha, Smith, Eck, D'Costa) concentrate their criticisms on Kraemer's theological standpoint, which they classify as an exclusive position. The pluralists oppose Kraemer's exclusivist position, claiming that it monopolizes the truth and does not allow room for others. They see it as irrelevant for the contemporary pluralistic environment. For different reasons, the inclusivists also oppose Kraemer's exclusivism, because it limits the grace of God and allows no salvation outside the realm of the gospel. The second group of scholars (Chao, Hogg, Thomas) criticizes its theological framework. They raise the question about God's presence in other religions and cultures and are critical of Kraemer's negative answer to this question.

Kraemer's theology of religions, however, is not without its defenders. Two noteworthy scholars who stand with Kraemer's position are Lesslie Newbigin and Tim Perry. For Newbigin, the exclusivist/inclusivist/pluralist typology is an inadequate category. The terms (i.e. exclusive, inclusive, and pluralist) are not self-explanatory. Each term needs a specific reference. One needs to know in what sense one's position is said to be exclusive, inclusive, or pluralist. One could be exclusivist in one sense, inclusivist in another sense, and still pluralist in another sense. It will be helpful for us to see how Newbigin describes his position as follows:

---

34. D'Costa, *Theology and Religious Pluralism*, 70.

> The position which I have outlined is exclusivist in the sense that it affirms the unique truth of the revelation in Jesus Christ, but it is not exclusivist in the sense of denying the possibility of the salvation of the non-Christian. It is inclusivist in the sense that it refuses to limit the saving grace of God to the members of the Christian Church, but it rejects the inclusivism which regards the non-Christian religions as vehicles of salvation. It is pluralist in the sense of acknowledging the gracious work of God in the lives of all human beings, but it rejects a pluralism which denies the uniqueness and decisiveness of what God has done in Jesus Christ.[35]

To claim simply that Kraemer's position is exclusive is neither sufficient nor clear. Newbigin points out that D'Costa mistakenly characterized Kraemer's position. It is true that Kraemer's position is exclusive in the sense that it refuses "to recognize any of the world religions as ways of salvation alternative to Christ." However, D'Costa assumed that "Kraemer regards all who have not accepted the gospel as lost."[36] This assumption is not correct. Kraemer is rather agnostic about the fate of those who have never heard the gospel. So Newbigin contends that D'Costa has misrepresented Kraemer's exclusivism by including the sense which does not belong to it.

Perry takes one step further than Newbigin. For Perry, the typology is not only misguiding but also "too narrow," "ineffective," and "functionally incoherent."[37] It is too narrow and cannot do justice to the positions labeled with the terms. For example, the positions of Newbigin, Barth, and George Lindbeck, are all labeled as exclusivist. It is true that they all maintain salvation within the Christian community, but they have different views on the fate of those who have not heard the gospel in their lifetime. Newbigin, as we have mentioned above, is an eschatological agnostic. Lindbeck opens up the possibility of a second chance for people to encounter Christ after this life. Barth's position leans toward universal salvation. Hence, we could see that the term exclusivist is not able to capture this variety within the exclusivist camp. When we press further, we come to see that there are only subtle differences

---

35. Newbigin, *Gospel*, 182–183.
36. Newbigin, "Christian Faith," 330–331.
37. Perry, *Radical Difference*, 18, 20, 28.

between Barth's exclusivism and Karl Rahner's inclusivism. Both Barth and Rahner acknowledge salvation in Christ and hope for universal salvation. They differ only on the role of non-Christian religions for this salvation. Barth denies it and Rahner accepts it. So, it is debatable whether this typology is able to draw clear lines between exclusivist and inclusivist positions.

In addition, Perry argues that the pluralist position is simply another form of exclusivism or inclusivism. Paul Knitter's pluralist position, for example, maintains "*soteria*, or justice for the poor and oppressed" as "a common context for inter-religious dialogue."[38] Yet, this criterion is not neutral because he understands justice as that "which liberates the poor and oppressed."[39] This concept of justice, Perry argues, still resonates with the modern Western context. Hence, Knitter's pluralism is "exclusive in that its consciously embedded conception of justice reserves for itself the ability to evaluate accurately all other culturally embedded conceptions" and "it is inclusive in so far as it argues that only those religions sharing its commitment to *soteria* are ultimately saving."[40] So, according to Perry, exclusivist, inclusivist, and pluralist are not "three distinct approaches to religious truth but . . . two muddled varieties of exclusivism."[41] Each position is exclusive in its own term.[42] Therefore, the threefold typology should not hinder Christians to reflect on a theology of religions which maintains the uniqueness and the finality of Jesus Christ, such as that of Hendrik Kraemer.[43]

Kraemer's defenders have focused on answering the negative charge on Kraemer's exclusivism, but they seem to leave unanswered the concern about the presence of God in other religions and cultures. This concern is neither trivial nor illegitimate, for even Newbigin acknowledged that Kraemer did not deal with it adequately.[44] So, it is the intention of this study to attempt to fill this gap. Notwithstanding some important shortcomings of Kraemer's theology of religions, as the study will show later, I am convinced that it is still a valuable resource for contemporary theology and missiology. This

---

38. Perry, 21.
39. Perry, 22.
40. Perry, 18–22.
41. Perry, 28.
42. Perry, 28.
43. Perry, 4.
44. Newbigin, *Finality of Christ*, 38.

study will then examine Kraemer's theology of religions; assess its strengths and weaknesses; and provide corrections, additions, and suggestions to it by utilizing the "other Dutch Reformed"[45] theological and missiological traditions of the twentieth century.

In so doing we will attempt to answer the following questions: (1) What are the key elements of Kraemer's theology of religions and why are they still relevant and valuable for today's pluralistic world? (2) What critiques of Kraemer's theology of religions properly call attention to inadequacies in his understanding of God's presence in non-Christian religions? (3) What important doctrines from the Reformed tradition address the identified weaknesses in Kraemer's theology of religions? And (4) What would a theology of religions that is rooted in Kraemer's work but amended by the elements of question 3 look like?

1.2 Thesis Statement

This study argues, (1) that even though critics raised objections to Kraemer's theological framework, their objections could be answered sufficiently; and (2) that the shortcoming of Kraemer's theology of religions could be overcome without altering its basic structure by enhancing doctrines that are present but underdeveloped in Kraemer's writings, namely general revelation, common grace, and the work of the Holy Spirit. These doctrines, developed by twentieth-century Dutch Reformed theologians such as Herman Bavinck and Abraham Kuyper, and the missiologist Johan H. Bavinck, would address the shortcoming. After completing this analysis, this study proposes an amended version of Kraemer's theology of religions, which maintains the uniqueness of Christ, the integrity of the gospel, and the necessity of Christian mission, while also honoring the presence of God in the world's religions and cultures.

---

45. Hendrik Kraemer came from the Dutch Reformed Church (Nederlandse Hervormde Kerk). This study will look at the trajectory of theology and missiology of the Reformed churches in the Netherlands (Gereformeerde Kerken in Nederland) represented by Abraham Kuyper, Herman Bavinck, J. H. Bavinck, and Johannes Verkuyl.

1.3 Methodology

This study examines and evaluates Hendrik Kraemer's theology of religions. Following this examination and evaluation, I propose amendments to his thoughts drawing from various Reformed theologians, such as Herman Bavinck, Abraham Kuyper, and J. H. Bavinck. To accomplish this project, the following steps are taken.

Chapter 1 introduces the topic, the problem, and the thesis of this study. Chapter 2 and chapter 3 provide an exposition of Kraemer's theology of religions. Chapter 2 focuses on his theological framework and chapter 3 on the nature of religions. The primary source of this exposition is Kraemer's *The Christian Message* (1938). His other writings of the same subjects (e.g. *Religion and the Christian Faith* [1956], *World Cultures and World Religions* [1960], and *Why Christianity of All Religions?* [1962]) are also used to clarify and supplement *The Christian Message*.

Chapter 4 presents the critiques to Kraemer's theology of religions. Three critics – A. G. Hogg, M. M. Thomas, and Gavin D'Costa – are selected to represent different eras and traditions. Chapter 5 analyzes, evaluates and answers the objections raised by the critics in chapter 4. As a result, it also exposes the inadequacies of Kraemer's theology of religions, which need further treatment. Chapter 6 addresses the shortcoming of Kraemer's theology of religions exposed in chapter 5. It lays out Christian doctrines of revelation and grace which are necessary to supplement Kraemer's theology of religions. Here, I draw particularly from Herman Bavinck, J. H. Bavinck, and Abraham Kuyper.

Chapter 7 applies insights gained from the work in chapter 6 to correct, modify, and supplement Kraemer's theology of religions. Chapter 8 concludes this project and draws important lessons learned for contemporary Reformed missiology and a preview of additional work to be done.

CHAPTER 2

Kraemer's Theological Framework

In this and the following chapter, I will explain Kraemer's theology of religions. It is not the concern of this study, however, to deal with the development of Kraemer's thought. For this purpose, readers may consult Carl Hallencreutz's work *Kraemer towards Tambaram*.[1] This study will then focus on Kraemer's mature thought, doing so in a systematic way, hence a systematic theology. I will take the liberty to analyze, synthesize, and systematize various works of Kraemer on this subject, with an assumption that there are no fundamental changes of his thought in those works, and I will necessarily point out cases which are otherwise.[2]

In this chapter, I will deal with Kraemer's theological framework and save his view on the nature of religions for the chapter 3. This chapter will show that Kraemer argues for the following theses. First, the Christian revelation is absolutely *sui generis*; and second, there is a radical discontinuity between the Christian revelation and non-Christian religions. Kraemer's theses are a direct response to the theologies that were prevalent in his time. Two particular theologies to which he responded are the "fulfillment theology" of J. N. Farquhar and the "cooperation theology" of William Hocking. Kraemer

---

1. Hallencreutz, *Kraemer towards Tambaram*.

2. Most scholars agree that there is no fundamental change of Kraemer's position in his later works. See, Anderson, "Kraemer and After," 355; D'Costa, *Theology and Religious Pluralism*, 53–54; Hoedemaker, "Hendrik Kraemer," 513.

After scrutinizing and comparing Kraemer's various works, namely, *The Christian Message*, *Religions and the Christian Faith*, and *Why Christianity of All Religions?*, I find that Kraemer did not alter his fundamental theses, but, as some scholars (e.g. Walter Horton and Jan A. B. Jongeneel) have noticed, Kraemer indeed made some significant changes on some elements of the subject. These changes will be made clear in the presentation. See Horton, "Review of *Religion and the Christian Faith*," 205–206; Jongeneel, "Hendrik Kraemer," 375.

maintains his theses by proposing an "evangelistic approach" to other religions. This approach takes "the Christian revelation" as its standpoint and "biblical realism" as its specific way of approaching the Bible.

2.1 Historical Context

To understand correctly and to fully grasp the importance and impact of Kraemer's thought, it is necessary for us to place his theology in its historical setting, namely, the International Missionary Council (IMC) conference in Tambaram, Madras, in 1938. As a part of the preparatory work for this conference, Kraemer was asked by John Mott, then the chairman of the IMC, to prepare material discussion in regard to "The Witness of the Church," one of the themes of the conference. Kraemer's answer to this request is *The Christian Message in a Non-Christian World*, a nearly five-hundred-page in-depth study of evangelism.[3] The book immediately created fiery debates, especially over Kraemer's position in regard to non-Christian religions. Kraemer later produced other works on the same subject, but they did not change the course he set at Tambaram. His later works served mainly as a clarification to the theses presented in *The Christian Message*.

The heated reaction to Kraemer's position is understandable when his thought is placed in relation to two prominent theologies of religions, namely J. N. Farquhar's fulfillment theology and W. Hocking's cooperation theology, to which Kraemer's *Christian Message* responded.[4] As our presentation below will show, Kraemer's thought is a sharp rejection of their thought. It is intended to be a new alternative for Christians to relate to non-Christian religions. With this in mind, we will proceed to briefly discuss the thought of Farquhar and Hocking.

2.1.1 Fulfillment Theology

Historically, Farquhar's thought can be placed in relation to the 1910 World Missionary Conference in Edinburgh. This missionary conference was set in a very optimistic time.[5] Mission works around the world looked very prom-

---

3. Kraemer, *Christian Message*, v.
4. Kraemer, *Religion and the Christian Faith*, 222–224.
5. Hedlund, *Roots of the Great Debate*, 25.

ising and there was a sense that the non-Christian worlds would soon turn into the arms of Christianity.[6] Such spirit was echoed in the closing address by the chairman of the conference, John R. Mott. He began the address with this sentence: "The end of the Conference is the beginning of the conquest."[7] In spite of this triumphal mood, the conference, however, was filled with a rather sympathetic attitude toward non-Christian religions. Such an attitude is understandable when one considers the notion that other religions were regarded as preparation for the gospel, and Christianity was seen as the fulfillment of those religions.[8] This way of seeing the relationship of Christianity to non-Christian religions is known as fulfillment theology.[9] Even though fulfillment theology was not the only trend of thought prevalent in that conference, it was certainly well received there.[10] Now, we turn to the fulfillment theology as it is best represented in the thought of J. N. Farquhar.[11]

John Nicol Farquhar (1861–1929) was a Scottish missionary to India from 1891 to 1923. He was born in Aberdeen, Scotland, and was educated in Aberdeen University and Oxford University. It was in Oxford that he learned about India and after his study, he was sent to teach at the London Missionary Society's college at Bhowanipur, Calcutta. After teaching for a decade, he was recruited by John R. Mott to join the YMCA and spent the rest of his missionary career in writing and the student movement. He had to leave India due to his poor health in 1923 and spent his last six years as a professor of comparative religion at the University of Manchester.[12]

Farquhar approached his missionary work with a deep study of Hinduism and was convinced that the Indian cultural and religious heritage must be

---

6. Kraemer, *Christian Message*, 36.

7. John R. Mott's closing address of the World Missionary Conference, Edinburgh 1910, can be found in Hedlund, *Roots of the Great Debate*, 49–51.

8. See the report of Edinburgh 1910 "that the missionary should seek for the nobler elements in the non-Christian religions and use them as steps to higher things . . ." World Missionary Council, *Report of Commission IV*, 267.

9. For a historical treatment of fulfillment theology, see Hedges, *Preparation and Fulfilment*.

10. Scholars mostly agree that fulfillment theology was well represented in Edinburgh 1910. See, for example, Hedges, *Preparation and Fulfilment*, 271; Kärkkäinen, *Introduction to the Theology*, 104; Wood, *Faiths and Faithfulness*, 4.

11. Hedge's treatment of the history of fulfillment theology culminates in the thought of Farquhar. See Hedges, *Preparation and Fulfilment*, 341–342. See also Sharpe, "Legacy of J. N. Farquhar," 62; Wood, *Faiths and Faithfulness*, 4.

12. Sharpe, "Legacy of J. N. Farquhar," 62–64.

acknowledged and shape our Christian attitude toward non-Christian religions. It is not a surprise that his works are mainly on the subjects of Hinduism and India. One can find an in-depth study of Farquhar's thought in the seminal work of Eric J. Sharpe *Not to Destroy But to Fulfil*.[13] For the purpose of our study, we will focus only on *The Crown of Hinduism*,[14] published in 1913, which not only is the best summary of Farquhar's thought but the best exposition of fulfillment theology.

The aim of the book, as Farquhar states, is to discover the relationship between Christianity and Hinduism.[15] In so doing, he applies a comparative study of religion to show that Christianity is not only superior to other religions but is the fulfillment of them. The emphasis on fulfillment is intentional. According to Farquhar, the emphasis is necessary to mitigate rising opposition toward Christianity. Written not long after the Edinburgh Conference, *The Crown of Hinduism* still echoed its optimism and triumphal spirit, but it did not ignore challenges ahead. Christian missionaries faced many different attitudes toward non-Christian religions. He writes:

> Missionaries feel far more keenly than ever before the need of stating clearly how their work and their faith stand related to the systems they are face to face with, and they are in great perplexity as to how to put things. In many fields there is a divergence of opinion as to the attitude which the Christian ought to adopt to the non-Christian religions.[16]

Some Europeans had raised questions of the necessity of converting non-Christians to Christianity. If the adherents of other religions are happy with their beliefs, "why should they be disturbed?"[17] Western-educated non-Christians, having dug into their own spiritual heritage, were convinced that "[their] religion is as good as Christianity." Therefore, missionaries were regarded as intruders and Christian mission was perceived as "an act of unjust aggression upon the existing religions."[18]

---

13. Sharpe, *Not to Destroy*.
14. Farquhar, *Crown of Hinduism*.
15. Farquhar, 3.
16. Farquhar, 16.
17. Farquhar, 23.
18. Farquhar, 25.

Farquhar answered those challenges as follows. On the one hand, he says, Christianity must acknowledge the values of non-Christian religions because each of them "contains a considerable amount of truth."[19] On the other hand, he also maintains that differences between religions cannot be denied. So, when one does a comparative study of religions, one would discover "the superiority of Christianity to the rest of the great religions."[20] Still, Christianity has no intention to destroy other religions, at least not in the sense of displacement. Surely, other religions will die, but in their death, they will live in Christianity, as Farquhar succinctly states, "Hinduism must die in order to live. It must die into Christianity."[21] Here comes Farquhar's fulfillment theology. Christ does not come to destroy pagan religions and cultures but to fulfill them. He says: "[Christ] did not destroy the old civilization, philosophy, literature, and art. Everything of value that the old world contained has been preserved and has flowered once more in Christianity."[22] So, Farquhar concludes, Christianity is not the destroyer, but "the Crown of Hinduism."[23]

Here, we need to understand what Farquhar means by Christianity. For him, Christianity in this context is not various forms of Christianity that are practiced in many nations. Nor is it that which is "defined and elaborated in detail in the creed, preaching, ritual, liturgy, and discipline of any single church." But Christianity, which is superior to other religions, is that which is expressed by Christ himself.[24] Hence, it is more accurate to say that Christ is the fulfillment of all religions. He explains as follows: "Hence, in this volume, in setting forth Christianity as the Crown of Hinduism, we shall restrict ourselves to Christ Himself, drawing our evidence only from His own life and teaching, and from those parts of the Old Testament which He accepted without alteration."[25] With this clarification, Farquhar avoids the association of Christianity with Western Christianity and gives room for a possibility of establishing local expressions of Christianity.

---

19. Farquhar, 29.
20. Farquhar, 31.
21. Farquhar, 51.
22. Farquhar, 53.
23. Farquhar, 55.
24. Farquhar, 58.
25. Farquhar, 63.

2.1.2 Cooperation Theology

If Farquhar's fulfillment theology is somewhat related to the Edinburgh 1910 conference, Hocking's cooperation theology can be set around the IMC, Jerusalem 1928. The situation of this conference was very different from that of Edinburgh 1910. By this time, the spirit of optimism had disappeared.[26] The mood, as Kraemer observed, was "more introspective and observant than strategical." Reality and experience had taught the self-confident Western missionaries to be more realistic in their missionary goal. Still, the most acute change in Jerusalem was "the unequivocal disavowal . . . of all spiritual imperialism."[27] As the triumphal spirit subdued, evangelism seemed to be pushed into the background and the mood moved toward the spirit of cooperation. That is to say, non-Christian religions were no longer perceived as rivals to be conquered, but as allies to combat the common enemy, namely, secularism and materialism. Such a mood was certainly expressed vividly in the thought of Hocking.

William E. Hocking (1873–1966) was an American philosopher, teaching philosophy at Harvard University from 1914 to 1943. Having been brought up in a devout Methodist family, his early Christian life was deeply shaped by pietism, which emphasized knowing God through personal experience. This emphasis on experience left a long-lasting mark on his approach to the philosophy of religion. Hocking went to Harvard to study architecture but ended up studying philosophy, a subject that had gotten his attention since his youth. His particular interest was philosophy related to human life and later to the Christian missions. After graduating from Harvard, he had several teaching careers before he finally returned to Harvard.[28]

Two of his works that got Kraemer's attention are *Re-thinking Missions*[29] and *Living Religions and a World Faith*.[30] *Re-thinking Missions* is particularly important as Kraemer stressed that the debate in the Tambaram Conference

---

26. Hedlund gives at least three factors that might have contributed to the change of mood: (1) the outbreak of World War I, in which the "Christian" nations fought against each other; (2) the rise of communism with its atheistic ideology in Russia; and (3) the growing secularism in the West. See Hedlund, *Roots of the Great Debate*, 61.

27. Kraemer, *Christian Message*, 36.

28. A short biography of Hocking can be found in Rouner, "Making of a Philosopher," 5–22.

29. Hocking, *Re-thinking Missions*.

30. Hocking, *Living Religions*.

could not be properly understood without considering the thought of this book.³¹ For this reason, we will pay attention to it.

In 1930 Hocking had gathered a group of laymen from a variety of expertises and denominations of the churches in North America, with the purpose to investigate "the functions of [Christian] missions in the world of today."³² The investigation was carried out in various mission fields but limited to India, Burma, China, and Japan.³³ *Re-thinking Missions* is the report of that investigation. Hocking wrote the first four chapters of this report.³⁴ The report basically contains evaluation and criticism of Protestant foreign missions – the task that had been carried out fervently for more than a hundred years by Western churches. The criticism of Christian mission is based on his view of non-Christian religions. We will now see this briefly.

Hocking begins with an assertion that Christian missions to foreign lands are a necessary task. Christian mission is based on "an always valid impulse of love to men"³⁵ and this goodwill should not be terminated. He, however, maintains that the missions must be adjusted according to the changing situations, otherwise it "deserve(s) to perish."³⁶ Hocking, then, proposes changes to the foreign mission in terms of its functions and methods. In the earlier days, he explains, Christian mission emphasized evangelism and church planting. All other corollary activities, such as social, educational, and medical works and training national leaders are simply means of getting into evangelism. Hocking contends that it is time for the mission needs to shift away from evangelism to foreign service. This work will be carried out by "a relatively few highly equipped persons"³⁷ who will function as advisor and counselor for local churches and leaders of other religions. The goal is to maintain the value of local cultures and to mitigate the dangers resulting from the changes due to the penetration of Western civilization.³⁸

---

31. Kraemer, *Religion and the Christian Faith*, 222.
32. Hocking, *Re-thinking Missions*, xi.
33. Hocking, x.
34. Rouner, ed., *Philosophy, Religion*, 481.
35. Hocking, *Re-thinking Mission*, 3–4.
36. Hocking, 3–4.
37. Hocking, 26.
38. Hocking, 26–28.

Hocking's proposal is based on his prediction of "the emergence of a world-culture."[39] A world-culture is the result of the meeting of the East and the West and their sharing of common properties in science, technology, trade, literature, and art. The negative aspect of this trend is its tendency to run away from old traditions and to commit itself to secularism.[40] The threat of secularism along with its antireligious spirit is so great that it requires all religions to set aside their differences and to come together to combat their common enemy. He puts this as follows:

> What becomes of the issues between the merits of one sacred text and another when the sacredness of all texts is being denied? Why compare Mohammad and Buddha, when all the utterances of religious intuition are threatened with discard in the light of practical reason? It is no longer, Which prophet? Or Which book? It is whether any prophet, book, revelation, rite, church, is to be trusted. All the old oracles are seeing a new sign: the scorn on the faces of students who know the experiments in anti-religion in Russia and non-religion in Turkey, and the actual religionlessness of much western life. The chief foe of these oracles is not Christianity, but the anti-religious element of philosophies of Marx, Lenin, Russell. The case that must now be stated is the case for any religion at all.[41]

In addition to coming together as one force to fight secularism, all religions also need to build a new type of relationship. With this, all religions "have much to learn from each other and much to contribute to each other."[42] Hocking argues that this cooperative spirit of all religions does not betray the Christian faith. Nor does it compromise the uniqueness of Christianity. The argument is based on his conception of religious truth. All religions in this present state have only partial truth and each strives to have "a better grasp of truth." Yet, the final truth to which all religions aim still lies in the future and "whatever it may be, [it] is the New Testament of every existing

---

39. Hocking, 19.
40. Hocking, 20.
41. Hocking, 32–33.
42. Hocking, 34.

faith."[43] The final truth is the fulfillment or the unity of all religions. With this, Hocking contends that the goal of Christianity is not to seek "destruction of [non-Christian] religions," but to maintain "their continued co-existence with Christianity." Hocking is convinced that through living together, all religions will stimulate each other to grow "toward the ultimate goal, unity in the completest religious truth."[44]

The underlying principle of this religious cooperation is thus much deeper than mere religious tolerance. Hocking is convinced that all religions need to prepare themselves for "the religious aspect of the coming world-culture." Here, he does not refer to a particular positive religion, but "a world faith" – a universal religion for all. He defines this world faith as "a simpler, more universal, less contentious and less expressive religion coming into human consciousness."[45] This world faith is the true and absolute religion for all human beings. "No religion is good enough for any man but the true and universal religion," he writes, "and if it is true and universal, it will fit every man under all circumstances."[46] It is this kind of religion, he argues, which fits modern humans with their world-culture.

Again, Hocking argues that this development will not jeopardize "the uniqueness of Christianity." The uniqueness of Christianity, he explains, lies in the unique treatment of its doctrines. So, even though Christianity may share similar doctrines with other religions, yet it is unique in its particular way of gathering, assembling, and presenting the truths with clarity. To this, Hocking names simplicity and the richness of Christian symbolisms, rituals, and observances as its main uniqueness. In addition to this, Christianity holds on to a personal God with whom Christians could have fellowship. Yet, this union with God is not attained through meditation, in contrast to the Eastern religion, but through obedience to God's will to serve their neighbors. As such it is exemplified in the person of Jesus Christ. He is the highest expression of religious life.[47]

---

43. Hocking, 44.
44. Hocking, 44.
45. Hocking, 21.
46. Hocking, *Living Religions*, 147.
47. Hocking, *Re-thinking Missions*, 49–55.

I have briefly described Farquhar's fulfillment theology and Hocking's cooperation theology. Both men for different reasons advocate a "sympathetic approach" toward non-Christian faiths, and both maintain that the approach will not endanger the uniqueness of Christianity.

Kraemer certainly does not concur also with the thoughts of Farquhar and of Hocking. To Kraemer, Farquhar is "a modern version of Justin Martyr" who attempts to create "a synthesis of Christianity and higher Hinduism." Even though the attempt may have come out of "a genuine desire" to break with "the attitude of impatient scorn" and to have "generous appreciation" of other religions and cultures, theologically such an attempt is "too facile and . . . too complacent."[48] The same, if not harsher, attitude is spoken toward Hocking's thought. Kraemer notes that "the point of view advocated by *Rethinking Missions* and its chairman is devoid of real theological sense and is . . . a total distortion of the Christian message, its content and real meaning."[49]

For Kraemer, both approaches of Farquhar and Hocking have fallen into the trap of the "science of religion" in their evaluations of religions. The science of religion is a scientific approach which "conceives of religion and religions as one of the great representative expressions of human culture, and as constitutive element of human consciousness."[50] In short, the science of religion limits itself to religions as a human factor. For Kraemer, both Farquhar and Hocking failed to provide a theological evaluation of religions, and dealt with religions simply as a human phenomenon.

Kraemer, however, does not simply reject their theologies, but presents his own thought as an alternative. *The Christian Message* is indeed Kraemer's answer to the theologies of Farquhar and Hocking. In this work, Kraemer maintains two theses: (1) the Christian revelation is absolutely *sui generis*;[51] and (2) there is a radical discontinuity between the Christian revelation and non-Christian religions.[52] The two theses uphold the uniqueness of the Christian revelation. The term Christian revelation requires further qualification. In the first place, we need to point out that in Kraemer's corpus, the

---

48. Kraemer, *Religion and the Christian Faith*, 215.
49. Kraemer, 223–224.
50. Kraemer, 37.
51. Kraemer, "Continuity or Discontinuity," 1.
52. Kraemer, 5.

term Christian revelation is used interchangeably with the following terms: "the Biblical revelation," "the revelation in Christ," and "the Revelation of God in Jesus Christ."[53] For the purpose of this study, I will use the term Christian revelation, except in places which require me to quote verbatim.

What is Christian revelation? According to Kraemer, the Christian revelation is God's saving acts in Jesus Christ. In Kraemer's words, the Christian revelation is "the story of God's sovereign redeeming acts having become decisively and finally manifest in Jesus Christ, the Son of the Living God, in Whom God became flesh and revealed His grace and truth."[54] From this definition, Kraemer's understanding of Christian revelation is close to what we customarily refer as the gospel. Yet, this gospel is not a set of Christian doctrines, but God's acts in the person of Jesus Christ. In the following sections, we will explicate these two theses.

2.1.3 Missional Emphasis

To maintain the *sui generis* character of the Christian revelation, Kraemer emphasizes the necessity of the Christian mission that is rooted in the nature of the church as an apostolic body. With this emphasis, he aims to counter Hocking's agenda of reinterpreting Christian mission.

From the start of *The Christian Message* Kraemer sets his thought in contrast to that of Hocking. First, he debunks Hocking's analysis of the current situation of the world and thus rejects Hocking's theory of a world-culture. Kraemer argues that the world is not in the process of becoming together as a unified entity, but a confused one, marked by "two seemingly contradictory facts." He says, "never before in human history has the world and mankind been such a close unity, and never before has it been such a discordant unity." That the Western ways of life have impacted the whole world and created "an amazing uniformity of life" is irrefutable, but despite the display of unity on its surface, "the inner structure of [its] life has been imperceptibly but steadily undermined by forces of disruption and dissolution." Far from being ushered into a unified world with its world-culture, the Christian church, Kraemer

---

53. Kraemer, *Christian Message*, 101, 109; cf. "Continuity or Discontinuity," 13; *Religion and the Christian Faith*, 6, 17, 125.

54. Kraemer, "Continuity or Discontinuity," 1.

argues, indeed lives in a time of transition, marked by "a severe outward and inward crisis" both in the West and in the East.[55]

Second, the greatest enemy that the church faces in today's world is not so much secularism as relativism. It is this threat of relativism that constitutes the crises both in the West and in the East. Kraemer contends that "the outstanding characteristic of our time is the complete disappearance of all absolutes, and the victorious but dreadful dominion of the spirit and attitude of relativism."[56] Certainly, Kraemer agrees with Hocking that secularism is a burning issue in the West and in the East. He, however, sees that secularism is rather an outward manifestation of the crisis that creeps into the soul of Western life, namely, moving away from absolutes toward the spirit of relativism. It is this inward aspect that Hocking neglected in his analysis of the current situation. This spirit of relativism also presents the most challenging factor in dealing with Eastern religions. In the East, Kraemer explains, the problem of relativism is not as great as in the West. The reason is not that this problem does not exist. On the contrary, he argues, the East "virtually always lived on the theory of the relativity of all truth as formulated by man."[57] In other words, relativism is inherent in the thought of Eastern religious and cultural life. To conclude, the whole crisis is due to the changes faced by the West and the East. While the East has to face an outward change due to the penetration of the Western ways of life, the West has to face an inward change due to the penetration of the spirit of relativism into her soul.

The challenges posed by this changing situation require the Christian church to have a "fundamental re-orientation" of its mission. What Kraemer means is not adjusting the mission to secure its place in the world as dictated by the situation of this world, but that the church is called to return to its essential nature, namely, "an *apostolic* body." For Kraemer, this missional nature of the church is extremely important. In regard to the aim of *The Christian Message*, he bluntly says, "The highest ambition I foster is that it may prove to be a helpful contribution to the Church's rediscovery of its apostolic nature."[58] Kraemer's essential critique of Hocking's position is that

---

55. Kraemer, *Christian Message*, 1–6.
56. Kraemer, 6.
57. Kraemer, 23.
58. Kraemer, vii.

the latter has emphasized mission as "a Christian obligation" but "with a very weak sense of apostolic consciousness."[59] The necessity of Christian mission lies not in human goodwill, as Hocking argues,[60] but solely in God's will, for the church is indeed "founded on a divine commission."[61]

With the emphasis of the church as an apostolic body, Kraemer maintains that witnessing is an essential activity of the Christian mission. He thus rejects Hocking's proposal of substituting witnessing with Christian service. Furthermore, he also puts the "older churches" – the churches in the West – and the "younger churches" – the newly formed churches in the East – on the same footing. Both older and younger churches are called to witness to the world around them. With this Kraemer avoids placing the Western churches in a superior position to the churches in Asia and Africa. They are all equal partners in doing God's mission. With this, Kraemer also criticizes Hocking's proposal. By elevating the Western churches to be advisors of the younger churches, Hocking cannot avoid placing the Western churches as superior to their counterparts in Asia and Africa.

Kraemer's emphasis on the younger churches is also strategically important. On the one hand, it is important for the younger churches to be involved in the mission. This involvement will move the younger churches from passive partners to active participants in the whole mission enterprise. Furthermore, it is also important because the younger churches are in the front line of Christian mission. They exist among non-Christian religions. Thus, they have direct contact with the followers of other religions.[62] On the other hand, the fact that the younger churches live in an "overwhelming non-Christian atmosphere" requires a careful understanding of how to relate properly to other religions and cultures.[63] The concern here is how the churches may live according to the gospel and avoid syncretistic practices. We will deal with this topic later.

The *sui generis* character of the gospel demands the church to remain in its true nature, namely, an apostolic body. Christian mission is not only inherent

---

59. Kraemer, 36.
60. Hocking, *Re-thinking Missions*, 4.
61. Kraemer, *Christian Message*, 2.
62. Kraemer, 40.
63. Kraemer, 105.

but also demanded by the gospel. After establishing this point, Kraemer continues to deal with his methodology to derive the content of the gospel. Here we will observe his theological approach.

2.2 Theological Approach

In this section, I will give attention to his theological approach, standpoint, and "biblical realism." This choice is not arbitrary but follows Kraemer's own hint. On at least two occasions Kraemer complained that the critics were confused about his position in *The Christian Message* because they "neither understood nor accepted [his] standpoint."[64] Certainly, one is not obliged to accept his standpoint, but in order to understand his perspective, it is necessary to judge his position on this subject. I shall then proceed to carefully delineate his methodology.

In contrast to the approaches of Farquhar and Hocking, both of whom utilize the science of religion in dealing with the subject of religions, Kraemer argues for a theological approach. The choice of a theological approach is driven by the following reasons. First, Kraemer was convinced that a theological approach is a legitimate option in dealing with religions. A theological approach is not secondary to other approaches such as the phenomenology of religions, comparative study of religions, and philosophy of religions. One does not utilize theology simply because science and philosophy have failed to give satisfactory answers on this subject and that theology could do this task better.[65] It is applied in the first place because it is a valid and scientific approach in studying religions. Theology is not a supplementary approach to fill the gap left by the other approaches. It deserves a position on par with other approaches. Kramer says, "Theology is fully entitled to formulate the case and to say its personal word on the problem of religion, on the basis of its peculiar presuppositions."[66] Having its own presupposition does not

---

64. Kraemer, *Religion and the Christian Faith*, 145, 222; cf. "Continuity or Discontinuity," 7.

65. In the introduction to W. Brede Kristensen's book *The Meaning of Religion*, Kraemer showed the strength and the weakness of Kristensen's phenomenological approach to the study of religions. On the one hand, such approach was able to show "the seriousness and relevance of Religion," but on the other hand, it is inadequate in dealing with the ambiguous nature of religion. Kraemer argued that that ambiguity could only be explained by the theological approach. See Kraemer, "Introduction," xi–xxv.

66. Kraemer, *Religion and the Christian Faith*, 143.

necessarily make this approach less objective; instead, by being frank about its own presuppositions, a theological approach is enabled to give honest accounts about the truths and values of religions.

Second, Kraemer is also convinced that the theological approach is the proper method in dealing with this subject. Fundamentally, it is the approach that understands "men's spiritual expressions" as "what happens in the depth between God, the Creator and Redeemer, and man, His creature."[67] In other words, from the perspective of the theological approach, human religious experience is not a cultural, social, or psychological construction, but is anchored in human relationship with God, who is the ultimate truth. Consequently, a true and real interpretation of religion is necessarily theological.[68] We have seen factors that have driven Kraemer to give priority to the theological approach. We now proceed to see what he means by it.

Kraemer does not argue for a generic theological approach.[69] Instead, he argues for a theological approach that maintains a full commitment to the faith in Jesus Christ. One's standpoint in Christ will determine their approach to other religions. Kraemer writes:

> By the theological approach we mean that in his attempts to understand and interpret religion and religions, the Christian thinker must frankly confess that he can never behave simply as the adherent of *a* religion, taking, if he so chooses, a standpoint detached from the basic views implied in the Christian faith. Under all conditions, in all kinds of work (including this work of interpreting and evaluating non-Christian religions, which calls for a great amount of scholarly work), he remains primarily a disciple, a captive of Jesus Christ, in whom God disclosed Himself, full of grace and truth.[70]

Kraemer's theological approach has both subjective and objective dimensions. Subjectively, it demands Christian scholars to have a full "allegiance

---

67. Kraemer, 299.
68. Kraemer, 52.
69. See Kraemer's surveys of some theological approaches in *Religion and the Christian Faith*, 147–233.
70. Kraemer, *Religion and the Christian Faith*, 144.

to the Person of Jesus Christ" in their evaluation of religions.[71] A Christian cannot study religions from a perspective detached from their faith in Christ. Objectively, it seeks to judge religions from the perspective of Jesus Christ. The emphasis is that the theological approach is not a study of religions by a Christian scholar from a perspective of Christian theology. For Kraemer, to judge human religious consciousness by a set of Christian doctrines is still an anthropological, not a theological, endeavor. Both religions and Christian doctrines are "peculiar human embodiment of religious consciousness."[72] The *sui generis* character of the gospel, then, demands a Christian theologian to hold to the theological approach, which seeks evaluation of religions not from human's, but God's, perspective.

With this, we move to two principles that undergird this approach, namely, the "standpoint *within* the realm of the Christian revelation," and "a persistent and attentive listening to the Bible."[73] The second principle is also termed as "biblical realism." For the sake of clarity, I will deal with the second principle, biblical realism, first.

2.2.1 Biblical Realism

Biblical realism is a technical term coined by Kraemer and employed extensively in *The Christian Message*.[74] Unfortunately, he did not define the term. Later he regretted this shortcoming and acknowledged that it might have contributed to the confusion with which his thought was received by others.[75] In the essay "Continuity or Discontinuity," Kraemer tried to clarify and explain the term, but again he did not define it.[76] In his later works, Kraemer totally abandoned the term but maintained its principle.[77] Given this limitation,

---

71. Kraemer, 145.
72. Kraemer, 144.
73. Kraemer, "Continuity or Discontinuity," 7–8.
74. The word realism is used more than 160 times, and Kraemer devoted one section to deal with this concept. See, e.g. Kraemer, *Christian Message*, 40–41, 64–74.
75. Kraemer, "Continuity or Discontinuity," 2; *Religion and the Christian Faith*, 232.
76. Kraemer, "Continuity or Discontinuity," 1.
77. Eric Sharpe suggests that Kraemer's employment of the term biblical realism is "an effort to bypass reflection on the content of revelation." But Hoedemaker rejects such conjecture. Instead, he contends that the term is "the expression of the unique context of Christian revelation in the terms of life, challenge, conversion, and obedience." See Sharpe, *Faith Meets Faith*; Hoedemaker, "Hendrik Kraemer," 514 (footnote 10).

we will still use the term biblical realism. The alternative terms, if they are available for us, will not solve the problem we have. Therefore, rather than attempting to define the term, I will try to describe its underlying concept.

Scholars have given various definitions of this term.[78] I contend that the terms "realism" and "reality" do not contain philosophical properties.[79] In other words, Kraemer's biblical realism cannot be understood as a philosophical standpoint. Instead, I agree with Libertus Hoedemaker that biblical realism is an ethical principle, namely, a particular attitude of approaching the Scriptures.[80] Hoedemaker explains it as follows:

> "Biblical realism" does not refer to a fixed system of truth which has to be defended and maintained as superior to all other truth; it does not suggest that the Bible is "real" whereas all other religious sources are products of fancy. Kraemer uses the term as a designation which takes the implications of biblical revelation seriously in total life. It is a framework, an atmosphere, a way of life in which obedience to the word of God is central. It is an ethical concept, rather than a dogmatic concept.[81]

Kraemer himself gives two hints to support this understanding. In his essay "Continuity or Discontinuity," he mentions the need to have "a persistent and

---

78. Since Kraemer did not provide his own definition of biblical realism, some scholars have come out with their own interpretations of it. Carl Hallencreutz identifies biblical realism with the gospel. Damayanthi Niles sees it as the criterion of evaluation. See Hallencreutz, "Tambaram Revisited," 355; Niles, *Worshipping at the Feet*, 8. Others, such as Lesslie Newbigin, Tim Perry, Richard Plantinga, and Edmund D. Soper simply mention it without even trying to define it. See Newbigin, "Christian Faith," 330; Perry, *Radical Difference*, 55; Plantinga, "Missionary Thinking," 165; Soper, *Philosophy of the Christian*, 223.

For discussions about the meaning of this term, see Jathanna, *Decisiveness of the Christ-Event*, 512–520; Jongeneel, "Christianity and The-Isms," 19–23.

79. Sharpe points out that "in Kraemer's treatment, the words 'realism' and 'reality' are not used in any sense which might be described as properly philosophical"; instead, he contends that "they refer to Kraemer's own Calvinist interpretation of the contents of the biblical message, in which the sin and moral inadequacy of man is set over against the saving perfection of God." Even though the label "Calvinist" is unfortunately used here, yet Sharpe made a very good point in regard to the content of Kraemer's biblical realism. See Sharpe, *Faith Meets Faith*, 94.

80. John H. Yoder takes biblical realism as a hermeneutical principle. That is to say, biblical realism is a particular way of understanding the Bible. This understanding is indeed very close to our principle. That said, we see that an ethical concept is better than a hermeneutical one. The former refers to the disposition of will that Kraemer has emphasized much. For Yoder's biblical realism as a hermeneutical principle, see Yoder, *To Hear the Word*, 61.

81. Hoedemaker, "Kraemer Reassessed," 45.

attentive listening to the Bible."[82] Again, in his later work *The Christian Faith*, he notes that one needs a "radical biblical orientation."[83] Both assertions refer to a particular attitude of approaching the Bible.

What then is Kraemer's attitude of approaching the Bible? In the first place, Kraemer values the Bible highly and takes it as "the only legitimate source" of the Christian faith.[84] Yet, the Bible, for Kraemer, is not merely a collection of sacred documents, which one could investigate with one's own assumptions, and from which one could extract its thoughts accordingly. The Bible is not a philosophical or theological specimen. One should not manage the Bible, but allow it to confront them.[85] One must not treat the Bible in the same genre as other so-called sacred scriptures or philosophical books. Instead, one should approach the Bible with its own assumption and let it speak its own thoughts. Or, in Kraemer's words, we need "to try as best we can to take it as it wants to be understood, and so to find out what is its peculiar mode of thinking and to try to present this biblical thinking according to its peculiar genius."[86] This particular mode of thinking refers to a particular type of realism presented in the Bible.

Kraemer asserts that in the time of disillusionment people seek for a "sober" and "realistic" answer of their conditions. They cry for realism, but what they really need must go deeper than "mere optimism or pessimism or even a well-balanced equilibrium of both."[87] Kraemer is alluding to the optimism of the Edinburgh 1910 conference, the pessimism of the Jerusalem 1928 conference, and a realistic approach of Hocking. For Kraemer, all these ways of looking at reality are incorrect, for they are dependent on the situation of this world. Instead, what we really need is "divine realism." It is realism that is not dependent on the situation of the world and that "looks realities honestly in the face and exposes them to the light of the divine judgment."[88] In other words, it is realism that tells them the truth of the human condition and this

---

82. Kraemer, "Continuity or Discontinuity," 8.
83. Kraemer, *Religion and the Christian Faith*, 7.
84. Kraemer, *Christian Message*, 63.
85. Kraemer, 64–65.
86. Kraemer, *Religion and the Christian Faith*, 238.
87. Kraemer, *Christian Message*, 40.
88. Kraemer, 40–41.

world, and of the divine acts of redemption and condemnation. This type of realism is only found in the Bible, hence, biblical realism.

What then is the truth or the central message of the Bible according to biblical realism? It is not about human religious ideas, but about God's saving human beings. The message of the Bible is not about religions but the gospel. Kraemer writes: "The Bible . . . consistently testifies to divine acts and plans in regard to the salvation of mankind and the world, and not to religious experiences or ideas."[89] The gospel is about the divine plan for human beings, not about religious or philosophical thoughts. The Bible does not provide us with "definite guidance in regard to the political, social, cultural, and economic spheres of life."[90] Instead, it is "radically religious" for it is about the divine plan for humanity's salvation; it is "intensely ethical" as a guide for holy living; and it is "radically theocentric" for it presents us with "the fact that God is God, that He is the Absolute Sovereign and the only rightful Lord."[91] It does not present us a worldview, nor does it give us a theology, but rather "the witness of prophets and apostles," which "challenges man in his *total* being to confront himself with these realities and accordingly take decisions."[92] In this world filled with contending philosophies, worldviews, and religions, the solution of the Bible is not another worldview, nor theology, nor philosophy, but the gospel, or the divine action for the redemption of human beings in Jesus Christ, which demands human's proper response.

In sum, Kraemer argues that the right way to approach the Bible is to take it as radically religious. The Bible presents neither worldviews nor philosophies, but the gospel as the ultimate answer for human's longing of realism. With this, we turn to the next point.

2.2.2 The Standpoint in the Christian Revelation

This section will deal with what Kraemer considers as a standpoint, or criterion, of judgment or evaluation of all religions. On this issue Kraemer is unambiguous. The only proper standpoint for dealing with the subject of

---

89. Kraemer, "Continuity or Discontinuity," 1.
90. Kraemer, *Christian Message*, 93.
91. Kraemer, 63.
92. Kraemer, 64–65.

religions is "the Christian revelation."[93] He resolutely says: "In all my reasoning and in all my efforts to formulate my opinion, I take my standpoint *within* the realm of the Christian revelation. From it I take my standards of judgment and evaluation. The Christian revelation itself is my authoritative guide and no other principle or standpoint."[94]

Kraemer determines to evaluate and judge religions from a very specific viewpoint, namely, the Christian revelation.[95] The task of theology of religions is defined as "to investigate . . . Religion, in the light of Biblical Revelation, particularly in the light of Jesus Christ, the Way, the Truth and the Life."[96] This leaves us some questions to deal with. Why does Kraemer think that the task of theology of religions is to judge and evaluate religions, and not simply to describe them? Why does he think that it is proper to do so from the standpoint of the Christian revelation?

There exist many ways of studying the subject of religions. One could choose to describe, inform, or present to readers a concept of religion(s) or of a particular type of religion. However, for Kraemer, this is not the task of theology of religions. The primary interest of theology of religions is the relationship of Christianity and other religions. The central issue of this relationship is the question of truth. Consequently, in pursuing the truth, the task of theology of religions cannot be simply "to describe and inform" but "to analyse, criticize, and evaluate" its subject of study, and doing so from a particular viewpoint or standpoint.[97] This is understandably so, for one could not claim a truth simply by giving information or a description of a particular subject.

Choosing one's standpoint is of the highest priority in the study of religions. For many people there exist many standpoints, such as scientific principles, other religious principles, and the like. Kraemer, however, argues that for Christian scholars the standpoint cannot be other than the Christian

---

93. The term itself requires a full explanation which we shall do in the latter part of this section.

94. Kraemer, "Continuity or Discontinuity," 6–7.

95. Hallencreutz contends that even though Kraemer determined to take the Christian revelation as his standpoint, he was not totally free from an "evolutionistic frame of reference" in his dealing with this subject. See Hallencreutz, *Kraemer towards Tambaram*, 291.

96. Kraemer, *Religion and the Christian Faith*, 6.

97. Kraemer, *Why Christianity*, 12.

revelation. Every follower of Christ should choose their standpoint in the Christian revelation from which all religions, including Christianity, are judged.[98] There are three reasons for doing so.

First, one is either with Christ or with something else. It is simply impossible to stand on so-called neutral ground, for example, a "general idea of religion," and to judge the Christian revelation accordingly. One cannot be so naïve as to think that they are able to have a neutral standpoint, for in the first place, religious neutrality is an illusion. A human being is not "a neutrally thinking being," but "a willing, desiring and striving being."[99] They are a responsible being who has to choose and decide which ultimate point they hold to. In term of choosing one's standpoint, "everybody is prejudiced." Nobody has a totally objective standpoint. If this is the case, then it is natural for a Christian to stand with Christ. Second, since the most important question of studying religions is the question of truth, then Christ who is the way, the truth, and the life, is a proper standard of judgment.[100] Third, our relationship with God affects our understanding of truth and demands us to respond in obedience. Kraemer maintains that "our whole apprehension of religious life is molded and colored by our contact with and knowledge of Christ."[101] He does not explain further how our relationship with and the knowledge of God has an effect on our epistemic capability in apprehending spiritual matter. Yet, his point is clear that choosing the standpoint in Christ is essential. Not only is it natural for Christians to do so, but that choice will also somehow affect our understanding of the truth.

This standpoint, the Christian revelation, is "absolutely *sui generis*," and therefore stands above all human religious consciousness and thought. It is, therefore, the only criterion by which all religions, including Christianity, will be measured and judged. Kraemer rejects the idea of a neutral standpoint as the standard of judgment. The choice is either to let Christ be the judge or else to judge Christ by a human standard.[102]

---

98. Kraemer, "Continuity or Discontinuity," 7.
99. Kraemer, *Christian Message*, 158.
100. Kraemer, 100.
101. Kraemer, "Continuity or Discontinuity," 8.
102. Kraemer, *Religion and the Christian Faith*, 145.

To conclude, we see that both principles form a unity. Biblical realism is a right way to approach the Bible and with this approach, one will find that the central message of the Bible is the gospel, the Christian revelation, on which one will stand and judge all religions. With this we have described Kraemer's first thesis: the Christian revelation is absolutely *sui generis*. In the next section, we will describe his second thesis.

2.3 Divine Revelation

The second thesis of Kraemer's *Christian Message* maintains that there is a radical discontinuity between the Christian revelation and non-Christian religions. With this thesis, Kraemer rejects Farquhar's fulfillment theology, which argues for a continuity position. We will show that Kraemer's radical discontinuity position logically follows from his Christocentric understanding of divine revelation.

In the following, I will substantiate the above thesis according to this order. I will present Kraemer's concept of revelation and show that it is not only theocentric but particularly Christocentric in its nature. Then, I will show how Kraemer responds to a traditional division of general and special revelation. In regard to this matter, Kraemer seems to be very reluctant to adopt this distinction in dealing with divine revelation, for he thinks that the terms are misleading and at best they are not useful for the discussion.

2.3.1 Christocentric Concept of Revelation

Before we discuss Kraemer's Christocentric concept of revelation, we will first see two concepts of revelation that he speaks against. First, Kraemer opposes the idea of employing the term revelation in a loose and general sense, by which "enlightenment, a sudden intuitive insight, a luminous idea, or knowledge about so-called occult facts" is taken as a divine revelation.[103] To take a human self-realizing activity as a revelation is not proper, for revelation implies an action of God.[104] Second, Kraemer rejects dogmatic conceptions of revelation, by which revelation is taken as "a supernaturally communicated

---

103. Kraemer, *Christian Message*, 69.
104. Kraemer, *Religion and the Christian Faith*, 110.

doctrine or a set of precepts or truths given out as infallible."[105] For Kraemer, this concept is also not proper, for when revelation is taken in this sense, the truth is of human discovery and achievement. Consequently, divine grace is no longer necessary for human's encounter with divine revelation. In conclusion, both concepts are improper for they are anthropocentric in nature. It is against these anthropocentric concepts of revelation that Kraemer proposed a concept of revelation that centers on God's free acts.

From the perspective of biblical realism, Kraemer argues that revelation in its proper sense is "what is by its nature inaccessible and *remains so, even when it is revealed*."[106] This seemingly paradoxical statement could only make sense when we consider Kraemer's theocentric, or more accurately Christocentric,[107] concept of revelation. Kraemer writes: "Revelation in Biblical realism means, God constantly acting in holy sovereign freedom, conclusively embodied in the man Jesus Christ."[108] This loaded sentence needs to be unpacked. In the first place, he argues that revelation is fundamentally "a connected series of divine acts" that happened repeatedly and constantly in the course of human history.[109] The divine acts are of his free sovereignty. It is free in the sense that it is not bound to any necessities. It is the divine sovereign act, for it has no human part in it.[110] Still, the divine free and sovereign acts reveal not ideas, nor truths, but God himself. Those acts may have given rise to many thoughts and ideas, but as such, they are not the revelation itself.[111] Revelation is a "divine-self disclosure."[112] Having said this, the divine self-revelation is not so much of his essence or being but of his will. The divine being will remain concealed from us, but his redemptive will and plan are shown to us.[113]

Still, the revelation is not only theocentric, namely, God freely reveals himself, but also Christocentric. God reveals himself in the person of his

---

105. Kraemer, *Why Christianity*, 76; see also, *Christian Message*, 61.
106. Kraemer, *Christian Message*, 69.
107. Scholars used different expression to stress this point. See, Perry, *Radical Difference*, 55; Plantinga, "Missionary Thinking," 176; Hallencreutz, *Kraemer Towards Tambaram*, 280.
108. Kraemer, *Christian Message*, 217.
109. Kraemer, 69.
110. Kraemer, *Why Christianity*, 79.
111. Kraemer, *Christian Message*, 61; see also, *Religion and the Christian Faith*, 62.
112. Kraemer, *Religion and the Christian Faith*, 146.
113. Kraemer, *Christian Message*, 73.

Son Jesus Christ. Kraemer says: "Revelation in Biblical realism means, God constantly acting in holy sovereign freedom, *conclusively embodied in the man of Jesus Christ*."[114] That is to say, Jesus Christ is the ultimate and final revelation. In this sense, Kraemer could say that "the revelation is the Person of Jesus Christ."[115] It is in Jesus Christ that all other modes of revelation find their source, meaning, and criterion.[116] The revelation in Jesus Christ is wholly unique. It is "an incomprehensible miracle" as it is at the same time revealed and hidden.[117] Kraemer states: "God was truly revealed in Jesus Christ, but at the same time He hid and disguised Himself in the man Jesus Christ."[118] Because of this peculiarity, the revelation can never be placed under human control as to treat it to be an object of investigation. It is always up to God to reveal and conceal himself according to his free and sovereign act. Therefore, the only proper organ to respond to the revelation is not knowledge, or in Kraemer's word, "gnosis," but faith. This faith, even though a human act, is ultimately a gift of God.[119] Kraemer, thus, strives to maintain the centrality of God's act in this whole concept of revelation.

Moreover, the Christian revelation is also inherently soteriological and missional. It is soteriological in the sense that this revelation is not so much about religious ideas but God's redemptive plan for human beings.[120] Here the revelation moves beyond God's self-manifestation, for when it discloses God, it at the same time also discloses the true condition of human beings. The revelation reveals both God and man, namely, God's redemptive plan and human fallen condition. Having said that, this could not be understood simply as God's offering salvation, because this same revelation also displays God's condemnation upon human sins. Therefore, the revelation is "an act of divine salvation and of divine judgment."[121] The revelation with its soteriological character demands faith and witness. Without faith, one could not penetrate into the mystery of the gospel, yet after having apprehended

---

114. Kraemer, 217, emphasis added.
115. Kraemer, *Why Christianity*, 62.
116. Kraemer, *Religion and the Christian Faith*, 359.
117. Kraemer, *Christian Message*, 118.
118. Kraemer, 70.
119. Kraemer, 69, 118.
120. Kraemer, "Continuity or Discontinuity," 1–2.
121. Kraemer, *Christian Message*, 71.

it, one could not but witness it. Kraemer states: "Witness, faith, and revelation are indissolubly connected."¹²² There is an inherent relation between revelation, faith, and witness. The revelation demands faith, and faith leads to witness. Witness could not be done without obedience. As mentioned above, for Kraemer, God's self-revelation is not so much of his essence, but his will. The God who wills is the God who gives commands, and his commands demand human obedience.¹²³ Thus, there is unity of theology and ethics, faith and action. Johannes Verkuyl calls Kraemer's thought a "theology of obedience." He contends that with this position Kraemer does not deny a "theology of grace" or "theology of glory," but he emphasizes that the life in God's grace must be manifest in obedience.¹²⁴

2.3.2 General and Special Revelation¹²⁵

In *The Christian Message* Kramer's treatment of this subject is set to balance two opposite views in accordance to their acceptance or rejection of *theologia naturalis*.¹²⁶ On the one side, there are those who argue favorably for natural theology and general revelation. The two concepts are differentiated but closely identified, if not identical, in which general revelation is seen as "an introduction" to natural theology. In this view, natural theology and/or general revelation functions as "a *praembula fidei* and a *praeparatio evangelica*."¹²⁷ This view, Kraemer explains, has so much emphasis on general revelation that special revelation has been pushed into the background and consequently

---

122. Kraemer, 72.

123. Kraemer, 73.

124. Verkuyl, *Contemporary Missiology*, 50–51. See also Hallencreutz, *Kraemer towards Tambaram*, 295.

125. In *The Christian Message* Kraemer acknowledges that this topic was not treated sufficiently in *The Christian Message* and for that reason he dedicated a whole chapter in *Religion and the Christian Faith* to this topic. See Kraemer, *Religion and the Christian Faith*, 317, 340–359. And for Kraemer's treatment of this topic in *The Christian Message*, see pages 103–130.

126. The term natural theology means different things to different people. For example, Kraemer defines natural theology as "a science of God and man, conceived as an imperfect form of revelation, introductory to the world of divine grace in Christ." Meanwhile, for Barth it means "every (positive or negative) formulation of a system which claims to be theological, i.e., to interpret divine revelation, whose subject, however, differs fundamentally from the revelation in Jesus Christ and whose method therefore differs equally from the exposition of Holy Scripture." See Kraemer, "Continuity or Discontinuity," 4; Barth and Brunner, *Natural Theology*, 75.

127. Kraemer, *Religion and the Christian Faith*, 161.

is treated as both "irrational" and "irrelevant."[128] In relation to religions, this view disavows the concept of revelation as God's self-disclosure by turning God into a pedagogue who "does not create anything new but assists in and guarantees the self-unfolding of the human spirit in the sphere of religion" and treating all religions as "more or less worthy vehicles of divine revelation."[129]

On the other side, there is the position of Karl Barth, who, in response to the denigration of revelation, tries to return it into the center of theological discourse. This position maintains that revelation is "an act of God, an act of divine grace for forlorn man and a forlorn world" which "remains hidden except to the eye of faith, and even remains an incomprehensible miracle." Consequently, general revelation in the sense that "God revealing Himself with compelling lucidity in nature, history and reason" is seen as "a contradiction in terms, for what lies on the street has no need to be revealed."[130] Barth's position, in contrast to that of proponents of natural theology, emphasizes special revelation at the expense of general revelation. In terms of reemphasizing special revelation, Kraemer agrees with Barth, but he cannot accept Barth's categorical rejection of natural theology and general revelation. On this point, Kraemer sides with Emil Brunner to argue for "a critical and right kind of natural theology." Barth's rejection of the possibility of God's working outside the biblical sphere of revelation proves that his standpoint is on "pure doctrine" rather than biblical realism.[131]

Kraemer's position on this particular subject lies somewhere between the extreme positions. On the one hand, he maintains that the terms "natural theology" and "general revelation" need to be used properly. Hence, a categorical disavowal of those concepts is untenable. This is a rejection of Barth's position. But on the other hand, he also maintains that one cannot simply take "sublime religious and moral achievement" as evidence of the revelation in the same quality as that of Jesus Christ. It is then a rejection of the natural theology position. Even though Kraemer maintains the exclusivity and particularity of God's working in Jesus Christ, he never denies the possibility of God's working in other religions and cultures, because "no man . . . can claim

---

128. Kraemer, *Christian Message*, 115–116.
129. Kraemer, 117–118.
130. Kraemer, *Christian Message*, 118–119.
131. Kraemer, 120–121.

the power or right to limit God's revelatory working."[132] Still, those "glimpses of revelation and the religious intuitions of mankind"[133] cannot be taken as a preparatory stage for the revelation in Jesus Christ. Fulfillment theory is therefore rejected.

However, he does not categorically reject the use of the term "fulfillment" in describing the relationship of the Christian revelation and non-Christian religions. The objection is to use the term "fulfillment" in the "sense of bringing to perfection what had already naturally grown to a more or less successful approximation to the life and the truth revealed in Christ." Kraemer rejects such usage, arguing that in the biblical sense the term always means "the fulfillment of God's promises and His previous preparatory doings." That said, he acknowledges that in a certain sense Christ can be said to have fulfilled people's "deep aspirations, longings and intuitions," but in fulfilling them Christ also brings "the reverse" of them. In other words, Christ's fulfillment of those longings and expectations is surpassing and at the same time judging them, for the cross and its real meaning is always "antagonistic to all human religious aspirations and ends."[134] Kraemer calls this "subversive fulfillment."[135]

In contrast to the fulfillment theory, Kraemer maintains that there is a sheer discontinuity or "radical difference"[136] between the revelation in Jesus Christ and non-Christian religions.[137] There is an abyss separating human religions and the Christian revelation, and there is no manmade bridge sufficient to cross it but faith in Christ. In this regard, Kraemer sides with Barth.[138]

After carefully qualifying his position, Kraemer defines general revelation as God's revelatory works in creation and human conscience. Kraemer states:

---

132. Kraemer, 122.

133. Kraemer, 123.

134. Kraemer, 123–124.

135. Kraemer's concept of subversive fulfillment has been widely adopted by scholars (e.g. Visser 't Hooft, Newbigin, and more recently, Daniel Strange). Michael Goheen contends that J. H. Bavinck's concept of *possesio* is similar to Kraemer's subversive fulfillment. See Kraemer, "Continuity or Discontinuity," 5; Visser 't Hooft, "Accomodation," 13; Strange, "For Their Rock," 379–395; Goheen, "As the Father."

136. Perry has taken this term as the principal characteristic of Kraemer's theology of religions. See Perry, *Radical Difference*, 3.

137. Kraemer, *Christian Message*, 123, 301.

138. Kraemer, "Continuity or Discontinuity," 19–20.

> General revelation can henceforth only mean that God shines revealingly through the works of His creation (nature), through the thirst and quest for truth and beauty, through conscience and thirst and quest for goodness, which throbs in man even in his condition of forlorn sinfulness, because God is continuously occupying Himself and wrestling with man, in all ages and with all peoples.[139]

From this, it is clear that Kraemer affirms the reality of general revelation. He, however, quickly adds that "this 'general revelation' can only be effectually discovered in the light of the 'special revelation.'"[140] That is to say, general revelation cannot be known apart from special revelation. Quoting Hebrews 11:1, he argues that as special revelation is attainable only through faith, so it is with general revelation. The function of general revelation is not to be *praeparatio evangelica* but "to lay bare the dialectical condition" of all human beings. That is to say, through general revelation human beings become aware of their rather paradoxical nature, namely, that they have "sublime faculties and accomplishments" in all spheres of life; but at the same time that they are also in "blindness . . . perversion and corruption."[141] Religions are at the same time "man's achievement" and "God's wrestling with him." Closing the argument, Kraemer admits that one cannot concretely point out where God's wrestling with man happens in non-Christian religions.[142] Kraemer eventually amends this position in his later work.[143]

In *The Christian Faith*, Kraemer acknowledges that his treatment of this subject in *The Christian Message* is not sufficient and might contribute to confusion concerning the reception of his thought. Hence, here he dedicated a whole chapter to this subject. Yet, to avoid repetitions, I will only point out necessary clarifications and additions made in this book.

First, Kraemer made clear his dissatisfaction with the terminology special and general revelation, which he views as "one of the most misleading and

---

139. Kraemer, *Christian Message*, 125.
140. Kraemer, 125.
141. Kraemer, 125.
142. Kraemer, 127.
143. See discussion in chapter 3 §3.1.1

confusing terms possible and ought to be abolished."[144] The reason for his charge is twofold. On the one side, the terms have been "tainted by all kinds of notions, contrary to the way in which the Bible speaks about the revelation."[145] On the other side, if one takes seriously the biblical sense of revelation, namely, as "God's active self-disclosure out of direct, personal concern for man, and directed towards the creative re-establishment of the relation of God with man," then "every kind of revelation is a 'special' revelation."[146] However, since there is no better terminology available, then "the most feasible way is a persevering struggle for their purification."[147] That is to say, his objection is directed only to the terminology, not against the concept itself. For the later, he strives for its biblical sense, the point which we will see below.

Second, Kraemer maintains the centrality of the revelation in Christ without negating the existence of other modes of revelation but stresses the dependency of other modes of revelation on that of Christ. Having been troubled with the terms general and special revelation, Kraemer tries to avoid them. He, instead, talks about many types of modes of revelation, namely, in Christ, in nature, in history of human life and activity, and in human consciousness. Yet, again he emphasizes that all other modes of revelation cannot be interpreted independently from that of Christ.[148] Kraemer's position is made clear in his interpretation of Barth's concept of *Christomonismus* as we quote in full as follows:[149]

> *Christomonismus* is a horrible word, but one must judge discriminatingly what Barth does not say. If Barth says – and he does – that the Bible knows no other mode of revelation than Christ, he has the Bible against him. If he says that all modes of revelation find their source, their meaning and criterion in Jesus Christ, and that the revelation of God's righteousness in Christ is the final revelation in the light of which Jesus Christ is the Truth,

---

144. Kraemer, *Religion and the Christian Faith*, 342.
145. Kraemer, 343.
146. Kraemer, 353.
147. Kraemer, 355.
148. Kraemer, 353.
149. Scholars (e.g. G. C. Berkouwer and Paul Knitter) contend that Christomonism is the heart of Barth's concept of revelation. See Berkouwer, *General Revelation*, 25; Knitter, "Christomonism," 100.

the *only* Truth, without whom no man comes to the Father – then he is quite right and we ought all to be *Christomonists*.[150]

Summary

In this chapter we have shown that Kraemer's position is a direct response to Farquhar's fulfillment theology and Hocking's cooperation theology. Fulfillment theology emphasizes that there is continuity between Christianity and non-Christian religions. Yet, Christianity is superior to other religions because it is the fulfillment of them. Cooperation theology maintains that Christianity is on par with other religions. Christianity and other religions have to work together to fight their common enemies, namely, secularism and materialism. With this stand, Christian mission in its traditional sense needs to be oriented.

In contrast to both theologies, Kraemer maintains the *sui generis* character of the Christian revelation and a radical discontinuity between the Christian revelation and non-Christian religions. With these theses, Kraemer aims for two goals. First, Kraemer wants to safeguard the decisiveness and the finality of the revelation in Jesus Christ. He is the only way, the truth, and the life. Second, this uniqueness of the gospel requires Christians to respond in faith and obedience. Christian mission in its traditional sense is therefore necessary.

Kraemer's position is based on his theological approach. Two important aspects of this approach are biblical realism and the standpoint of the Christian revelation. The former is Kraemer's unique way of approaching the Bible and the later the central message of the Bible itself. It is from the standpoint of the Christian revelation, Kraemer argues, that non-Christian religions have to be evaluated and judged.

I have also shown that Kraemer maintains a Christocentric view of revelation. The self-revelation of God is embodied in the person of Jesus Christ. Yet, unlike Barth, Kraemer does not reject the reality of general revelation. Still,

---

150. From this quotation it is clear that the term Christomonism or *Christomonismus* may carry different meanings to different people. Karl Barth himself does not reject this label applied to his thought. But it is not clear to us in what sense he understands this term. See Kraemer, *Religion and the Christian Faith*, 359; Barth, *Church Dogmatics* III/3, xi.

in this regard, he maintains two important points. First, general revelation cannot be separated from special revelation in Christ. In other words, general revelation has no independent status by itself. Second, general revelation cannot serve as *praeparatio evangelica*. Kraemer, therefore, maintains a radical discontinuity between the Christian revelation and non-Christian religions.

CHAPTER 3

Kraemer's Understanding of the Nature of Religions

In the previous chapter, I described Kraemer's theological framework, in which he argues for the *sui generis* character of the Christian revelation (thesis 1) and the radical discontinuity between the Christian revelation and non-Christian religions (thesis 2). In this chapter, I will deal with Kraemer's view on the nature of religions and present two more theses Kraemer argued.

I will divide this chapter into two sections: his view on the nature of religions and the Christian attitude to other religions. The first section will show that Kraemer maintains three characteristics of religions: they are universal, dialectical, and "totalitarian" or holistic[1] (thesis 3). Furthermore, Kraemer also maintains that Christians must carry out evangelism and adaptation without being trapped into syncretism, and practice tolerance without minimizing Christian mission (thesis 4). As mentioned previously, Kraemer's theological framework is set as an alternative to those of Farquhar and Hocking. In this chapter, I will show that Kraemer's concept of religions, in particular, his view of the holistic nature of non-Christian religions, is also a rejection of fulfillment theology.

---

1. In his *The Christian Message*, Kraemer uses the term "totalitarian." The adjective totalitarian should not be confused with its political usage, by which it describes a total control of the government under a dictatorship; but Kraemer uses it to describe the comprehensive and interconnected character of religions. In short, by totalitarian, he means to approach religion in its totality. To avoid misunderstanding of its meaning, I follow Tim Perry to use the term "holistic." See footnote 1 in Perry, *Radical Difference*, 112.

3.1 Nature of Religions

In this section, I will deal with the concept of religions in general. According to Kraemer, religions bear the following characteristics: universal, particular, holistic, and dialectical. This thesis is particularly applied to non-Christian religions. But with some qualifications, it is also applied to "empirical Christianity." By this term, Kraemer refers to various forms of Christianities as they appear in history in contrast to the Christianity that is presented in the Scriptures. So, for Kraemer, empirical Christianity shares similar features with non-Christian religions. That said, it is advisable not to conclude that empirical Christianity is just one of many religions. Kraemer's understanding of the Christian religion is rather complex as our discussion will show.

As seen in chapter 2, Kraemer prefers the theological approach to modern scientific approaches. He, however, does not discredit scientific methods but sees them as useful tools, provided they are used in their proper place.[2] This is true when he discusses the nature of religions. In this point, one could see that Kraemer's conception of religion is a combination of scientific and theological approaches.[3]

3.1.1 The Universality of Religious Consciousness

In regard to the nature of religions, the first emphasis Kraemer makes is that even though there are many religions, each religion has its particular features. Each religion is unique by itself. What unifies religions is not a general idea of religion, but the biblical idea of religious consciousness. By maintaining the particularity of religion and putting the universality of religions on religious consciousness, Kraemer intends to cast away any foundations for the idea of fulfillment.

Kraemer contends that there are two empirical facts of religions. Religions are plural and each religion is particular. Those facts are affirmed by the science of religion. Kraemer gets the insights from scholars of religions, such as

---

2. Kraemer, *Religion and the Christian Faith*, 298–299.

3. Alan Race has questioned whether Kraemer has ever succeeded in utilizing the phenomenological study of religions in forming his exclusivist position. His answer is certainly negative. He states that "ultimately, it is to claim, the exclusivist theory functions independently of the knowledge of other faiths." See Race, *Christians and Religious Pluralism*, 24–25. However, as this study will show, Race's claim seems to be inaccurate. Kraemer indeed gives genuine attention to the study of other faiths and this knowledge certainly shapes his theology of religions.

John Dewey, Friedrich Schleiermacher, and William Hocking. Kraemer agrees with their view that religions are found only in their multifarious forms. For him, there is no such thing as "religion" in its singular form. So, in line with Dewey, Kraemer agrees that whenever the singular form of religion is used, it is used simply as "a strictly collective term."[4] In conclusion, he quotes Schleiermacher to say that "religion is only real in religions."[5] Yet, Hocking also asserts that "religion *must* be particular."[6] That is to say, despite the fact that there are many religions, each religion exists in its particularity.[7] The plurality and the particularity of religions are empirical facts.

That said, Kraemer does not agree with these scholars' assessment of those facts. Looking beyond this empirical reality of religious plurality, some have attempted to find "a general idea of religion," "a natural religion," or, what they believe as, "*the* normative, original, universal and genuine religion, hidden under the corrupted forms of the positive religion."[8] By positive religion, Kraemer means religion in its concrete form, such as Christianity, Islam, Buddhism, and Hinduism. Others have tried to reduce multifarious forms of religions into what they call "the essence of religion." Kraemer rejects both ideas. In the first place, the general idea of religion is only "an artificial abstraction" of philosophical minds that does not fit with the fact of religious plurality. Moreover, what scholars consider as the essence of religion may not necessarily be central to a particular religion, even though it may reflect more or less some aspect of the religious life of that religion. The problem, Kraemer argues, lies in their attempts to generalize ideas completely detached from all positive religions. When one carefully looks through many religions, they will find that each religion is particular in its character. The similarities that are seen in those religions become less significant when the particularity of each religion is taken account. Kraemer writes, "The more one penetrates different religions and tries to understand them in their total, peculiar entity,

---

4. Kraemer, *Religion and the Christian Faith*, 73. The quotation is taken from Dewey, *Common Faith*, 7.

5. Kraemer, 73–74. Schleiermacher's arguments for the plurality of religions can be seen in the Fifth Speech in Schleiermacher, *On Religion*, 95–124.

6. Kraemer, *Religion and the Christian Faith*, 73. Yet, what Kraemer does not mention here is that Hocking also maintains the universality of religion. See Hocking, *Living Religions*, 59.

7. Kraemer, *Religion and the Christian Faith*, 73–74.

8. Kraemer, 74.

the more one sees that they are worlds in themselves, with their own centres, axes, and structures, not reducible to each other or to a common denominator which expresses their inner core and makes them all translucent."[9] In other words, every religion is unique. Later in this chapter, we will consider the uniqueness of Christianity.

In sum, Kraemer maintains both empirical facts: the plurality of religions and the particularity of each religion. In contrast to the scholars of religion who have attempted to find "a common denominator" behind the fact of religious plurality in the notions of the general idea of religion, the natural religion, or the essence of religion, Kraemer instead finds it on the notion of "the universal religious consciousness." To this topic, I will now turn.

Why are there so many religions in this world? How do we account for the similarities and dissimilarities of religions? Or, in other words, how could we explain that religions are both convergent and divergent? Kraemer answers this question in two ways. First, Kraemer contends that all religions, together with philosophies and worldviews, are "the various efforts of man to apprehend the totality of existence." Since religions are universal human efforts to apprehend the totality of existence, then naturally "there should be an amazing amount of concurrence as to the aspirations, ideas, institutions, symbols and intuitions." Their particularities are, however, "caused by differences of environment, mental structure and historical development."[10] Still, Kraemer moves beyond this philosophical explanation and proposes a theological explanation for the unity and disunity of religions. From a theological perspective, he argues that the unity behind the multiformities of religions lies not merely on human efforts but primarily on "a universal religious consciousness" that exists "amongst men of all ages and climes and races."[11] There is no universal religion, nor natural religion, but "there is only universal religious consciousness that produces many similarities."[12]

To elaborate this point Kraemer does not shy away from utilizing the thoughts of scholars of religions. Explaining the universality of the religious consciousness, Kraemer, employing the thought of William James, asserts

---

9. Kraemer, 76.
10. Kraemer, *Christian Message*, 111.
11. Kraemer, 111.
12. Kraemer, 112.

that religious consciousness is "an empirical reality" which manifests into both "objective" and "subjective" religiosity. Objectively, the religious consciousness embodies and manifests itself in a variety of positive religions. Subjectively, it expresses itself in the form of individual religiosity, without necessarily transforming itself into a positive religion.[13] In this way, religious consciousness exists even among those who do not profess a positive religion. Again, Kraemer also finds support from Johan H. Bavinck, a Dutch missiologist with whom he had worked during his tenure in the Dutch East Indies.[14] Religious consciousness is something mysteriously present in human life. Bavinck contends that religious consciousness is a "persistent force" that operates in human beings with or without apparent positive religions.[15] This religious consciousness centers on what Bavinck calls "magnetic points," namely, certain religious senses that all human beings have experienced in a more or lesser degree. Kraemer agrees with Bavinck that the similarities and dissimilarities of religions lie in their "peculiar combination of emphases" of these magnetic points. That is to say, human religious expressions share all those magnetic points, but some emphasize one over the others.[16]

Kraemer contends that there is divine work behind this universal religious consciousness. "What is the meaning of the universal religious consciousness?" he asks. "Does it in some way testify to a real relation to God in the biblical sense?"[17] The phrase "God in the biblical sense" is crucial in this sentence. The question is not intended to find out whether religious consciousness is somehow related to god(s) in general, but to God the Father of Jesus Christ. That is to say, it is the question of whether one could assume the presence of the Christian God behind human religiousness. Kraemer's answer to this question is affirmative and it is explained in two ways. First, religious consciousness is inherent in human nature.[18] In other words, God has implanted religious consciousness as an essential part of human makeup.

---

13. Kraemer, *Religion and the Christian Faith*, 78–79. For James's objective and subjective parts of religious experiences, see James, *Varieties of Religious Experience*, 498–499.

14. The work of J. H. Bavinck mentioned in this part is *Religieus besef en Christelijk geloof*. Fortunately, this work is recently available in English and can be found in Bolt, Pratt, and Visser, eds., *J. H. Bavinck Reader*.

15. Bolt, Pratt, and Viser, *Bavinck Reader*, 148.

16. Kraemer, *Religion and the Christian Faith*, 80–81.

17. Kraemer, 190.

18. Kraemer, 140.

In this point, Kraemer finds support from John Calvin's concept of *sensus divinitatis* or *semen religionis*.[19] God has inscribed this sense of divinity in human hearts and continues to renew this awareness in them.[20] The sense of divinity is intended to lead human beings to the knowledge of God, but due to human sin, this natural light of God is insufficient to lead them to the true knowledge of God. Still, Kraemer does not stop at this point as to be satisfied with the affirmation of God's inscribing and renewing the sense of divinity in human hearts. Instead, he goes further to inquire whether "there [is] evident in this religious consciousness a drama between God . . . and man."[21] That is to say, whether one could postulate that there are ongoing and active divine interactions, positive or negative, with human beings in or through their religious consciousness. Or, to put in a more direct way of saying: Is there a divine revelation in the religious life of non-Christian religions?

Here, it is necessary to point out that on this specific point Kraemer has changed his mind. In *The Christian Message*, he posed the question: "Does God . . . reveal Himself in the religious life as present in the non-Christian religions?"[22] The answer given in the book is vague.[23] At best, he indicated that it was not feasible to pin down where concretely the divine work is found within the religious life of non-Christian religions.[24] In his later work, *Religion and Christian Faith*, Kraemer modified this view as to affirm that such divine activity is manifest in human religious consciousness.[25] This is not to say that he abandons his previous thesis, but, as he admits, affirms the dialectical

---

19. In his *Institutes* John Calvin writes as follow: "There is within the human mind, and indeed by natural instinct, an awareness of divinity. This we take to be beyond controversy. To prevent anyone from taking refuge in the pretense of ignorance, God himself has implanted in all men a certain understanding of his divine majesty." See Calvin, *Institutes*, I.iii.1. Hereafter, all references to Calvin's *Institutes* is taken from this edition. For Kraemer's allusion to Calvin's *sensus divinitatis*, see Kraemer, *Religion and the Christian Faith*, 121.

20. Kraemer, *Religion and the Christian Faith*, 169.

21. Kraemer, 6.

22. Kraemer, *Christian Message*, 111.

23. He acknowledged this deficiency in his *Religion and the Christian Faith* and attempted to amend it accordingly. See Kraemer, *Religion and the Christian Faith*, 233, 317.

24. Kraemer, *Christian Message*, 127; see also, *Religion and the Christian Faith*, 8.

25. In addition to this change, Walter Horton also notices that Kraemer also softened his view on syncretism. See Horton, "Tambaram," 232.

character of religious consciousness, which he did not stress enough in his previous works.[26] To this topic, we now turn.

3.1.2 Dialectical Character of Religions

All sympathetic approaches to non-Christian religions have a tendency to emphasize the positive side of religions. Kraemer does not reject this positive idea but strives to bring out the whole picture, namely, religions with their dialectical character – positive and negative. Hence, when asked, "are religions good or evil?," for Kraemer, the answer is both. Religions are at the same time good and evil, noble and corrupt. This dialectical character of religions is manifest in two relations: human and divine. Religions are of man and of God. In the first place, Kraemer maintains that religions are "human achievement."[27] In this respect, religions are placed in the same category as other human cultural achievements, such as ideologies, philosophies, and worldviews. All these, including religions, are all human "efforts to apprehend to totality of existence."[28] Here religion is considered generally, and in this sense, it also includes the Christian religion, namely, "Christianity as a historical religious body."[29] Such differentiation should be noted, for it is only in this particular sense that Christianity is on a par with other religions. This matter will be discussed later.

Kraemer contends that all human efforts to apprehend to the totality of existence, including religions, succumb to the dialectic conditions of human beings. Human beings are created in the image of God and yet this image is corrupted by sins.[30] As God's image, they are *homo adorans*,[31] created beings who worship their Creator. As fallen creatures, they are *fabrica idolorum*,[32]

---

26. Kraemer, *Religion and the Christian Faith*, 8.
27. Kraemer, *Christian Message*, 126.
28. Kraemer, 111.
29. Kraemer, 108.
30. Kraemer, 125.
31. Alexander Schmemann maintains that humans are first of all beings that worship God. He writes: "All rational, spiritual and other qualities of man, distinguishing him from other creatures, have their focus and ultimate fulfillment in this capacity to bless God, to know, so to speak, the meaning of the thirst and hunger that constitutes his life. '*Homo sapiens*,' '*homo faber*'... yes, but, first of all, '*homo adorans*.'" See Schmemann, *For the Life*, 15.
32. Calvin writes: "Man's nature, so to speak, is a perpetual factory of idols." See Calvin, *Institutes*, I.ii.7.

created beings who make idols for themselves. In religions, human beings cannot but seek to worship their Creator. However, due to their sins, their noble intention has become perverted so that they worship created things instead of the Creator.

However, religions are not simply of human origin, but of divine origin as well. As discussed above, the divine work in the religious consciousness is not only that God has implanted the sense of divinity in humans, but also that he works actively and continuously in their religious life. Kraemer succinctly says, "the religious and moral life of man is man's achievement, but also God's wrestling with him."[33] In religions, humans do not simply wrestle with themselves, they wrestle with God, or more accurately, God wrestles with them in their pursuit of him. There is a drama involving both God and man. Religion is a monologue of humans seeking after God, but at the same time, it is a dialogue of God and man. Still, this drama displays its dialectical character. Kraemer continues to say, "[The drama] manifests a receptivity to God, but at the same time an inexcusable disobedience and blindness to God."[34] In their seeking after him, they also reject and disobey him. They are inescapably related to him, and yet separated from him.[35]

In addition to the works of humans and God, Kraemer brings one more player into the scene, namely, evil spirits.[36] He says, "It must . . . never be forgotten that in this divine-human drama the demonic has a very significant place. The devil is active everywhere, and has a special ability to pervert the best into the worst."[37] For that matter, the negative responses to the divine work in human religious life are not solely due to human perverted nature, but are also due to external forces, in this case, the influence and assistance of demonic powers. In their religions, human beings are not only

---

33. Johannes Aagaard charges that "in Kraemer revelation is isolated from religion. Revelation is 'solely and exclusively divine possibility and divine reality.'" Yet, we can see that Aagaard's charge cannot be justified. He is certainly right to say that for Kraemer revelation is solely the divine possibility, yet it is not isolated from religion. For in religion, God is also wrestling with man. See Kraemer, *Christian Message*, 126; Aagaard, "Revelation and Religion," 158.

34. Kraemer, *Christian Message*, 126.

35. Kraemer, *Religion and the Christian Faith*, 251–252.

36. On many occasions Kraemer mentions satanic activities in human religious life. See, for example, Kraemer, *Christian Message*, 113, 286; *Religion and the Christian Faith*, 321, 364, 379–380; *Why Christianity*, 90.

37. Kraemer, *Religion and the Christian Faith*, 321.

subjected to their sins, but also to satanic forces.[38] Hence, there exist three powers – human, divine, and demonic – interplayed in religions. Kraemer's conviction of the demonic influences in human religions is primarily due to his reading of the Bible from the perspective of biblical realism, but also grew from his experiences as a missionary in Indonesia. That is to say, he takes seriously biblical assertions of the demonic activities in various texts of the Bible. Kraemer repeatedly warns the readers of the apostle's injunction that Christians should be vigilant of the work of the devil who is like a roaring lion, seeking to devour the faithful, and who also disguises himself as an angel of light, seeking to deceive them.[39] He does not take lightly Jesus's rebuke of Peter's suggestion and calling him Satan. Kraemer dares to imply that behind Peter's friendly reminder of his master, there is the work of the devil, seeking to distort the divine will.[40] Still, he gives much attention to the frequent biblical mentioning of "hardening of hearts." Kraemer contends that the hardening comes from humans and God, but there is also the influence of the devil.[41] Again, this biblical understanding of the demonic factor in human religions is confirmed by his personal experience as a missionary in Indonesia. For example, in discussing the Balinese cultures and religions, Kraemer writes that their ritual of the dead displays the demonic aspect of Balinese religions.[42]

Still, it is necessary to point out that for Kraemer the demonic influences are not limited to non-Christian religions. Instead, it is in empirical Christianity that "the demonic aspect of religion . . . appears in its most dangerous and damnable form."[43] There are two reasons – internal and external factors – that put the Christian religion in this acutely vulnerable position. First, the church is both the body of Christ and at the same time a human institution. The church is the sphere where the world of new life meets with the world of man. Second, it is because "the Evil One is more interested and more active in tempting the Church in order to destroy it."[44] So, internally, the

---

38. Kraemer, *Christian Message*, 113.
39. See for example, Kraemer, *Religion and the Christian Faith*, 337, 379–380.
40. Kraemer, *Religion and the Christian Faith*, 379.
41. Kraemer, 379–380; see also Kraemer, *Communication of the Christian*, 31.
42. Kraemer, *From Missionfield to Independent*, 169, 175–176.
43. Kraemer, *Religion and the Christian Faith*, 335.
44. Kraemer, 337.

church is a mixing of believers and unbelievers; and externally, it becomes the prime target of the devil. The two reasons place Christianity in a dangerous position for demonic attacks.[45]

In this point, it will be helpful to compare and contrast Peter Beyerhaus's thought with that of Kraemer. Beyerhaus has proposed what he calls a "tripolar" view of religions, which is very likely taken from Kraemer.[46] Although Beyerhaus's tripolar view of religions is somewhat similar to that of Kraemer, in which he also maintains the three factors in human religions (human, divine, and demonic), yet the two views have at least two fundamental differences. First, Beyerhaus applies his concept only to non-Christian religions, while Kraemer applies the concept to all religions, including Christianity. Second, Beyerhaus considers each of the three factors, human, divine, and demonic, with the same weight. Hence, he could unhesitatingly say that there are "*three* constitutive elements or sources of origin" pertaining to human religions.[47] Kraemer is more cautious at this point. Kraemer would not be hesitant to say that all religions are of human and of God. He, however, will not put the demonic factor on the same plane as those of human and God. That is to say, Kraemer's position is solidly bipolar, namely, that religions are human achievements at the same time God's wrestling with man. The satanic factor functions merely as external influences to intensify human negative responses to God's works in man's religious life. In other words, the demonic factor serves only to heighten the dialectical character of human religions.

More recently, Daniel Strange, following Kraemer and Beyerhaus, argues that "non-Christian religions are sovereignly directed . . ., collective human idolatrous responses to divine revelation behind which stand deceiving demonic forces."[48] He, then, also maintains three factors, divine, human, and demonic, in non-Christian religions. Strange, however, overemphasizes the human and demonic factors. The divine factor seems to be put aside. In the final analysis, Strange's view on non-Christian religions is wholly negative and parts ways with the dialectical character that Kraemer attempts to stress.[49]

---

45. Kraemer, 335–337.
46. Beyerhaus, "My Pilgrimage," 174.
47. Beyerhaus, "Authority of the Gospel," 142.
48. Strange, *Their Rock*, 42.
49. See Djung, "Review of *Their Rock*," 421.

3.1.3 Holistic Approach of Religions

The proponents of fulfillment theology emphasize the similarities that non-Christian religions share with Christianity. They also contend that those similarities could function as points of contact for Christian missionaries to relate to adherents of other religions. Kraemer, however, sees the futility of this effort. Not only are those similarities superficial when one considers the particularity and dialecticity of religions, but they are "dangerous" when one considers the indivisibility of religions and cultures.

This section will deal with the relationship of religion to other spheres of life, such as social, cultural, political, and economic life. In the first place, it is important to point out that Kraemer deals with this topic particularly in regard to non-Christian religions. Even so, the religions that he has in mind are those of Asian heritage, namely of India and China.[50] Having said that, Christianity is not totally excluded from this discussion. Yet, for the sake of a smooth discussion, I will first concentrate on non-Christian religions and address Christianity later.

In discussing the attitude towards non-Christian religions, Kraemer reminds us that non-Christian religions cannot be treated as "merely sets of speculative ideas about the destiny of man." In this modern world, religion has been treated a mere object of study. It could be sectioned, observed, and analyzed unrelated to other spheres of life as if it is "a laboratory of spiritual chemistry."[51] Such treatment does not do justice to what Kraemer sees as an inclusive character of religions. "Non-Christian religions," he observes, "are all inclusive systems and theories of life, rooted in a religious basis, and therefore at the same time embrace a system of culture and civilization and a definite structure and society and state."[52] Religions are inclusive, functioning as an umbrella that covers all other spheres of life and under which they operate accordingly. In other words, all other spheres of life are more or less permeated by religions and vice versa. Consequently, religions should not be treated in a segmented and isolated way.

---

50. Kraemer, *World Cultures*, 20.
51. Kraemer, *Christian Message*, 127.
52. Kraemer, 102.

In contrast to the modern study of religions, Kraemer proposes a holistic approach to religions.[53] By this, he means to approach religion in its totality. Kraemer says: "The [holistic] approach . . . take(s) a religion as one whole of religious life and expression, of which all the component parts are inseparably interrelated to each other and animated by the same apprehension of the totality of existence peculiar to it."[54]

According to Kraemer, there is a twofold internal unity in each religion. First, there is unity of all components of a religion. Every element of a religion is related to another. Next, there is also unity between components of a religion with its core, namely, a peculiar existential apprehension of reality, on which all parts of a religion depend. Kraemer explains this twofold unity:

> Every religion is a living, indivisible unity. Every part of it – a dogma, a rite, a myth, an institution, a cult – is so vitally related to the whole that it can never be understood in its real function, significance and tendency, as these occur in the reality of life, without keeping constantly in mind the vast and living unity of existential apprehension in which this part moves and has its being.[55]

Still, he moves further to postulate the unity between religion and all other spheres of life. Non-Christian religions and other spheres of life, he says, are intertwined so tightly as to be an "indissoluble unity."[56] This characteristic is "organic" in its nature. In other words, "the symbiosis of culture and religion belongs to their essence."[57] What he means here is that both religions and cultures share the same underlying principle, namely, "primitive systems of cosmic naturalism," which, Kraemer contends, spread throughout the whole of South and South-Eastern Asia, from India, China, Japan, and the

---

53. Hallencreutz points out that the holistic nature of non-Christian religions is an important feature of Kraemer's "missionary study of non-Christian religions." Even though in his years as a student in the University of Leiden, Kraemer was aware of the holistic nature of religions, the young Kraemer did not give much attention to this concept. Kraemer's holistic view of religions was then fully developed during his years as a missionary in the Dutch East Indies. Hallencreutz, *Kraemer Towards Tambaram*, 100–104, 286–287.

54. Kraemer, *Christian Message*, 146.

55. Kraemer, 135.

56. Kraemer, *World Cultures*, 20.

57. Kraemer, 20.

archipelago of Indonesia.[58] This primitive system[59] is characterized by "the absolute interdependence of all the spheres of life . . . and consequently the total absence of conscious differentiation and specialization."[60] There is "no absolute contrast" and everything is relativistic in its nature. This "naturalistic monism" is the root of the primitive apprehension of reality.[61]

Noted above, this holistic approach to religions particularly refers to non-Christian religions. Still, Kraemer maintains that the holistic character also applies to empirical Christianity. This is especially true when the Christian religion is tainted with a "pagan ideal of religion" as in the case of *Corpus Christianum* of medieval Europe.[62] Kraemer, therefore, implies that the holistic character does not belong to the essence of Christian religion. It is rather an element that is imported into it.

The implication of this idea is clear. If all elements of cultures and religions are related closely to their kernel or tainted by it, then they could not safely be used as points of contact. Here, Kraemer reminds us of the dangers of syncretism. On this point, we will hold our judgment of this view. We will return to it when we evaluate his view later.

3.1.4 The Intractability of Christianity

In the preceding section, I have dealt with Kraemer's understanding of the nature of religions in general. On various occasions, I have pointed out that for Kraemer the subjects being discussed could, to a certain extent, be applied as well to Christianity. That said, this does not mean that Christianity is simply one of many religions and could, therefore, be subsumed under the general notion of a religion. For Kraemer, Christianity is unique in its proper sense. To this, we now turn.

Edmund D. Soper in his chapter on "the uniqueness of Christianity" mentions two senses by which uniqueness may be understood. First, it is

---

58. Kraemer, 20.

59. Kraemer warns the readers that the term primitive is not used pejoratively. Here it does not involve value judgment. Instead, it only refers to that which belongs to tribal religions. Hence, primitive apprehension of reality is that of tribal religions, in contrast to the other two types of existential apprehensions, namely, the rational apprehension of the Greeks and the prophetic apprehension of biblical realism. See Kraemer, *Christian Message*, 149.

60. Kraemer, *Christian Message*, 150.

61. Kraemer, 156.

62. Kraemer, 26–27.

understood in the sense of "distinctive" or "unusual," "one and only." Every religion is therefore unique in this sense. Hocking's understanding of the uniqueness of Christianity certainly falls under this category. Kraemer points out that Hocking's *Re-thinking Missions* "placed Christianity more or less on an equal footing with other religions."[63] Still, Christianity is unique as it is distinct from other religions. Second, uniqueness could also be understood in the sense of "superior," "unrivalled," "having no equal," or "single in excellence." To a certain extent, one could say that Farquhar's uniqueness of Christianity comes under this category.[64]

Yet, for Kraemer, the uniqueness of Christianity cannot be merely understood in the above two senses. Here, we have a third sense of uniqueness. For Kraemer, Christianity is unique in the sense that it is "intractable," "wholly other," "one of its kind," or in Kraemer's favorite term *sui generis*. Christianity is unique not merely in the sense that every particular religion is unique in itself, nor is it superior to other religions, but it is unique in the sense that it possesses certain virtues by which it is extremely hard to compare it with other religions or to put it under the general notion of religion. Kraemer calls it the "intractable character of Christianity."[65] Repeatedly, Kraemer reminds us that the nature of biblical religious truth, such as the Christian revelation and the Christian church, is *sui generis*.[66]

Still, for Kraemer, Christianity is necessarily distinguished from the Christian revelation or the gospel. The latter is absolute and on which the Christian religion stands or falls. The former, however, is not absolute. Christianity is a religion understood in two senses. First, it refers to the religion that Jesus Christ prescribes for his followers. It is the ideal expression of Christianity, to which all forms of Christianities ought to point to. Kraemer calls it the "New Testament Christianity."[67] Second, it refers to Christianity as a historical phenomenon, or as Kraemer calls it, "empirical Christianity."[68]

---

63. Kraemer, *Religion and the Christian Faith*, 222.
64. Soper, *Philosophy of the Christian World*, 212.
65. Kraemer, *Religion and the Christian Faith*, 77.
66. See, for example, Kraemer, *Christian Message*, 116, 121, 415.
67. Kraemer, *Christian Message*, 324.
68. Kraemer, 108.

In this sense, it is more or less comparable to other religions and naturally, both dialectical and holistic characters of religions are applied to it as well.[69]

That said, we may not quickly conclude that empirical Christianity is therefore totally identical with other religions. For Kraemer, even as a religion, Christianity is not fully equal with other religions. The position of the gospel is clear-cut. It is *sui generis*. It is absolute. The position of empirical Christianity is rather ambiguous. In the one sense, it stands on par with others, but in the other sense, it is not so. This somewhat incommensurable quality of empirical Christianity does not rest on itself, but only by virtue of its special relationship with the Christian revelation. For this reason, Kraemer repeatedly calls Christianity the religion of revelation.[70] Certainly, he does not think that Christianity is the only locus of revelation, but that it is the only religion that rests on revelation in its strictest sense.[71]

There are two features of Christianity as the religion of revelation. First, Christianity does not fit with the modern understanding of religion, which treats it as just one of many religions subsumed under the general idea of religion. "All religions," Kraemer argues, to a certain extent, "are distorted and misrepresented [forms] of some general Idea of Religion."[72] To the Christian religion, we cannot say so. Nor can we say that it is the perfect form of it. The Bible is not a philosophical, nor a theological specimen. Therefore, Christianity, which stems out of it, bears the same features as the Bible does. As such, it can't fit with the modern sense of religion which is after all a human philosophical construction. In other words, the biblical idea of religion is not that of religion as understood today. Second, Christianity continuously stands under "direct influence and judgment" of the divine revelation

---

69. Kraemer, 145.

70. See for example, Kraemer, *Christian Message*, 23, 62, 72, 114.

71. Kraemer indeed classifies religions into two groups – prophetic religions of revelation and naturalist religions of trans-empirical realization. By the term "trans-empirical realization," Kraemer means that "man conceives all his efforts of meditation, religious practices, concentration, asceticism, etc., as means towards realizing and grasping the identity of his real self with divine reality." The first group includes Christianity, Judaism, and Islam. All other religions fall under the second group. Yet, it does not mean that the first group is purely the work of divine revelation and the second group is totally ignorant of or absent from the idea of revelation. In a certain sense all religions are religions of revelation for their reliance on sacred books that are considered revelation. But the first group is called as such, for they "belong all within the periphery of Biblical realism and have their centre of gravity wholly in revelation." See Kraemer, *Christian Message*, 142–143.

72. Kraemer, *Religion and the Christian Faith*, 77.

in Christ.[73] As a result, it acquires "radical self criticism" as "one of its chief characteristics."[74] That is to say, Christianity stands in a special position to the revelation in Christ in that it is continually being corrected by it so as not to stray away into the erroneous path.[75] Such quality makes Christianity radically different from other religions.

Still, Kraemer never supports the idea that empirical Christianity is in any way superior to other religions. On this point, Kraemer is not ambivalent at all. The feeling of superiority is negative and offensive. Such a feeling is never a religious notion, but rather a cultural product. He even rejects Ernst Troeltsch's notion of the "relative absoluteness of Christianity,"[76] which, he believes, is still an expression of "innate feeling of Western cultural achievement."[77] When asked whether Christianity is absolute, Kraemer resolutely says, "No!" What is absolute is not Christianity but Jesus Christ.[78] Following this line of thought, he contends that "there is no true religion."[79] Certainly, this assertion cannot be confused with a scholastic distinction of *religio vera* and *falsa*. Kraemer does not reject this notion but understands that *religio vera* refers to the religious life that honors God the Father of Jesus Christ and *religio falsa* to religions that fail to meet this criterion.[80] Or to put it another way, *religio vera* is the way of worshipping the triune God as prescribed in the Bible and this is not identical with Christianity as a concrete religion.[81] It is New Testament

---

73. Kraemer, *Christian Message*, 145.

74. Kraemer, 109.

75. Kraemer, *Why Christianity*, 114.

76. Troeltsch argues for a relative absoluteness of Christianity in the sense that it is superior to other religions, understood in two aspects. In the first aspect, unlike other religions, Christianity is not bound to a particular race or nation. In addition, this, he maintains that Christianity is "the loftiest and most spiritual revelation." See Troeltsch, "Christianity among World Religions," 35–63.

77. Kraemer, *Christian Message*, 109.

78. Kraemer, *Why Christianity*, 115–116.

79. Kraemer, 110.

80. This distinction of *religio vera* and *religio falsa* is a perspective given from the Christian revelation. See Kraemer, *Religion and the Christian Faith*, 340.

81. This way of understanding *religio vera* is somewhat in line with Protestant orthodoxy. Richard Muller explains as follow: "true religion is most simply defined by the Protestant scholastics as the right way of knowing and honoring God . . ., involving knowledge of God . . ., love of God . . ., and fear of God . . . leading to an honoring or veneration . . . of God." See Muller, *Dictionary of Latin*, 261.

Christianity. But empirical Christianity in its varied expressions cannot be said to be *religio vera* because it is still a mixture of truth and error.

I have dealt with the nature of religions as Kraemer has seen it. I have shown that for Kraemer, religions display the following characteristics: universal, particular, dialectical, and holistic. There is no religion in its singularity. However, the plurality of religions could be traced back to a singular source, namely, human religious consciousness which is universal and has a divine origin. Kraemer also maintains the dialectical character of religions. That is to say, religions are both human and divine. To approach a religion, one needs to take it in its totality. Religion cannot be separated from all aspects of human life. These characteristics of religion are particularly applied to non-Christian religions. Christianity has its particular place among other religions. It is not totally the same as others, nor is it totally different. Its particular status is due to its special relationship with the revelation in Jesus.

In the next section, we will see how the principles drawn from this section are applied to the way Christians relate to other religions.

3.2 Christian Attitude toward Non-Christian Religions

This section deals with the application of the above principles. We will deal with what practices Christianity needs to undertake in its relationship to other religions and cultures. In this part, we are reminded again that, for Kraemer, the church is an apostolic body. The church is called to do God's mission in this world. Theology of religions is to support this very purpose. This is obvious from what he calls an "evangelistic approach"[82] to non-Christian religions and cultures.

Kraemer rejects both aggressive and sympathetic approaches to other religions. The former is psychologically "unwise and unfair" and religiously "contradictory to the radical humility" required of Christ's followers. A sympathetic approach, which tries to build bridges between non-Christian religions and Christianity on the assumption that Christianity is the crown of all religions, is also rejected because such an approach fails to take into account

---

82. Kraemer explains that the phrase "evangelistic approach" was taken from the minutes of the Ad Interim Committee of the IMC. See Kraemer, *Christian Message*, v.

the radical difference between the Christian revelation and non-Christian religions. Furthermore, such an approach also implies a sense of superiority that does not comport with the Christian faith.[83]

According to Kraemer, the search for a new approach to non-Christian religions is therefore necessary. Such an approach ought to maintain the "essential character" of Christianity and at the same time also recognize the dialectical character of human religions.[84] In other words, it is to proclaim the Christian truth, which is unalterable in its nature in such a manner that is "persuasive and winning," but also shows the "real Christian spirit" of serving God and man.[85] Here, one can see that Kraemer adopts the positive elements of both aggressive and sympathetic approaches and discards their negative elements.

Kraemer's approach consists of three aspects: evangelism, adaptation, and service.[86] Even though Kraemer widens his approach so as not to be limited to the proclamation of the gospel,[87] he considers it as the core of this approach. Hence, the aspects of adaptation and service cannot be treated separately from the aspect of evangelism, for they are intended to support the first aspect.[88] The following section will explicate this evangelistic approach following this order: evangelism and point of contact, syncretism and adaptation, tolerance and interreligious cooperation.

3.2.1 Evangelism and Points of Contact

Kraemer contends that the proper attitude to non-Christian religions has to be put in a wider context of the relation of the church to the world. That is to say, the way in which the church, including Christians corporately or individually, relates to non-Christian religions and their adherents, is the way the church is called to relate to the world. To this, Kraemer says: "The right attitude of the Church . . . is essentially a missionary one."[89] Thus, as the church is sent to the world to proclaim the good news in it, so the church must approach

---

83. Kraemer, *Christian Message*, 301–302.
84. Kraemer, 301–302.
85. Kraemer, 302.
86. Kraemer, 302.
87. Cf. Kraemer, vi.
88. Kraemer, 302.
89. Kraemer, 129.

the adherents of non-Christian religions. Kraemer's emphasis on evangelism is a direct answer to Hocking's *Rethinking Mission*, which showed a decrease in evangelistic zeal amongst churches.[90] Add to this, missionaries were also discouraged by "meager results" on the mission field.[91] Hocking's proposal was to reorient Christian mission to interreligious cooperation. But Kraemer's response is to return the true nature of the church and Christian obedience to God's great commission. Mission is not driven by human support nor by the result of our work, but only by obedience to the will of God.[92]

Kraemer emphasizes that conversion is never merely a human work. This principle has some implications as follows. First, missionaries do not strive simply for the sake of replacing non-Christian religions with Christianity. This is a direct answer to Hocking's charge. In reference to various missionary approaches, Hocking rejects a "radical displacement" approach, by which Christian missions' primary aim is to replace non-Christian religions with Christianity. Hocking cites Kraemer as an example of such an approach.[93] Kraemer certainly does not deny the possibility that Christianity may replace other religions. However, when the replacement indeed happens, it is "the outcome of a definite concatenation of these indirect factors, which is not in human hands."[94] Kraemer implies the work of the Spirit at this point. Instead, missionary activity should aim for "the clear and persevering witness in words and acts to Christian truth and life and the building up of living Christian communities, trustfully leaving to God what He will do with the work of His servants."[95] The emphasis is on the witness: first through the missionaries and then through the indigenous churches. Second, the mission has to "strive for a purely religious revolution through moral and religious persuasion."[96] To hope for success on political and social influences such as that of the Constantine era is no longer viable. The "process of permeation," namely, the saturation of

---

90. Kraemer, 36.

91. Kraemer, 49.

92. Kraemer, 146.

93. In his book *Living Religions and a World Faith*, Hocking proposes three ways by which a world faith could be accomplished: (1) Radical Displacement, (2) Synthesis, and (3) Reconception. Hocking rejects the first two and considers the way of reconception the best option. See Hocking, *Living Religions*, 190–208, 165.

94. Kraemer, *Christian Message*, 287.

95. Kraemer, 287.

96. Kraemer, 287–288.

Christian ideas through various works in non-Christian worlds in the hope that it will become "an embryonic form of Christianity" is naïve.[97] Practically, the people of the East will happily grant Christ as a noble man. But, to accept him as the only truth and Savior is a matter of conversion. Christ is not the fulfillment of, but the crisis of, all religions. In this point, we need to turn to the topic of points of contact.

In discussing Christian attitudes to non-Christian religions and practices that Christians ought to adopt in relating to them, it is necessary for us to discuss the subject of points of contact. To understand correctly Kraemer's position on this subject, we need to consider two issues involved in this discussion, namely, truth and evangelism.[98]

Pertaining to the question of truth, the topic of points of contact is discussed within the theological debate between Barth and Brunner.[99] The possibility of points of contact is one of its contentious subjects, with the two theologians holding opposite positions and Kraemer affirming both. This can only be true when points of contact are taken in a different sense for the respective positions. Barth's concern is whether there is a contact between the realm of grace and the realm of nature, whether there is a possibility to bridge the wisdom of God with the wisdom of man, or whether it is possible to accept God's grace by human effort. Barth's answer is resolutely "No!"[100] Kraemer wholeheartedly agrees with Barth on this score. There is no theological contact between grace and nature. There is only the Holy Spirit who can open human hearts for receiving God's grace. Still, he also accepts Brunner's emphasis on human responsibility in responding to the word of God and sees this emphasis as a legitimate concern. It is an undeniable fact that human beings are able to respond and therefore are responsible for their choice. This implies that points of contact indeed exist between grace and nature.[101] Even though Kraemer shares Brunner's concern, and sees that there has to be some form of points of contact between grace and nature, he does not follow Brunner's take of human "capacity for words" (*Wortmächtigkeit*) as points of

---

97. Kraemer, 289.

98. Kraemer, *Religion and the Christian Faith*, 232.

99. It will not be necessary to deal with the debate comprehensively in this study. For this matter, readers may refer to Barth and Brunner, *Natural Theology*.

100. Kraemer, *Christian Message*, 131–132.

101. Kraemer, 133–134.

contact.¹⁰² Indeed, in his later work, he seems to drop Brunner's thought on this issue. Hence, he can freely say that there is no point of contact in Barth's sense of the term and affirms the existence of points of contact only in terms of communication of the gospel.¹⁰³

In regard to evangelism, however, Kraemer's position is straightforward. The search for points of contact, he explains, is naturally driven by the desire to bring the message of the gospel to an environment that is foreign to its nature, and consequently needs to find a port of entry for that message. In this context, he affirms the necessity of points of contact. He states, "there is here undeniably a point of contact for the Message of the Gospel."¹⁰⁴ The question is "where . . . are the concrete points of contact to be found?" Here, Kraemer's answer takes a different path from that of his contemporaries as shall be discussed below.

Kraemer explains that it is customary for people to think of points of contact in terms of finding similarities between Christianity and non-Christian religions. Such endeavor is certainly futile and mainly comes out of an intellectual approach. It fails to account for a religion in its totality. Here, we are reminded again of Kraemer's holistic approach to religions. When one considers religions as a whole and takes into account each's peculiar core, namely, particular existential apprehension of reality upon which a religion is built, the similarities between Christianity and non-Christian religions become superficial. Under the light of the Christian revelation, "all 'similarities' and points of contact become dissimilarities."¹⁰⁵ Again, he explains, when one takes "Christianity as a total religious system approaching the non-Christian religions as total religious systems, there is only difference and antithesis, and this must be so because they are radically different."¹⁰⁶ With this sheer discontinuity between Christianity and non-Christian religions, theologically there is no point of contact between them.

That said, the points of contact for the communication of the gospel are possible in two ways. Negatively, the points of contact are not found in the

---

102. For Brunner's view of points of contact, see Hart, "Capacity for Ambiguity?," 289–305.
103. Kraemer, *Religion and the Christian Faith*, 363–364.
104. Kraemer, *Christian Message*, 130.
105. Kraemer, 136.
106. Kraemer, 301.

similarities between Christianity and non-Christian religions, but in their antitheses. That is to say, under the light of the Christian revelation, it reveals "the fundamental misdirection that dominates all religious life and the same time the groping for God which throbs in this misdirection, and which finds an unsuspected divine solution in Christ."[107] In other words, those similarities do not function as real "bridges" for the gospel, but as "mirrors" to show the futility of human effort to come to God. Non-Christian religious aspirations, even in their best forms, cannot pave a way to find fulfillment in Christ, but they only show human groping for God and find fulfillment in Christ in an unexpected manner. To put in another way, there is only "subversive fulfillment."

Positively, there exists only one point of contact for the communication of the gospel, namely, missionary workers, or we can say, Christians as messengers of the gospel. Here, Kraemer argues, the contacts are created by Christians who show genuine interest in other human beings. The contact is not between two different religious thoughts, but between two fellow human beings. Thus, for Kraemer, there is no positive and concrete theological point of contact, but a practical one.[108]

3.2.2 Syncretism and Adaptation[109]

I will deal with the topics of syncretism and adaptation together because they represent two opposite aspects of the same problem when the gospel enters a new environment, saturated by non-Christian beliefs and cultures. The church is called to avoid syncretism and to practice adaptation. The two concepts, as familiar as they may be to us, need to be explicated carefully since they have been interpreted in many ways. My aim is to present Kraemer's understanding of them.

The problem of syncretism and adaptation is unavoidable. When Christianity enters a new land, people of non-Christian backgrounds convert to Christianity and a new community of believers is formed in that place. They unavoidably need to apply their new found faith in response to their pagan

---

107. Kraemer, 139.

108. Kraemer, 140–141; *Religion and the Christian Faith*, 364.

109. Various terms are used to convey the same concept: accommodation, contextualization, etc. See for example, Visser 't Hooft, "Accomodation," 5–18.

cultures, customs, and practices. I quote here at length Kraemer's description of the problem of syncretism and adaptation.

> What really *happens* when two religions, two spiritual worlds, meet and enter into a relation of give-and-take, whether in an irenic or in a bellicose way? What really *happens* when a people, or a group of a people, who for centuries have lived in a specific climate, with their own roots, norms and values, leave this spiritual world and *enter a different religion*? What does this transition mean? It means at any rate these people are ready to adopt this new religion as their new spiritual home; and to set out to live through an entirely different rootage and an entirely new orientation, *in the old and familiar environment*, is one of the most formidable experiences that an individual or a group can undergo.[110]

Now, both missionaries and the younger churches need to face these problems. When missionaries bring Christianity to other parts of the world, they do not enter a land devoid of customs and cultures.[111] Hence, missionaries need to be aware of the foreign "spiritual home" they enter, and of the relativity of the type of Christianity they bring with them. To avoid syncretism, the mission has to aim for conversion, namely, "the convert leaves his original spiritual home and enters a new, different home."[112] When a new community of believers is formed in this place, they face the problem of adaptation. Missionaries must not impose the type of Christianity they bring within to the younger churches, since "Western Christianities, theologies, and ecclesiastical forms are adaptations and consequently relative, and often not very successful, expressions of the biblical religion of revelation."[113] Instead, the younger churches seek to express Christianity in their indigenous way. The younger churches need to face the "foreignness of Christianity" which comes to them in foreign forms, namely, Western Christianities.[114] As the religion that is anchored in the revelation in Jesus Christ, Christianity is wholly other.

---

110. Kraemer, "Syncretism," 254.
111. Kraemer, 249–250.
112. Kraemer, 255.
113. Kraemer, *Christian Message*, 316.
114. Kraemer, 314.

It is radically foreign to the religiosity that the converts left behind. Christians in the younger churches have no choice but to accept this foreign gospel. But they must strive to have indigenous Christianities. Kraemer describes this as follows: "The smell of the earth, the brightness of the sky, the natural and spiritual atmosphere which, in the course of ages, wrought the soul of a people, manifest themselves in the kind of Christianity that grows there."[115] It is in this context, the problem of adaptation takes place. In this point, we need to flash back to the problem of syncretism.

What is syncretism? For Kraemer, syncretism is not simply "*illegitimate mingling of different religious elements.*"[116] Nor is it simply "absorption and digestion of extraneous elements" of one religion into another.[117] It is only when such a process reaches the core of a religion it can be labeled genuine syncretism. In other words, as Kramer put it, syncretism happens when "the imported or digested elements are essentially contrary to the authentic 'soul' of the absorbing religion."[118] That is to say, syncretism happens at the level of the core of a religion, or what Kraemer terms as its apprehension of reality. Kraemer differentiates this apprehension of reality into three big groups: the primitive or naturalist apprehension, the rationalist and idealist, and the prophetic one. Certainly, Christianity falls under the third category, but to be exact, one can say that the core of Christianity is the gospel or the self-disclosure of God in Jesus Christ. So, syncretism does not happen, so long as in the process of absorbing non-Christian elements into Christian practices the gospel is kept wholly intact. This thought is important as it opens the possibility of relating to other religions and cultures without having to compromise the core beliefs of the Christian religion.

In describing syncretism in terms of the core of a religion, Kraemer also shows how a colossal syncretism may happen spontaneously among religions. To be sure, an amalgamation of religions may happen either deliberately or spontaneously. Manichaeism is a form of deliberate synthesis of Zoroastrianism, Buddhism, and Christianity. This type of syncretism presented a great threat to Christianity centuries ago. Today, however, the threat

---

115. Kraemer, "Syncretism," 256.
116. Kraemer, *Christian Message*, 203.
117. Kraemer, *Religion and the Christian Faith*, 397.
118. Kraemer, 398.

is coming from what Kraemer calls "spontaneous primitive syncretism"[119] such as the amalgamation of the three religions Confucianism, Taoism, and Buddhism in China, and Ryubo-Shinto which is the synthesis of Buddhism and Shinto in Japan. This type of syncretism happens with the religions of the East because they are "all the natural products of the naturalistic monism."[120] In this naturalistic atmosphere, religions do not compete against each other, because each form of religion is simply "one of the many possible and available ways and methods for the *realization* of a purpose or end that man has set himself."[121] The question of truth is never a problem in this setting. What they really seek is not so much "truth-value" but "experience value." In this world, everything is unreal and relative. Therefore, religions that are born out of this worldview are also relative in their nature. Religious doctrines are never taken in an absolute sense.[122] Hence, this whole scheme of a naturalistic monistic worldview explains how religious syncretism can take place in a natural way.

Syncretism is not a problem at all for non-Christian religions of the East since it is natural and inherent in their nature. But it becomes a great problem for prophetic religions, especially Christianity, whose core is the self-disclosure of God in Jesus Christ. As Christianity comes into contact with the religions whose cores are different and whose religious environment is naturally syncretistic, it inevitably faces the problem of syncretism. Hence, younger churches in Asia and Africa are "called to fight the spiritual battles inherent in *her* situation," because it is their privilege to be given this task and only by doing so can their witness be taken seriously in that environment.[123]

Kraemer argues that the proper answer to syncretism is an indirect one, namely, that the church remains true to its nature, doing so in obedience to Christ.[124] This is translated as to build a community, "reborn in Christ, conscious of being under His rule, discipline and grace." The emphasis is that it is not simply a community of Christians, but rather that which produces "the quality of life of the community . . . taken in the Biblical sense."[125]

---

119. Kraemer, 399.
120. Kraemer, *Christian Message*, 204.
121. Kraemer, 204.
122. Kraemer, 204–205.
123. Kraemer, *Religion and the Christian Faith*, 404–405.
124. Kraemer, 409.
125. Kraemer, 409.

Inevitably, to have such quality of life, this community needs "to make a genuine knowledge of and regular intercourse with the Bible in all spiritual nurture and education."[126] The emphasis is not to have knowledge about the Bible, but to enter deeply into the Bible as to have "a real inner grasp of the prophetic-apostolic message of the Bible,"[127] which will produce "a far more living spiritual consciousness and discernment"[128] by which that community will be able to resist temptation of syncretism. We now move on to the problem of adaptation.

The church is also reminded of its true nature, namely, an apostolic body. It is sent to the world to witness for Christ. In this context, the problem of adaptation becomes crucial and necessary. The church needs to adapt in order to carry out its missionary task. Now, in case of the younger churches, this means they need to grow to be a true church, not only in terms of being independent and self-governing but also in terms of being free and not as "Western spiritual colonies." That is to say, the younger churches are still "to a great extent, in their structure and style of expression, spiritual colonies of the West, copies of something, but not grown-up."[129] The problem is that those younger churches seem to be feeling comfortable with this condition, unaware that being Western spiritual colonies hinders their missionary task. Behind this thought of Kraemer lies an assumption that as the church becomes less and less foreign to its environment, and adapts well to the soil in which it grows, the church will carry out its missionary task more and more effectively.

How can adaptation enhance the church in doing its missionary task? On this point we proceed to see Kraemer's definition of adaptation. What is adaptation? Kraemer's answer is not as obvious as the term "adapt" implies, namely, to change or adjust to new or changed circumstances.[130] He does not talk about changing or adjusting to something. Instead, he focuses on the communication of "the cardinal facts of the revelation in Christ" or, in a more familiar word, the gospel. In this communication, the aim is not "to assimilate" the gospel to a non-Christian religious environment. In other words, it

---

126. Kraemer, 411.
127. Kraemer, 411.
128. Kraemer, 411.
129. Kraemer, 410.
130. See Webster's New World Dictionary.

is not to make the gospel look familiar to them. Instead, it is to present the gospel as concretely as to reveal the two folds of truth – the sufficiency of the gospel in Christ and the insufficiency of human religious efforts. I quote here his full sentence:

> Adaptation in the deepest sense does not mean to assimilate the cardinal facts of the revelation in Christ as much as possible to fundamental religious ideas and tastes of the pre-Christian past, but to *express* these facts by wrestling with them concretely, and so to present the Christian truth and reveal at the same time the intrinsic inadequacy of man's religious efforts for the solution of his crucial religious and moral problems.[131]

Or, to say it differently, adaptation is a "genuine translation of Christianity into indigenous terms so that its relevancy to their concrete situations becomes evident."[132]

Kraemer argues that the New Testament, especially the writings of John and Paul, is the supreme example of adaptation of the early church. John and Paul were fully aware of various religious ideas in their time. Yet, in communicating the gospel, they freely employed words, expressions, ideas, or thoughts, available to them and in doing so "their minds were neither bent on assimilation to these elements, nor on intentional refutation of them, but on presenting and formulating vigorously the revelation."[133] This practice was taken with two underlying principles. In the first place, they took those non-Christian elements simply as "tools for their witness and message."[134] Still, in addition to that, they also believed that it is possible for those elements to go through "conversion" and "filling" with new content or meaning, which can be done only by "the converted mind of the *indigenous employers*" of those elements.[135]

Kraemer calls the adaptation of the New Testament as the first "incarnation" of the gospel. In the course of history, many incarnations have already taken place as the gospel came into contact with different worlds, ideas, and

---

131. Kraemer, *Christian Message*, 308.
132. Kraemer, 323.
133. Kraemer, 309.
134. Kraemer, 313.
135. Kraemer, 326.

contexts. To be sure, not all those incarnations are of the same quality. Some are "vigorous assertions of [the gospel's] true character" and some "represent more a dimming and suppression of the true character of the [gospel] by the alien forms and instruments than an expression of it."[136] But, Kraemer asserts, the point is that "new incarnations and adaptations of Christianity in the concrete Asiatic and African settings are natural and legitimate."[137] That said, the implementation of adaptation in those settings is a formidable task.

Why is adaptation such a big problem for modern missions? Or, in other words, how could it be harder in the present day than in the New Testament time? Kraemer gives a succinct answer: "Christianity was entirely new."[138] That is to say, Christians of that era had a "naked gospel" which only needed to be "clothed" as it entered a new environment. Nowadays, however, Christianity, after going through centuries of history and development, has taken a particular form. What we have today is a "clothed gospel" of one kind or another. Hence, for Christians of younger churches, "as to its content as well to its form, [Christianity] is utterly foreign."[139] In other words, Christians in mission fields need to go through a double adaptation process. They need to unclothe the gospel before putting new clothing on it. In addition to this, they also face the challenge of the identification of community with religion. That is to say, in order to be part of a particular community, it is necessary to hold religion(s) that are considered native to that community. Christianity, due to its association with Western political powers, is considered as a foreign religion.

Despite the challenges, Kraemer argues that adaptation is inescapable for Christianity never comes into "a social and cultural vacuum."[140] When indigenous people accept the gospel, a Western form by which the gospel comes into contact with its indigenous form is already in the process of interchange. But that process must happen "naturally." That means it cannot come from outside, planned and imposed by missionaries, most of whom "are unable to emancipate themselves from the cultural, mental, emotional and social frame in which they are accustomed to live and to express their religious life."[141]

---

136. Kraemer, 312–313.
137. Kraemer, 313.
138. Kraemer, 314.
139. Kraemer, 314.
140. Kraemer, 318.
141. Kraemer, 316.

Instead, it has to come from and by indigenous Christians and be done with "real creativity"[142] in which the form and content of the gospel are carefully differentiated. The ultimate aim is never to be outwardly acceptable to their environments but rather to be "good Christians."[143]

3.2.3 Tolerance and Interreligious Cooperation

We are now living in a religiously pluralistic society, in which religions coexist and their adherents need to learn to live together in a more or less peaceful way. Here, we need to discuss two important concepts, namely, tolerance and interreligious dialogue.

The term "tolerance" is fluid in its definition. Societies ruled by a naturalist monist worldview, such as in India, China, and Japan, are extremely tolerant in regard to religious truth, but at the same time are also extremely intolerant in regard to religious social life. Members of this society are absolutely required to observe and to conform to "the traditional religious behavior of the group." To do otherwise is considered as "unpardonable sin and *défaitism*." Hence, it is hard to label this phenomenon as religious tolerance in its real sense. What this society display are not religious tolerance, but "truth-equalitarianism."[144]

In contrast to that "pseudo tolerance," Kraemer explains, real tolerance "presupposes the combination of unswerving obedience to, and vindication of, the authority of absolute and evident truth with acceptance of the liberty of others to reject it or to adhere to other convictions, even though they be considered erroneous."[145] There are two aspects of tolerance, namely, to hold one's own claim of truth and to respect others' liberty to reject such a claim. This implies that "[Christianity's] intolerant exclusivism as to the ultimate truth" is not real tolerance. As offensive as the claim may be to other religions, it cannot be said as intolerant to others, since it reserves the right and freedom of others to reject such a claim without having impending persecution or

---

142. Kraemer, 315.
143. Kraemer, 319.
144. Kraemer, 207.
145. Kraemer, 208.

threat of any sort. Nor is it religious arrogance to claim so, because Christians do not possess such truth, but simply witness to it.[146]

The motive for Christians to practice religious tolerance comes from their faith in Jesus Christ. To be intolerant is "against God's character ad His whole way of dealing with men," and it is also "against the life, work and death of Christ," for "God's way, Jesus' way, is not the fight for truth, either by power or violence, but by love."[147] Kraemer points out that there is no direct teaching of religious tolerance, but it is implied in God's forbearance. The almighty God never forces people to follow him, but in bringing people to himself, he persuades, invites, and calls them to come to him. So, he respects "man's full freedom" whether to put his faith in him. So, "in principle Christianity is the only tolerant religion," because its tolerance comes from "a divine love and respect for man."[148] With this concept of tolerance, we now move to consider interreligious cooperation and dialogue.

Kraemer points out that Christians should seek opportunity and take initiative to have sincere meetings with followers of other religions to discuss "problems of social life in one's common country and society."[149] However, this ought to be done properly. Kraemer warns that such meetings cannot be done "on the assumption that there is some future catholic Church or religion which, as a result of mutual co-operation and inter-religious communication, transcends the religion represented . . . is the future common religious fatherland." Nor can it be acceptable "in the name of tolerance . . . to hide one's Christian self-identity" for "a Christian can only be loyal to Christ . . . and to nothing and nobody else."[150] The emphasis is on obedience to Christ. When such a claim is not granted or respected, real interreligious cooperation fails. Here, what Christians should seek is genuine interreligious cooperation and dialogue, in which there is "a frank and open-minded respect of each other as sincere men and women, behaving oneself as a sincere Christian, Hindu, Buddhist, etc." In such cooperation, the intention is not "to convert

---

146. Kraemer, *Religion and the Christian Faith*, 373.
147. Kraemer, 372.
148. Kraemer, 372–373.
149. Kraemer, 366.
150. Kraemer, 366.

them into mutually proselytizing societies, but rather to make the necessary moral and social co-operation intense and realistic."[151]

As we have shown above, in relation to other religions, Kraemer emphasized evangelism, adaptation, and tolerance as well as cooperation with the adherents of other religions. With these approaches, Kraemer attempts to achieve two aims. On the one hand, he argues for faithful obedience of the church to its calling as an apostolic body. This is certainly done through evangelism and adaptation of the church without succumbing to syncretism. On the other hand, he also sees the reality of the plurality of religions and the need to maintain peaceful co-existence with adherents of other religions. Yet, tolerance and cooperation with other religions must not be done at the expense of evangelism.

Summary

In this chapter, I have described Kraemer's view on the nature of religions and on Christian attitudes to other religions. On the nature of religions, Kraemer argues that religions are universal, particular, dialectical, and holistic (thesis 3). Applying these characteristics, Christians must take the following attitude toward non-Christians. They carry out evangelism without falling into syncretism and practice religious tolerance without minimizing the necessity of the proclamation the gospel (thesis 4).

I argued in the first chapter, Kraemer's theological framework is set to be an alternative to the thought of Farquhar and of Hocking. This is also applied to his view on the nature of religions and its praxis. For example, in contrast to the scholars of religions, including here Hocking, who argue for natural religion as the essence of all religions, Kraemer argues for the universality of religious consciousness. In contrast to those who argue for points of contact found in the similarities among religions, Kraemer argues for a holistic nature of religions, and thus rejects the simplicity of making similarities points of contact. Again, to those who argue for a sympathetic approach to other religions, and by which all religions are to be treated as allies to combat secularism and materialism, Kraemer sees that the fundamental problem lies not in secularism but in relativism. Still, while maintaining the necessity of

---

151. Kraemer, 367–368.

the Christian mission, he argues for a real tolerance and cooperation with the adherents of other religions.

As Kraemer seeks to provide a breakthrough for the church in his time, his own thought turned to be controversial. In the next chapter, we will discuss critiques launched against Kraemer's thought.

CHAPTER 4

Critiques of Kraemer's Theology of Religions

In chapters 2 and 3, I delineated Kraemer's theology of religions. I showed that Kraemer's thought is a sharp response to and intended to be an alternative to the positions of Farquhar and Hocking. In this chapter, I will examine selected critiques of Kraemer's position and consider the proposals given to address the alleged deficiencies. This chapter will show that Kraemer's position receives both positive and negative appraisals from its onset to the present time.

In the foreword to Kramer's *The Christian Message*, William Temple, the then Archbishop of York (later the Archbishop of Canterbury), envisioned that Kraemer's book would play an important role for future discussion. He says, "This volume is a product of his knowledge, experience and vision. It is likely to remain for many years to come the classical treatment of its theme."[1] Temple's words proved to be true as this work of Kraemer and the view he argued are still being discussed to the present day. Yet, with the limitation of space, it will not be possible to deal with all available responses.[2]

I select critiques that are helpful for this study. In the first place, the critiques are given from a theological standpoint that shares Kraemer's commitment to the uniqueness of Christ and the necessity of Christian mission in its traditional sense. In addition, these critiques not only represent various

---

1. Temple, "Foreword."
2. For a nice summary of various responses given to Kraemer's thought, see Plantinga, "Missionary Thinking," 159–190.

theological traditions and eras but also attempt to overcome deficiencies they see in Kraemer's thought.

The first pool of responses is from what I call the Tambaram circle. This circle is represented by two groups. The first group is from the participants of the IMC at Tambaram in 1938. Their responses were captured in its post-conference series *The Authority of the Faith*.[3] The second group is composed of several Indian scholars, represented in their work *Rethinking Christianity in India*. This work was published in advance of the Tambaram Conference and made available to its participants. The responses in *Rethinking Christianity* are unanimously negative to Kraemer's thought, especially in regard to his view on Hinduism, Indian philosophy, and cultures. The responses in *The Authority of the Faith*, however, are rather mixed. D. G. Moses and K. Hartenstein basically agreed with Kraemer's view;[4] T. C. Chao, H. H. Farmer, A. G. Hogg, and K. L. Reichelt opposed it; and Walter M. Horton tried to navigate between the two conflicting views of Kraemer and Hocking. Out of this pool, it is A. G. Hogg who gives the most penetrating response and we will consider him first.

The second pool of responses is found in *Tambaram Revisited*, a special issue of *International Review of Mission*, which contains selected essays presented in the consultation of mission in connection with the fiftieth anniversary of the Tambaram Conference. The consultation was held at Madras Christian College, the location where the conference was held in 1938. The responses were still mixed. We have Diana L. Eck, Wilfred C. Smith, and Stanley J. Samartha in opposition to and Lesslie Newbigin in defense of Kraemer's position. However, the most nuanced position was offered by M. M. Thomas, who was sympathetic to Kraemer's view and now sought a "Post-Kraemerian" position. From this pool, I will select Thomas's position.

Outside the two pools, I will add Gavin D'Costa who has given critiques to Kraemer's view from a Roman Catholic's perspective. That said, in the presentation, I will deal with first Hogg and D'Costa because they both focus on

---

3. Paton, ed., *Authority of the Faith*.

4. In his later work *Religious Truth and the Relation between Religions* Moses clarifies his position. He agrees with Kraemer in regard to the emphasis of the problem of truth, but contends that Kraemer has answered it "in a too dogmatic a fashion." Hence, he does not agree with Kraemer's discontinuity position in regard to the relation between the Christian faith and non-Christian religions. See Moses, *Religious Truth*, 143–159.

theological aspects of Kraemer's thought, in contrast to Thomas who focuses on practical aspects of Kraemer's view.

4.1 A. G. Hogg: "Faith and Faiths"

Alfred George Hogg (1875–1954) was a Scottish missionary to India.[5] He was born to a missionary family and brought up on the mission field. His parents were pioneer missionaries in Egypt. Following in the steps of his parents, Hogg returned to Scotland to prepare himself to be a missionary. He entered Edinburgh University and completed his study in philosophy and then continued to the study of theology. At this point, he was introduced to the thought of Albrecht Ritschl. Later Ritschl's philosophy played a significant role in his analysis of religion.[6] Hogg was sent to India to be a missionary and arrived there in 1903. He spent his thirty-five missionary years exclusively in teaching philosophy at Madras Christian College in Tambaram, India. At the time when IMC 1938 was held at his college, Hogg had just completed his task as the principal of that college. Soon after the conference, he returned to Scotland for his retirement.

To better understand Hogg's critique of Kraemer's position, we need to see briefly his theology of religion. Hogg's thought on this subject is found in the following works: *Karma and Redemption* (1909) and *The Christian Message to the Hindu* (1947).[7] In addition to Hogg's works, Eric Sharpe's *The Theology of A. G. Hogg*[8] and James L. Cox's essay "Faith and Faiths"[9] also provide helpful summaries of Hogg's thought.

Sharpe points out that the fundamental element of Hogg's dealing with religion is his distinction between *faith* and *beliefs*,[10] or in Cox's words, between *faith* and *faiths*. Faith is the internal principle of a religion. It is an immediate "trust in God"; whereas beliefs are intellectual expressions of the faith. Sharpe explains:

---

5. For a brief biography of A. G. Hogg, see Sharpe, "Legacy of A.G. Hogg," 65–69.
6. See Sharpe, "Legacy of A. G. Hogg," 65; also Hedges, *Preparation and Fulfilment*, 348–349.
7. Hogg, *Karma and Redemption*; *Christian Message to the Hindu*.
8. Sharpe, *Theology of A. G. Hogg*.
9. Cox, "Faith and Faiths," 241–256.
10. Sharpe, *Theology of A. G. Hogg*, 34.

> Faith is immediate and existential: basically trust in God, a living relationship with God, a desire for intelligent fellowship with God. Beliefs are those intellectual expressions to which men resort in order to express implications and consequences of their faith, to protect their faith, to perpetuate their faith and to attempt to communicate their faith. And as such, they are liable to change; indeed, they must change as a condition life.[11]

Beliefs differ from faith in several aspects. First, beliefs are external, but faith is internal. Second, beliefs are not only prone to change but have to change in accordance with the change of one's life condition. When a belief does not change, it becomes superstition.[12] Faith, however, is less susceptible to change. Third, beliefs may vary, but faith remains one. Hogg asserts that "the innermost faith of all religions which are still, at any time, worthy of the name must be one and the same."[13] This point is very important. For Hogg, despite many religions or beliefs, they all share one common faith. Or, to put it more blatantly, despite, for example, that Christianity and Hinduism look so differently from one another in their doctrines, rituals, or worships, they share the same faith in their cores.

That said, Hogg does not disregard the differences in beliefs. Those differences are "an immensely important matter" for him.[14] So, to say reversely, despite Christianity and Hinduism sharing the same faith in their cores, what they believe still matters. Differences between religions are important because beliefs affect faith. Human beings need an "intelligent fellowship" with God. As such this cannot happen, if beliefs are false.[15] In other words, for a faith to function well, it requires a true belief. In this aspect, Christianity is superior to other religions. Here, Hogg compares two cardinal concepts: karma of Hinduism and redemption of Christianity. Even though karma can function well in Hinduism, where the purpose of life is not required, it cannot do so in the universe of moral order. In the universe that demands the purpose of life, Christian redemption is superior to Hindu karma.

---

11. Sharpe, 34.
12. Sharpe, 34.
13. Hogg, *Karma and Redemption*, xix.
14. Hogg, xix.
15. Cox, "Faith and Faiths," 242.

Hogg responded to Kraemer's *The Christian Message* in a pamphlet entitled *Towards Clarifying My Reactions to Dr. Kraemer's Book*.[16] This pamphlet was published before the Tambaram Conference and was made available for the participants of the conference. After the conference, he also penned an essay "The Christian Attitude to Non-Christian Faith"[17] to state his position. We will examine both works accordingly.

In his pamphlet *Towards Clarifying*, Hogg begins by pointing out two points on which he agrees with Kraemer. First, he agrees that Christ is not the fulfillment of Hinduism. Thus, Hogg rejects Farquhar's fulfillment theology. For Hogg, to say Christianity is the crown of Hinduism is to smack of Christian superiority. By this, it also gives emphasis in the wrong place, namely, doctrinal similarity over the system of thought. Hogg contends that what Christ has fulfilled is not Hinduism, but the very need of human beings. The sense of this need does not come from Hinduism but from God himself. In his review of Farquhar's works, he explained as follows:

> We feel that Mr. Farquhar proves that Christ, working on India through the impact of Christendom in all its forms, has brought her to the point at which none but He can satisfy her need. On the other hand, we feel that the claim that Christ is the crown of Hinduism is little more than a debating-point. Doubtless Christ fulfils what is good in Hinduism. But then He leaves out so much of what was in Hinduism, and He fulfils so much of what was never in Hinduism, that Mr. Farquhar's tracing out of the aspect of fulfillment sometimes seems far-fetched. What Christ directly fulfils is not Hinduism but the need of which India has begun to be conscious, the need of which He has made her begin to feel conscious, the need, by making her feel conscious of which, He has made her no longer quite Hindu.[18]

Second, Hogg accepts Kraemer's holistic nature of religions. He contends that similarities between religions will turn to be superficial when one considers each as a system of thought. From this standpoint, both religions are

---

16. Hogg, *Towards Clarifying*.
17. Hogg, "Christian Attitude," 94–116.
18. Hogg, "Review," 172–173.

antithetical.[19] In his essay "Christian Attitude" Hogg carries further this notion of the holistic nature of religions and points out its implication for evangelism. He again agrees with Kraemer that "points of contact" for evangelism face the danger of syncretism. When a religion is taken in its unity, no part of it is safe to use as a point of contact. As for the religions in India, "they all have suffered impregnation with the dye of a monistic mysticism."[20] But, this unity, he qualifies, is rather "an inevitable and persistent process" not "an achieved" one. Therefore, he cannot agree with Kraemer to take Hinduism as an organic unity. Still, the impregnation of monistic mysticism in Hinduism cannot be taken lightly. The "dye" has tainted the whole system. He explains: "This dye has become so 'fixed' as to render it doubtful whether any strands of Hindu conceptual thought can be safely woven into the web of an Indian formulation of Christian doctrine."[21] Hogg, again, agrees with Kraemer that points of contact for evangelism can be found only in its antithesis.

After presenting his points of agreement with Kraemer's thought, Hogg continues with his critiques. His main objection is to Kraemer's concept of revelation. According to Hogg, Kraemer fails to affirm God's revelation outside the sphere of Christian revelation. Hogg says that

> the chief defects of Kraemer's distinguished and wonderfully instructive book seem to be connected with the extent to which the concept of Revelation determines the structure of its argument, and with his timidity about admitting a genuine activity of Divine self-revelation outside the range of Biblical religion. And I fear that the result will be harmful if K.'s book leads the Christian evangelist or missionary to lay a similar stress upon the concept of Revelation *in his approach to the non-Christian*.[22]

In short, to Hogg, Kraemer's concept of revelation is too narrow. Revelation is a constraint within the religions of Judaism and Christianity. That is to say, only Judaism and Christianity are considered as the product of divine revelation and other religions are of human "religious consciousness."[23]

---

19. Hogg, *Towards Clarifying*, 1.
20. Hogg, "Christian Attitude," 101.
21. Hogg, 100–101; see also, Hogg, *Towards Clarifying*, 11.
22. Hogg, *Towards Clarifying*, 6.
23. Hogg, 2–3.

Kraemer's failure to affirm God's revelation in other religions troubles Hogg. We may point out two reasons. First, as James Cox correctly points out, the contrast between Hogg and Kraemer is due to their different conceptions of revelation.[24] Whereas Kraemer emphasizes the revelation in Christ, Hogg maintains the universality of divine revelation. He asserts that "God is *always* seeking to reveal Himself to *every* man, and that the limited measure (or the no-measure) in which the revelation succeeds in breaking through is man's fault and not God's decree."[25] Theologically, Kraemer's concept of revelation does not square with that of Hogg.

Second, limiting revelation to the religion of Christianity may lead others to suspect Christianity of having "an intolerant religious superiority." Hogg contends that "it is not enough that, in actual fact, the missionary should be free from any attitude of superiority; it is essential that he should not even be suspected of that attitude."[26] He attempts to free Christianity from any potentiality to be suspected as such. Kraemer's theology in his view does not serve this purpose.

Hogg proposes two ways to overcome Kraemer's deficiency. First, he contends that it is necessary to make a distinction between the occurrence and the content of revelation. Kraemer, however, fails to make this distinction.[27] On this point, D. G. Moses agrees with Hogg. Moses argues that Kraemer's judgment on this subject is based on the "mere occurrence of revelation." Therefore, Kraemer has difficulty affirming God's revelation in other religions. If he has taken into account "the content of revelation," he will not face such a problem. The difference between Christianity and non-Christian religions will eventually lie not in the occurrence of revelation but in their contents.[28]

With this distinction, Hogg argues that both the universality of God's revelation and the uniqueness of the Christian revelation could be safeguarded. Hogg agrees with Kraemer concerning the uniqueness and the absoluteness of the Christian gospel. As such, this point is "vital" for "effectual missionary effort." He, however, does not agree that it should be grounded on the

---

24. Cox, "Faith and Faiths," 247.
25. Hogg, *Towards Clarifying*, 3.
26. Hogg, 4.
27. Hogg, 7.
28. Moses, *Religious Truth*, 154–155.

occurrence of revelation but on its content. The occurrence of revelation is universal. All religions are founded on the divine revelation, in the sense that they all experience the occurrence of the revelation. But the contents of the revelation experienced in non-Christian religions differ from that in Christianity. God speaks in human language to all human beings, but in the Christian gospel he speaks in a medium superior to human language, in the word made flesh. He explains as follows:

> But it must be rightly grounded, and it is not rightly grounded when the uniqueness and the absoluteness of the Gospel is ascribed to its having come by revelation. The Christian Gospel is unique and absolute not because it is God speaking but because it is the Word made flesh . . . when He reveals Himself by speaking, what He says can only be the nearest approximation possible in human language to what He wants to convey to our apprehension. But the Christian Gospel witnesses to God's making for Himself a more perfect medium of self-revelation than language . . . In the Incarnation we have a divine self-revelation that is final but at the same time ever inexhaustibly new.[29]

In other words, what makes Christianity different from other religions is its content, namely, the incarnated Son of God, Jesus Christ, the "perfect expression of [God] toward our race in the medium of action and human personality."[30]

Second, Hogg maintains the distinction between *faiths* and *faith*. This approach is found in his essay "Christian Attitude to non-Christian Faith." According to Hogg, Kraemer fails to make this distinction. Kraemer's discussion touches only non-Christian *faiths* (plural) or religions, not a non-Christian *faith* (singular). Hogg contends that his distinction of faith and faiths is parallel with Kraemer's distinction of the Christian revelation and empirical Christianity. If Kraemer could make a distinction between the Christian revelation with empirical Christianity, how could he not distinguish between non-Christian faith and non-Christian religions? Hogg says,

---

29. Hogg, *Towards Clarifying*, 7–8.
30. Hogg, 8.

Dr. Kraemer has referred to "the rash and erroneous identification of empirical Christianity with the revelation in Christ." Is it equally rash and erroneous to identify other religions with their empirical forms, or are they, as Christianity is not, merely phenomena belonging to "the relative sphere of history" with no basis in a Divine initiative of self-disclosure?"[31]

According to Hogg, by the phrase "the religious life as present in the non-Christian religions," Kraemer seems to refer to the reality of a non-Christian faith.[32] In Christianity, Hogg continues, this faith is what Paul refers to as life "hidden with Christ in God" (Col 3:3). Now, Hogg indicates that this faith may also be present even amongst non-Christian religions. "Can there be," he asks, "a life which, although without Christ, is yet somehow a life 'hid in God'?" To put it another way, can we find "a religious faith" outside the sphere of Christianity, before which one needs "to put the shoes off the feet, recognizing that one is on the holy ground of a two-sided commerce between God and man"?[33]

Our previous discussion of the object of faith is helpful to illuminate the case here. The question is on the quality of faith and as such, it is related to its object. In other words, the quality of faith is determined by its object. In this scenario, Smith's paradigm does not work at all. Even if we grant that the transcendent is taken as the object of Smith's faith, still it would not satisfy Hogg's inquiry. In Hogg's question, the object that determines such a quality of faith is not any god or gods, but the Christian God, the God who reveals himself in Christ. The real question then is: Can we say that this God whom Christians know through Christ also reveals himself in the religious life, or the faith, of non-Christian religions?

Hogg's answer is affirmative. For him, non-Christian religions are not simply of human product. Based on his experience as a missionary, he was sure that divine revelation is also present in other religions. It is at this point that Hogg finds Kraemer's answer unsatisfactory. Hogg acknowledges that although at times Kraemer wants to maintain a dialectical character

---

31. Hogg, "Christian Attitude," 96.

32. The quotation is taken from Kraemer, *Christian Message*, 111. The accuracy of Hogg's interpretation on Kraemer will be dealt with later in our discussion.

33. Hogg, "Christian Attitude," 94–95.

of non-Christian religions, the overall tone of Kraemer's approach to non-Christian religions is negative.[34] Hogg's fundamental reservation is Kraemer's unwillingness to affirm fully and positively God's revelation in non-Christian religions. For Hogg, every religion is based on divine revelation. "Is not every religion," he rhetorically asks, "found on what is, in some sense, revelation . . . Divine effort of self-disclosure?"[35]

Furthermore, Hogg cannot concur with Kraemer's distinction between the form and content of a revelation. According to Hogg, Kraemer has attempted to make a distinction between revelation and its content, namely, the ideas, concepts, and experiences that are derived from it. However, Hogg contends that such a distinction is too "elusive" to handle. Unless one takes revelation as the communication of divine truths and ideas (a notion which both Hogg and Kraemer do not embrace), Hogg thinks that it is impossible to separate between pure content of the revelation with one's human interpretation. To try to grasp the pure content of the revelation is "as vain as to hope to seize 'matter' without 'form.'" Hence, the content of revelation is always expressed in human fallible and imperfect ideas and concepts.[36] This implies that behind those imperfect ideas and concepts, God is still at work. Hogg asserts that

> what we Christians . . . regard as the unsound and misleading character of the religious and philosophical conceptions in which the founder of a non-Christian faith couched his message . . . does not require us to deny that a divine activity of self-revelation had any part in the creation of that message.[37]

In other words, a divine revelation cannot be disqualified by a distorted form with which the revelation is grasped. Instead, we need to carefully distinguish "pure fragments of divinely revealed truth" from those corrupted "doctrinal tenets of such religions."[38] Having said this, Hogg concludes that the continuity is found in *faith* not in *faiths* because God reveals himself in faith – both in the Christian faith and in non-Christian faith. Hogg emphatically says that

---

34. Hogg, 97.
35. Hogg, 98.
36. Hogg, 98–99.
37. Hogg, 99.
38. Hogg, 99.

whether to Christian faith or to non-Christian faith, God reveals *Himself*; He does not reveal ready-made truths about Himself. And the thought and language in which a man expresses to Himself or others his apprehension of that supernatural self-disclosure has to be human thought, human language – always defective, sometimes gravely distorting.[39]

Hogg's conviction of the existence of non-Christian faith is based on his personal experience. As a missionary, he acknowledges that he has "known and had fellowship with some from whom Christ was not absolute Lord and only Savior . . . and yet who manifestly were no strangers to the life 'hid in God.'"[40] Many missionaries, he adds, could testify the same story as he had. Yet, this conviction of non-Christian faith is not simply an intellectual exercise. It has an important implication. It opens up a possibility for non-Christians to have a true and real relationship with God apart from faith in Jesus Christ. Or, more explicitly, there is a possibility of salvation outside the revelation in Jesus Christ.

Hogg is convinced that God is the Father who is always willing to save his children. In Hogg's words, "Almighty God is the kind of Father who longs to make of His human children little comrades and is ever taking the initiative toward that end."[41] God "is so great as to have room for" those who don't have mature knowledge of him. Yet, lacking such knowledge, God could still have a real fellowship with them as a human parent can have real communion with their infants. Still, Hogg acknowledges, the Bible teaches that faith is a "necessary condition" for human beings to come to God. But, he continues, "in a world that is full of enigmas, this belief [in God] can often be difficult." The enigmas of life may cloud our vision of God. When this happens, there has to be "a new point of view," namely, a "doctrinal concept that will, by resolving or evading the enigma, restore some experience of His radiance."[42] In other words, Hogg argues that our doctrines have to be flexible enough to accommodate the varieties of life experiences. The circumstances before and

---

39. Hogg, 99–100.
40. Hogg, 101.
41. Hogg, 107.
42. Hogg, 113.

after our experience with Christ require two different sets of belief.[43] Hogg's analogy of a sleep walker is helpful to illustrate his case here. Hogg states that

> A sleep-walker may safely cross a chasm by the narrowest of shaking planks. He is too absorbed in his dream to realize the full threat of the gulf beneath. But let him wake and he will fall. Now in soul and conscience men are prone to be as inappreciative as the sleep-walker of the abysses they think to pass. And so it may befall that, by narrowest and crookedest of doctrinal bridges, they win across the gulf of doubt to that trustful and obedient faith which the Father loves to reward. But when once Christ has stirred them to wakeful perception of the engulfing depths that divide the guilty conscience from trust in God's liberty and readiness to forgive, then by no other bridge than His Cross can they win again "to joy and peace in believing."[44]

With this, Hogg proposes a possibility of gaining salvation through other means before one meets personally with the gospel of Christ. He explains as follows:

> Where Christ has not yet been spiritually apprehended, there may be other ways than He to the trust in God which enables our Heavenly Father to bestow on a man some measure of communion with Himself. But when Christ succeeds in unveiling for any man the judgment of God on sin, in this very act He cannot help making Himself, for that man, the one and only way. Christ is the only way to God that can remain permanently a thoroughfare.[45]

To summarize, Hogg criticizes Kraemer for his failure to affirm God's revelation in other religions. This failure happens because Kraemer does not make the following distinctions: first, between the occurrence and content of revelation, and second, between faith and faiths. According to Hogg, with the distinction between occurrence and content of revelation, one can confirm God's revelation in other religions without jeopardizing the uniqueness of

---

43. Hogg, 113.
44. Hogg, 114.
45. Hogg, 114.

Christ. What makes Christianity different from other religions is not the occurrence of revelation, but the content of revelation, namely, the incarnation of Christ. Furthermore, with the distinction between faith and faiths, Hogg is able to maintain the discontinuity between Christianity and other religions, and at the same time to maintain the continuity between them. Christianity and other religions differ in terms of their faiths, but they are similar in term of their faith. For Hogg, "Christian and non-Christian *faith* ... cannot ... be wholly 'incommensurable.'"[46]

Hogg sees that Kraemer's problem lies in his conception of revelation, which he perceives as too narrow, due to the influence of Barthian theology. As a result, it is not able to acknowledge the divine revelation in non-Christian faith. To recognize the presence of God's activity in other faiths is never contradictory to the commitment to the uniqueness of the revelation in Christ if one differentiates occurrence of revelation from its content, which Kraemer fails again to do. Finally, Hogg's pursuit of the existence of non-Christian faith has a profound implication to Christian mission, for it may open up a possibility of gaining salvation outside the special revelation in Jesus Christ.

4.2 Gavin D'Costa: "Karl Rahner's Anonymous Christians"

Gavin D'Costa (born 1958) is a Roman Catholic theologian. An Indian by descent, he was born in Kenya and moved to England in 1968. Since 1991, he has taught Catholic Theology in the University of Bristol, UK. D'Costa's critique of Kraemer's position is found in his early work *Theology and Religious Pluralism* published in 1986.[47] In this work, D'Costa utilized Alan Race's threefold typology – exclusivism, inclusivism, and pluralism – to present his case.[48] He positioned Kraemer's view as exclusivist, John Hick's as pluralist, and sided himself with Karl Rahner as inclusivist. Since then, D'Costa abandoned this typology. D'Costa contends that since both pluralism and inclusivism will eventually collapse into one or another type of exclusivist position, then the threefold typology is no longer a helpful category to label certain types of

---

46. Hogg, 100.
47. D'Costa, *Theology and Religious Pluralism*.
48. Race, *Christians and Religious Pluralism*.

theologies of religions.[49] As a consequence of the invalidation of the typology, D'Costa treats his view as a type of exclusivism. His position is, however, fundamentally unchanged. In other words, the exclusivist version of D'Costa still fits as the inclusivist in the threefold typology. As Veli-Matti Kärkkäinen points out, D'Costa remains a faithful follower of "the inclusivist theology of religions of Vatican II."[50] Thus, his criticism against Kraemer's position does not change with the abandonment of this threefold typology. In other words, the absence of particular labels affects neither his fundamental view nor the essence of his critiques of Kraemer's view.

That said, for the sake of consistent argument, we will still apply this threefold typology as presented in this work. With this clarification, we shall then proceed to see his critique.

The central issue which D'Costa attempted to deal with in this book is the possibility of salvation outside of Christianity. The issue is placed within two axioms: salvation is available only through Jesus Christ and God desires salvation for all mankind.[51] When one answers the question affirmatively, they need to face the challenge of the first axiom. If there is salvation outside Christianity, how could this happen without undermining the decisiveness of Christ's salvific work? Furthermore, they also need to deal with the question of the necessity of Christian mission. That is to say if there is salvation outside Christianity, what is Christian mission for? The negative answer, however, faces the challenge of the second axiom. If God wills for all to be saved, how could he restrict salvation within the sphere of Christianity? To put in another way, how could a loving God let those who have never heard the gospel enter into damnation? Also, how could we account for the religious experiences of other religions? Are they simply psychological or cultural phenomena? The challenge is therefore to find a theology of religions that could satisfy the demand posed by the two axioms. For D'Costa, pluralism and exclusivism fail to meet the demand. Pluralism cannot satisfy the first axiom. For pluralists, all religions could provide a means of gaining salvation. Christianity is simply one of many ways. Exclusivism, however, cannot satisfy the second axiom. By restricting salvation through Christ alone and with an

---

49. See D'Costa, "Impossibility of a Pluralist View," 223–232; *Meeting of Religions*, 22.
50. See Kärkkäinen, *Introduction to the Theology*, 216.
51. D'Costa, *Theology and Religious Pluralism*, 4.

explicit acknowledgment of faith in Christ, exclusivism negates God's salvific will for all nations. D'Costa, therefore, contends that the best option falls into the inclusivist camp. Inclusivism could affirm both axioms. It could do so by not requiring an explicit acknowledgment of faith in Christ. Now we turn to D'Costa's critiques of Kraemer's exclusivist position.

In the first place, D'Costa considers Kraemer's view from its phenomenological and theological aspects. In regard to the phenomenological aspect, Kraemer, unlike Barth, was knowledgeable about non-Christian religions. Kraemer's exclusivism rejects the superiority of Christianity and sees non-Christian religions as a mixture of noble and abject elements. In this regard, his position is much more nuanced than that of Barth. Theologically, in contrast to pluralism, Kraemer emphasizes salvation by the grace of God alone through Jesus Christ and takes Christian mission as an imperative task of the church. That said, contrary to common charges against exclusivists, Kraemer encourages "practical cooperation" with others and displays "an openness and willingness to learn from non-Christian religions." In conclusion, D'Costa admits that Kraemer "is more broadminded than some exclusivists."[52]

D'Costa, however, raised objections to Kraemer's view on the nature of religions. In the first place, Kraemer neglected the dynamicity of religion. D'Costa asserts that "Kraemer underestimates the dynamic and changing nature of religions because of his overemphasis on their [holistic] nature."[53] For example, Kraemer is mistaken to lump the *bhakti* traditions under the umbrella of Hinduism and regards them all as "fundamentally anthropocentric... *monistic, mystic*" religions.[54] Due to his "Christologically exclusivist starting point," he is "often insensitive" and disregard the possibility of "the principle of faith in grace alone" outside the sphere of Christianity as in the case of Shinran's Japanese Shin-Shu Amida religion.[55] For D'Costa, Kraemer's problem lies in "his reductive hermeneutic."[56]

In addition to disregarding the complexity of religions, as D'Costa points out, Kraemer does not pay attention enough to the discrepancy between

---

52. D'Costa, 54–58.
53. D'Costa, 62.
54. D'Costa, 62.
55. D'Costa, 63.
56. D'Costa, 63.

doctrines and practices of religions. In other words, it is possible that a religion may change when it is practiced or applied in a different context. D'Costa cites an example of Theravada Buddhism in Magala, Sri Lanka. Buddhism, as practiced in this place, has changed radically from its classical form.[57] Masatoshi Doi adds a similar point. Kraemer is mistaken in his judgment on Buddhism because it is based on dogmatic rather than on factual observation. Doi states that

> no good scholar in Buddhism would approve Kraemer's assertion that "the Bodhisattva-ideal is the apotheosis of anthropocentric self-assertion in the guise of a religion of grace and divine deliverance." This kind of dogmatic assertion betrays Kraemer's Biblical realism which is based upon the principle of factuality.[58]

According to Doi, it is necessary to maintain two principles: the factuality of revelation and that of religious phenomena. The first principle is based on faith, and the second on the scientific method. Still, Doi argues that the two principles need to go hand in hand. A Christian scholar is justified when they hold to faith as their starting point, but they cannot "distort the scientific factuality of religious phenomena." Doi charges that Kraemer has violated these principles by subjugating the second principle under the first principle. In other words, Kraemer's judgment of other religions is dictated by his faith rather than based on scientific analysis of religious phenomena. This is also D'Costa's complaint.

The second objection of D'Costa pertains to Kraemer's theological framework. D'Costa detects incoherency in Kraemer's thought. Kraemer maintains both the *sui generis* nature of Christ and openness to other religions. But, according to D'Costa, the two axioms are mutually exclusive. D'Costa says, "Kraemer's *exclusivist* Christological truth criterion is in serious conflict with his attempted phenomenological openness."[59] Kraemer has to deny any points of contact because of his emphasis on salvation in Christ alone. In other words, Kraemer's view on the first axiom (i.e. salvation through Christ alone) is mistaken, because his view is held "at the cost of the axiom of the

---

57. D'Costa, 60–64.
58. Doi, "From Tambaram," 142. Cf. Kraemer, *Christian Message*, 175.
59. D'Costa, *Theology and Religious Pluralism*, 64.

universal salvific will of God." This problem, D'Costa explains, is rooted in Kraemer's view of revelation. Kraemer maintains both the *sui generis* event of Christ's revelation and the notion that God is also working in nature, history, conscience and religious consciousness. For D'Costa, such assertions are contradictory.[60]

The charge is only plausible when one operates with a belief that the divine revelation is concomitant with divine grace. To admit the existence of divine revelation in other religions is, therefore, to be open to the possibility of salvation in them. To restrict salvation to the sphere of Christianity and to maintain divine working in other religions are therefore inconsistent. Operating with this belief, D'Costa contends that the test case is God's working in Israel's history. The question is how to count the nature of that revelation. Is it revelation or not? And if it is, is it adequate for salvation? D'Costa argues that exclusivists cannot deny that it is indeed a divine revelation, but they take it as inadequate for salvation. D'Costa contends that it is in this point, exclusivists have an internal tension. If Christ's revelation is the *sui generis* event, how can exclusivists justify their acceptance God's working in the history of Israel as revelation? If it is the divine revelation, how can they maintain salvation through explicit confession to Jesus Christ, for that revelation happened long before the coming of Christ?[61]

In addition to the above objections, D'Costa also points out that Kraemer, and other exclusivists, cannot satisfactorily deal with the following question being placed by pluralists. "Can we really accept that the God revealed in Christ, a loving of 'generous, unlimited Divine love,' has denied so many millions the means to salvation – through no fault of their own?" Kraemer never answers this question directly. According to the logic of his thought, one will assume that he will take an agnostic position. But, for D'Costa, Kraemer's assumed agnosticism in this matter is neither helpful for this pressing issue, nor is it adequate as it cannot square properly with the test case of God's working in the history of Israel.[62]

D'Costa's solution to overcome what he sees as deficiencies of pluralists and exclusivists is an inclusivist position, represented here by Rahner's position.

---

60. D'Costa, 64–65.
61. D'Costa, 66–67.
62. D'Costa, 68.

D'Costa summarizes Rahner's position as follow. First, Rahner affirms the absoluteness of both Christianity and Christ. Christianity is an absolute religion and demands others to join in. Yet, the affirmation of Christianity as an absolute religion is tempered with the sensitivity to "the fact that the Christian Gospel has not reached all people." Second, until the gospel reaches them, non-Christian religions are vehicles of God's "gratuitous gift on account of Christ." Here, Rahner takes very seriously the salvific will of God for all people. Third, in regard to Christian mission, non-Christians cannot be regarded as persons "deprived of salvific grace" for they have already been touched by divine grace, and therefore should be regarded as "anonymous Christians." The emphasis is on salvation through Christ alone even though without explicit confession of faith in him. The third confirms the necessity of Christian mission. Finally, the church is not a community of the redeemed elite as opposed to the unredeemed mass, but "a tangible sign of the faith, hope and love made visible, present and irresistible in Christ." This last point affirms the role and status of the church.[63]

In conclusion, D'Costa sees that Kraemer's view cannot affirm revelation in other religions, and as such entails its denial of the possibility of salvation outside the sphere of Christianity. The problem lies in Kraemer's *sui generis* nature of the revelation in Christ. In the end, it is Kraemer's "narrow Christological understanding" that causes him to neglect "the fatherly love of God."[64] D'Costa points out that in contrast to pluralists, exclusivists are right to maintain Christ as the criterion to evaluate other religions. But this criterion cannot be applied narrowly as in the position presented by Kraemer. The solution offered is an inclusivist position, which, D'Costa argues, maintains the two axioms properly.

4.3 M. M. Thomas: "New Humanity of Christ"

Madathilparampil Mammen Thomas (1916–1996) was an Indian lay theologian and a world ecumenical leader. He was raised in the Mar Thoma Syrian Church and, as he testified, went through "an evangelical spiritual experience"

---

63. D'Costa, 84–89.
64. D'Costa, 73.

in his college years.⁶⁵ A natural activist, he became involved in various kinds of activism and movements throughout his life – freedom fighter in support of Mahatma Gandhi in the 1930s, student movement in the 1940s, and Governor of Nagaland for a short period (1990–1992). His interest in religious studies, mission, and churches was channeled through The Christian Institute for the Study of Religion and Society, an organization he cofounded with Paul Devanandan in Bangalore in 1956, and through decades of involvement with the World Council of Churches (1953–1975).⁶⁶ This rather detailed background of Thomas will help to give us insights to the nature of his critiques of Kraemer's theology.

Thomas knew Kraemer personally. He acknowledged his indebtedness to Kraemer for his spiritual life and theology.⁶⁷ Here is what Thomas says of the benefits of reading Kraemer's work:

> I had read Kraemer's *Christian Message in a Non-Christian World* while in India, and it had opened up for me a whole new vista of the theology of Biblical Realism, initiated by Karl Barth and Emil Brunner. Besides confirming my faith in Jesus Christ as the one and only Saviour, its insight into the reality of the tragedy of self-righteousness at the core of all religions and all struggles for human values became part of my religious and social philosophy.⁶⁸

Unlike Hogg and D'Costa who operated with rather different theological frameworks in their arguments against Kraemer, Thomas was initially a follower of Kraemer. Later he was dissatisfied with Kraemer's thought and sought to establish a "post-Kraemer theology," namely, "a position which accepts the substance of the main emphasis of Kraemer but seeks to go beyond it."⁶⁹ In this section, I will deal with what Thomas considers as the substance of

---

65. See Thomas, "My Pilgrimage," 28–31.

66. For a short biography and legacy of M. M. Thomas see Joseph, "M. M. Thomas," 666–667.

67. Damayanthi Niles contends that Thomas's theology was heavily shaped by Reformed thought and neo-Orthodoxy, and due to his closeness in following Kraemer's theology, he was unable to free himself from it. See Niles, *Worshipping at the Feet*, xxiii, 34–39.

68. Thomas, "Rewarding Correspondence," 5. See Thomas's correspondence with Kraemer in Thomas, *Some Theological Dialogues*, 22–23. The correspondence itself was dated from 1961 to 1963.

69. Thomas, *Some Theological Dialogues*, 31; "Absoluteness of Jesus Christ," 134.

Kraemer's thought, what he considers as Kraemer's deficiency, and his own proposal to overcome that deficiency.

In his essay presented in the fiftieth anniversary of Tambaram Conference, Thomas points out that a corrective theology has a tendency to be one-sided. Thomas says, "Theological emphases of ecumenical conferences are always correctives of existing one-sided theologies and tend themselves to be one-sided."[70] According to Thomas, this also applies to Kramer's thought. Thomas appreciates Kraemer's emphasis on the transcendence of the divine revelation in Christ over western Christianity. Such transcendence "makes Asian and African incarnations of Christianity not only legitimate but also imperative."[71] He was also sure that Kraemer was an adaptationist. Adaptation is a process by which all forms of Christianity, including western Christianity, go through "incarnations," namely, being radically transformed by the power of the gospel. In other words, "the total person with his/her culture and religion . . . is to undergo conversion to Christ."[72] Up to this point, Thomas is in total agreement with Kraemer.

However, Thomas notices that the effect of Kraemer's theology is not in line with what he intended to convey. As a result, in spite of Kraemer's positioning himself as an adaptationist, it was anti-adaptationists who eventually got the upper hand among the missionary movement and younger churches. Thomas charges that the blame falls partly on Kraemer because of his one-sided theology. Here, we need to point out what Thomas considers as the ultimate and the penultimate matter. The ultimate matter is concerned about the truth in Christ and the penultimate matter the values of non-Christian religions and cultures. According to Thomas, Kraemer has emphasized the ultimate matter to the expense of the penultimate matter. Thomas writes, "Kraemer gives the impression in the book of separating the ultimate Truth from penultimate Values so absolutely that sharing in values appears to have no ultimate significance."[73]

Thomas brings up a matter that Indian theologians are deeply concerned with, namely, the relation of Christianity with other religions and cultures. For

---

70. Thomas, "Assessment of Tambaram's Contribution," 393.
71. Thomas, 394.
72. Thomas, 394.
73. Thomas, 395.

some of them, the interreligious relationship is so important that it is taken as a matter of life and death. One's relationship with God cannot be separated from their relationship with others. Here is how Pandippedi Chenchiah puts it:

> The Indian Christian's interest in the theme is not merely theological or intellectual. *To us in India the inter-relations of religions have become a matter of life and death.* We can have no peace here or hereafter and our nation can have no future till we find the key to the mystery. The Christian in India, and for this he may praise the Lord with a full heart, has yet no Church or theology, which he feels bound to defend and maintain. He still struggles with the Lord, seeking to understand the why and where-fore of Him. *He still feels he can never understand Jesus till he understands the drama of God's dealing with man in and through the other religions of the world.*[74]

Thomas does not go as far as Chenchiah does. He does not place interreligious relationship as "a matter of life and death." Nor does he say that Christians cannot understand their faith without relating it with other religions. For Thomas, relationship with other religions and cultures remains as a penultimate matter, subordinate to the ultimate truth in Christ. Pertaining to the ultimate, Thomas is solidly with Kraemer. Yet, the penultimate matter is not insignificant. Here, we need to consider the context in which Thomas's theology was set, namely, post-colonial India. In this context, Christians and other adherents of religions were called to participate in nation building. Here, Christians faced not only social change but also the renascence of non-Christian religions. Thomas contends that Christians need a theology which fits this context. They need a "theology of nation-building." This theology needs to strive for "a pluralistic consciousness," namely, an "awareness of our common responsibility to a common historical human destiny."[75] Physical nearness among adherents of different religions, he explains, does not naturally create this pluralistic consciousness. People of different religious backgrounds will have "a common language of discourse at spiritual depth," when they "begin

---

74. Chenchiah, "Christian Message," 144, emphasis added.
75. Thomas, "Christology," 106.

to respond together to the challenge of the common struggle for nationhood and nation-building."[76] It is for this reason that Thomas sees the need to pay attention to the penultimate matter. For Thomas, Kraemer has neglected this penultimate matter because of his overemphasis on the ultimate matter.

According to Thomas, Kraemer's one-sided theology is manifest in two ways: first, "[Kraemer's] opposition to the Jerusalem 1928 call to Asian Christians to a life of 'sharing' with non-Christians in values," and, second, "his concentration on the dangers of syncretism."[77] The latter is particularly acute, because with his definition of syncretism as "illegitimate mingling of religious elements,"[78] Kraemer gives "a purely negative theological meaning" to the term. Consequently, it creates "fear rather than courage for interfaith relations."[79] Kraemer's emphasis on the danger of syncretism has created a double-edged sword effect. Positively, it helps to keep the purity of the gospel. Negatively, it hinders Christians from practicing necessary adaptation. Thomas says, "Kraemer was quite right to show the red light to the heavy traffic across religious boundaries going in wrong directions, but the red light never changed to green in any direction so that there was practical cessation of all traffic for a long long time."[80] As a result, his thought hinders courageous experiments to create "the Asian incarnation of Christianity" and solidifies "the established syncretism of Western and denominational Christianity."[81] This is the deficiency Thomas sees in Kraemer's theological framework.

Thomas's own proposal to overcome this deficiency is to give a proper place for human values by reconnecting them with the truth in Christ. Thomas explains, "Human values do become idolatrous and tragic precisely when they are disconnected from an encounter with Christ the Truth."[82] The disconnection between the truth and the values not only makes the values to be idolatrous, but it also turns the truth to be "a most 'invidious [sic] form of syncretism.'"[83] Thomas acknowledges that Christ as the ultimate truth is

---

76. Thomas, 106.
77. Thomas, "Assessment of Tambaram's Contribution," 395.
78. Cf. Kraemer, *Christian Message*, 203.
79. Thomas, "Assessment of Tambaram's Contribution," 395.
80. Here, Thomas is quoting Newbigin. See Thomas, "Absoluteness of Jesus Christ," 135.
81. Thomas, "Absoluteness of Jesus Christ," 135.
82. Thomas, "Assessment of Tambaram's Contribution," 396.
83. Thomas, 396.

transcendent. The eternal Logos is ahistorical. But this transcendent truth has taken "form in the realm of spiritual, ideological and cultural values."[84] In other words, the eternal Logos has become incarnated Logos. The word has become flesh. The truth has connected with human values. To disconnect the truth from human values is a form of syncretism because it is not in line with the truth presented in the Scriptures. For this reason, the connection between truth and values is necessary. In addition to this, human values need "redemption and renewal in Christ."[85] Here, Thomas opens up a possibility of Christ redeeming non-Christian values. With this, he argues that syncretism is not inherently negative and proposes what he calls "Christ-centered Syncretism."

First, Thomas's approach is to focus on Christology, particularly on the humanity of Christ. He points out that the gospel "is from God and should ever remain in the Christ of God," but it is also "for the human person."[86] Hence, Christology should not be in opposition to anthropology. This is especially true in terms of "new anthropology." The term certainly needs a fuller explanation which will be discussed below.

Thomas does not oppose Kraemer's view of a radical difference between the revelation in Christ and non-Christian religions. That said, Thomas cannot concur with Kraemer's negative response to a possibility of the knowledge of Christ in other religions. Kraemer has missed the point, Thomas charges, because he does not count non-Christian religions in their renascent forms. Here, Thomas is in agreement with D'Costa that religions are dynamic and changing, but he adds that the changes happen "under the stimulus of Christianity and Western secular humanism."[87] As such it also includes "a radical attempt on their part to 'convert' Christian religious elements and human values into their own system."[88] Hence, the change occurs in both forms and content, or to use Hogg's terms, in both their *faiths* and *faith*. As a result, they are "no more a totality integrated with their monistic spiritual center."[89] Hence, Thomas concludes that in today's pluralistic world in which sharing ideas between religious communities is inevitable, "no religion or ideology

---

84. Thomas, 396.
85. Thomas, 396.
86. Thomas, "Absoluteness of Jesus Christ," 136.
87. Thomas, 137.
88. Thomas, 137.
89. Thomas, 136.

today is wholly [holistic] or monolithic."[90] Kraemer's holistic character of religions is no longer valid, or at least it needs qualification.

Second, Thomas points out that in this modern world where there is so much "interpenetration and intermingling" syncretism is inevitable. He says, "every religion must accept a good deal of unprincipled mixture and elements from various religions and secular faiths."[91] Syncretism is not only inevitable, but it is also legitimate so long as it leads to adaptation according to Christian principles. Thomas asserts, "In this sense the unintegrated mixtures of religious, ideological and cultural elements, which Kraemer calls syncretistic, are inevitable; they are legitimate for the Christian and the church so long as they are not seen as a goal in themselves but indicate a movement towards a new integration or adaption based on Christian fundamentals."[92]

Thomas contends that we do not have pure Christianity in the present time. Christianity in its pure sense remains an eschatological reality. In the present time, "all Christians are pagan in parts." But it does not matter, because these syncretistic elements do not make us un-Christian. Instead, what makes us Christian is our decision for Christ.[93] In other words, our identity as Christians does not depend on those pagan elements which saturate our belief, but the central decision for Christ is the decisive factor.

Positive engagement with non-Christian religions and secular faiths in this concept of Christ-centered syncretism is based on Thomas's eschatological Christology. Thomas argues that the renascence of non-Christian religions evidences that Christ is working in other religions and that he "is breaking down the wall of partition between Christians and others even as Christ destroyed the wall of partition between Jews and Gentiles."[94] Utilizing Barth's neo-orthodoxy framework, Thomas argues that religions, which Barth considers as unbelief, are possible to be redeemed and sanctified in Christ. Christ has the power to change religions. As such, it is not only applicable to the religion of Christianity, but also to all religions.[95] This possibility will become reality in the eschaton, namely, in the new humanity in Christ. Indeed, in

---

90. Thomas, 137.
91. Thomas, 137.
92. Thomas, 137.
93. Thomas, 137.
94. Thomas, 137.
95. Thomas, 138.

the end, religions will be fulfilled and abrogated in Christ. The abolition of religion as Barth says will eventually be realized in the end.[96] At the present time, we are living in its partial realization of that new reality.

The response that should be taken by Christians today is to have interreligious dialogue in the hope that all will be caught up by the new humanity of Christ and be changed by it. Thomas explains, as follow:

> Therefore the only path open for us is . . . to be involved in religion with the hope of its abolition in Christ always present. It means a theological relativisation of all religions in the name of the Grace of God in Jesus Christ. That is, people are "already" released from the absolute claims of religions and quasi-religions, in so far as they are caught up in the New Humanity of Christ through implicit or explicit faith; in being opened to the judgment of God at the Cross, they become increasingly receptive to the power of the Risen Christ and His humanity, and to entering into dialogue with other religions within the context of a concern for "human" fellowship.[97]

The relation between Christianity and other religions is based on the new humanity of Christ in which all religions will be reconciled. In this scheme, Christ and Christianity are sharply differentiated. The latter together with all religions will be abrogated and reconciled in Christ. With this Thomas affirms the possibility of the knowledge of Christ in other religions and redemption of Christ in them. He explains as follows:

> If Jesus Christ transcends the Christian religion, as its judge and redeemer, it opens up the possibility of Christ redeeming all religions and in-forming Himself in them. Herein we are acknowledging the theological validity of attempts at expressing the meaning of the Cross in terms of the indigenous religious traditions other than Christian, and in that process renewing the indigenous traditions themselves to become the vehicle of Christ and His divine humanity.[98]

---

96. Thomas, *Man and the Universe*, 148.
97. Thomas, 149.
98. Thomas, 151.

In sum, Thomas agrees with Kraemer that the truth in Christ is the substance that needs to be kept. He, however, disagrees with Kraemer in regard to the penultimate matter. Thomas contends that Kraemer has neglected human values because of his overemphasis on the truth in Christ. Kraemer does so by overemphasizing the danger of syncretism. Thomas argues that Kraemer's theological framework is insufficient because it fails to take seriously the power of the new humanity of Christ. Thomas believes that the new humanity of Christ has the power to transform all religions. In the end, all will be absorbed into Christ. Since this power is already at work, then a positive attitude toward other religions is appropriate, for they are also "the vehicle of Christ and His divine humanity" and in them, he is also "informing Himself."[99] Christians should not then fear to interact with other religions, for syncretism is legitimate in so far as they are centered in Christ.

Summary

We have seen three critiques of Kraemer's position. The critics, in agreement with Kraemer, all see the importance of maintaining the uniqueness of Christ and the necessity of Christian mission. Their concerns are, however, on Kraemer's negative view of non-Christian religions, which are rooted in his concept of revelation, salvation, and religion.

Kraemer's concept of revelation, they argue, is narrow and centered in the person of Christ. With this Christocentric revelation, Kraemer fails to affirm divine revelation in other religions and salvation in and through other religions. Pertaining to both aspects – revelation and salvation – the critics are basically in agreement, namely, they all argue against Kraemer. All affirm that non-Christian religions are to a certain extent embedded in the divine revelation of God, yet this acknowledgment would not put the uniqueness of Christ's revelation at risk. Even though different in their forms and solutions, they all agree that salvation is available outside the sphere of Christianity.

In respect to Kraemer's holistic character of religions, however, the critics are not of one voice. Hogg is in agreement with Kraemer, but both D'Costa and Thomas are against it, arguing that Kraemer fails to account for the dynamic and changing nature of religions. In regard to Kraemer's emphasis on

---

99. Thomas, 151.

the danger of syncretism, they have different opinions as well. Hogg sees that Kraemer's warning about syncretism is helpful. Thomas, however, sees that warning as a hindrance for younger churches to experiment with adaptations so as to create indigenous churches in Asia.

The solutions offered involve several strategies. The first one is to enlarge the scope of divine revelation outside the sphere of Christianity. One cannot treat non-Christian religions as simply human products. The experiences of missionaries as they encountered the religious life of non-Christian religions tend to confirm the divine work in them. However, this strategy leads to a question of the uniqueness of Christ's revelation. How could it be unique if revelation is found anywhere and anytime?

Hogg's answer is to distinguish between form and content, faiths and faith. This is the second strategy they employed. This distinction is indeed an important contribution of Hogg in this discussion. Both D'Costa and Thomas, to a certain extent, also apply this distinction in their theological framework. Although all locate the important aspect of faith or the content of religions, they do not concur with the importance of the forms. Hogg and D'Costa maintain the importance of the form of Christian faith. Christianity as a religion is therefore absolute. And this demands conversion of other religions into the Christian religion. For Kraemer, Christianity as a religion is certainly not absolute. But the form is still important and syncretism, therefore, needs to be avoided. Thomas, however, presses further than Kraemer; he considers syncretism to be legitimate as long as it centers in Christ. Thomas even sees the redemption of religions in Christ in the eschaton. In this point, Thomas is close to Smith's idea of the end of religion.

Finally, we come to the question of Christology. If salvation is found outside the sphere of Christianity, then how does it relate to the work of Christ? Hogg is rather obscure in this aspect. D'Costa provides the answer through Rahner's anonymous Christian. Those who are saved outside the visible body of Christ are saved through Christ who works within non-Christian religions. Thomas sees this happening in the eschaton when all are redeemed into the new humanity of Christ.

CHAPTER 5

Evaluations of Kraemer's Theology of Religions

In the previous chapter I have dealt with the critiques of Kraemer's theology of religions. I have shown that Kraemer's position received both positive and negative appraisals. Hogg, D'Costa, and Thomas both praise and criticize Kraemer's thought. In this chapter, I will analyze and evaluate those critiques. I will show that the objections raised by Kraemer's critics can be addressed sufficiently. However, some internal tensions remain and require further treatment.

5.1 Analysis of the Critiques

There are two paradigms that are useful for our analysis of the critiques. First, I will utilize Kraemer's four theses. He argues that: the Christian revelation is absolutely *sui generis* (thesis 1); there is a radical discontinuity between the Christian revelation and non-Christian religions (thesis 2); the nature of religions is universal, particular, dialectical, and holistic (thesis 3); and finally, the Christian attitude toward non-Christian religions is evangelistic but not syncretistic, and tolerant but not timid (thesis 4). In addition, I will also utilize Thomas's distinction of the ultimate and the penultimate matter. For Kraemer, the ultimate matter is the uniqueness of Christianity and the necessity of the Christian mission in its traditional sense. The penultimate pertains to the relationship between Christianity and non-Christian religions. With these two paradigms, I will now analyze the critiques given by Hogg, D'Costa, and Thomas.

We begin with Thomas's distinction of the ultimate and the penultimate matter. Here, we see that Hogg, D'Costa, and Thomas generally agree with Kraemer in regard to the ultimate matter. They all maintain the uniqueness of Christianity and the necessity of the Christian mission in its traditional sense. Yet, some qualifications are necessary here. First, they understand differently the uniqueness of Christianity. In the previous discussion, I have said that the uniqueness of Christianity can be understood in three senses: (1) distinct from others, (2) superior to others, and (3) wholly other. Kraemer adopts the third sense. Yet, this is said only relatively. Its uniqueness is due to its special relationship with the Christian revelation. It is the Christian revelation that is absolutely *sui generis* or wholly other. Hogg, D'Costa, and Thomas, however, adopt the second sense of uniqueness. Christianity is unique because it is superior to other religions.

Pertaining to the penultimate matter, however, the critics disagree with Kraemer. They argue that Kraemer's position does not provide a favorable ground to foster the relationship between Christianity and other religions. Having said that, they differ in regard to what they see as Kraemer's deficiencies. Here, I will analyze their objections according to Kraemer's four theses.

Hogg accepts all of Kraemer's theses except the second one. He particularly likes Kraemer's holistic view of religions (thesis 3) and appreciates his warning of the danger of syncretism (thesis 4). But he cannot agree with Kraemer's radical discontinuity view (thesis 2). Yet, this still requires a qualification. Hogg rejects Farquhar's fulfillment theology. In other words, he cannot accept either a radical continuity position or a radical discontinuity position. Instead, he maintains a both-and position. That is to say, there is both continuity and discontinuity between Christianity and other religions.

D'Costa, however, sees Kraemer's problems lying in his first and third thesis. According to D'Costa, Kraemer's *sui generis* character of the Christian revelation (thesis 1) contradicts his openness to other religions and cultures (thesis 4). For D'Costa, the blame lies in thesis 1. It is mistaken to take the divine revelation as absolutely *sui generis*. Such a narrow concept cannot fit with a broadminded attitude toward others. In addition, D'Costa also has a problem with Kraemer's holistic view of religions (thesis 3). He sees this as too rigid. It fails to account for the dynamicity of religions.

Finally, the biggest problem Thomas has with Kraemer's position is on Kraemer's view of syncretism (thesis 4). Due to Kraemer's one-sided theology, syncretism is overemphasized. Consequently, adaptation is neglected. Kraemer's position is therefore charged to be anti-cultures. Thomas also supports D'Costa's opinion that Kraemer's holistic view of religions is too rigid (thesis 3).

We see that the critics were able to locate deficiencies in all of Kraemer's four theses. I summarize their objections in accordance with Kraemer's theses:

1. As a concept, the *sui generis* character of the Christian revelation is too narrow. As such it cannot square with his attempted openness to non-Christian religions. In other words, Kraemer has taken salvation in Christ alone at the expense of God's universal salvific will.
2. It is mistaken to maintain a radical discontinuity between the Christian revelation and non-Christian religions. Some sorts of continuity must exist between them.
3. The holistic view of religions is too rigid as it fails to account for the dynamicity and changes of religions.
4. The danger of syncretism is overemphasized to the point that it hinders the practice of adaptation. As a result, Kraemer's theological framework is insufficient to deal with the penultimate matter.

In the following section, I will examine those critiques and deal with their objections accordingly.

5.2 Examination of Thesis 1: *Sui Generis* Character of the Gospel

In thesis 1, Kraemer maintains that the Christian revelation is absolutely *sui generis*. With this thesis, he argues for the uniqueness of Christ as the only way to God. Salvation is therefore through Christ alone. D'Costa agrees that salvation belongs to Christ alone, but disagrees that the Christian revelation is *sui generis*. For D'Costa, the *sui generis* character of revelation is incoherent with the openness to other religions. Kraemer maintains both the *sui generis* character of the Christian revelation and God's revelation in nature, conscience, and human religious consciousness. D'Costa argues that these two positions cannot hold together. In the end, Kraemer has to sacrifice the latter.

Or, to say this differently, Kraemer's position requires an explicit expression of faith in Christ. For D'Costa, this narrow Christology is inconsistent with the universal salvific will of God. Salvation through Christ alone is safeguarded to the expense of God's universal salvific will.

D'Costa uses Israel as the test case. The question, he explains, is how to consider the divine work in the people of Israel. Is it a revelation? If it is, then is it adequate for salvation? D'Costa contends that the exclusivists, including here Kraemer, will acknowledge that there is revelation outside Jesus Christ, but it is inadequate for salvation. But, according to D'Costa, this creates a contradiction. If there is revelation outside Jesus Christ, then the revelation in Jesus Christ cannot be *sui generis*. If the divine work in the people of Israel is accepted as revelation, then how can it be said that salvation requires an explicit confession of faith in Jesus Christ? If salvation requires an explicit confession in Jesus Christ, then how about those who have not heard the gospel? How could we fathom that "God . . ., a loving father of 'generous, unlimited Divine love,' has denied so many millions the means to salvation – through no fault of their own?"[1] D'Costa contends that Kraemer's agnostic position in dealing with this issue is neither helpful nor adequate to answer this urgent question.

Hence, D'Costa argues that the *sui generis* character of the divine revelation is inadequate because, first, it contradicts with God's revelation in nature, conscience, and religious consciousness; and, second, it cannot provide an answer for the salvation of those who have never heard the good news of Jesus Christ.

To deal with D'Costa's objection I will first consider Tim Perry's response. Perry argues that the success of D'Costa charge is dependent on how one understands the term *sui generis* as it is applied to the Christ event. For D'Costa, the term *sui generis* is used to mean "both that the revelation in Christ is the only revelation and that salvation is possible only by responding in faith to this revelation."[2] If this meaning is correct, then the charge is justified. But this is not what Kraemer means by it. Instead, Perry continues, the term is used "to emphasize that a properly Christian evaluation of other religions takes

---

1. D'Costa, *Theology and Religious Pluralism*, 66–67.
2. Perry, *Radical Difference*, 99.

as its ultimate criterion the revelation in Christ."[3] In other words, the term refers to the revelation in Christ as the sole criterion of judgment, not as the only revelation. Hence, it is not contradictory to maintain both the *sui generis* character of the Christian revelation and God's revelation outside Christ.

Next, Perry also contends that the affirmation of God's general revelation is not in conflict with Kraemer's discontinuity position. In other words, maintaining discontinuity between the Christian revelation in Christ (or the gospel) and non-Christian religions does not contradict with the affirmation of continuity between God's (general) revelation and non-Christian religions. In short, Kraemer maintains both continuity and discontinuity between the divine revelation and non-Christian religions. As such it can be explained from Kraemer's concept of "subversive fulfillment."[4] The fulfillment theology argues that there is continuity between non-Christian religions and the gospel, with the former serving as "a schoolmaster to Christ." Kraemer rejects this idea of fulfillment. Instead, he speaks of "contradictive or subversive fulfillment." By this, he means that "Christ may *in a certain sense* be called the fulfillment of some deep and persistent longings and apprehensions" of non-Christian religions, but "when we subject the facts to a close scrutiny," Christ's fulfillment "never represents the perfecting of what has been before."[5] In other words, Christ, in fulfilling their religious longings and expectations, at the same time also contradicts them.[6] Hence, there exists continuity and discontinuity at the same time.

Furthermore, according to Perry, Kraemer's agnostic position in regard to the salvation of those who have never heard the gospel is justified. D'Costa has charged that this position is "painfully inadequate," especially when one uses the revelation to the Jews as the test case. For Perry, with this statement, D'Costa implies that "God's covenant with Israel is a [test]-case for all non-Christian or pre-Christian religions." In other words, D'Costa regards the Jewish people on par with adherents of other religions. Consequently, the divine actions and promises toward the Jews can more or less be applied to them. Yet, this cannot be true. As also for Kraemer, the Jews stand in a unique

---

3. Perry, 99.
4. Perry, 100.
5. Kraemer, "Continuity or Discontinuity," 2–5.
6. Kraemer, 2–5.

relationship with Christ. Hence, "the religion of and revelation to Israel was and remains an important part of the world of Kraemer's biblical realism." In other words, the Jewish people cannot be treated in the same position as adherents of other religions. As such, Perry concludes that "D'Costa's use of Israel and the Old Testament as a salvific test case can be questioned."[7]

Having answered the Jewish question, Perry also maintains that to remain agnostic about the fate of those who have never heard the gospel is not "tantamount to being skeptical about the eternal destiny of the many faithful people listed in Hebrew 11." Again, since religions have proposed their own versions of salvation and way(s) to attain it, then refraining from judgment upon the fate of their adherents is a wise and cautious way to take. Finally, given an eschatological hope that there will be the restoration of all creation and humanity, it is also wise not to deny in advance their destiny. In the final analysis, salvation belongs to the mysterious work of the Spirit. We cannot speculate about how the Spirit works. With these arguments, Perry finds justification of Kraemer's agnostic position.[8]

Hence, in defense of Kraemer's position, Perry maintains that: first, the term *sui generis* does not entail that there is only one revelation; second, Kraemer's discontinuity position does not contradict God's general revelation, because, with the idea of subversive fulfillment, Kraemer indeed maintains both discontinuity and continuity; and finally, Kraemer's agnostic position is justified because it does not explicitly deny salvation to those who have never heard the gospel, but leaves it to the work of the Spirit.

Perry has rightly answered D'Costa's objections. Still, some points can be added here. First, the *sui generis* character of the Christian revelation is consistent with the affirmation of general revelation, when one makes a clear distinction between revelation and salvation. D'Costa's charge is only true when revelation and salvation are taken as a concomitant. With this notion, to affirm a revelation outside Christ also means to affirm a possibility of salvation outside him. As such, one cannot affirm God's general revelation without violating the *sui generis* character of the Christian revelation. One cannot hold that there is salvation in Christ alone and that there are other means of salvation. Yet, should this be the only way of interpreting the divine

---

7. Perry, *Radical Difference*, 101.
8. Perry, 101–102.

revelation outside Christ? Or, does revelation exist concomitantly with divine grace? Does revelation always entail salvation? D'Costa assumes that it does. I, however, disagree with D'Costa. As Kraemer noted, the Jews have received much of the divine revelation and yet, somehow, they still rejected God. So, the Bible testifies that Jews are not saved simply by being receivers of God's revelation. From this, we can say that revelation does not always entail salvation. The two need to be distinguished clearly.

Second, I contend that an agnostic position on the fate of those who have never heard the gospel is not only justified but also theologically wise. A Christian theologian shall refrain from dealing with a matter that is hidden from them. Kraemer does not directly deal with the question about the fate of those who have never heard the gospel. Yet, in his essay "Continuity or Discontinuity," we may find the direction which he intends to go in regard to this matter. Here, Kraemer maintains that his rejection of natural theology does not include "denying that God has been working in the minds of men outside the sphere of the Christian revelation," and, he adds that, "there have been, and may be now, acceptable men of faith who live under the sway of non-Christian religions." But he quickly clarifies that they are "products, however, not of these non-Christian religions but of the mysterious workings of God's Spirit."[9] It is clear from this assertion that Kraemer does not categorically deny the possibility of salvation of those who do not have explicit faith in Christ. But, if there is salvation such as this, it is never by way of non-Christian religions, but of the work of the Spirit. Still, he further clarifies, "God forbid that we mortal men should be so irreverent as to dispose of how and where the Sovereign God of grace and love has to act."[10] Kraemer is saying that one should refrain from passing judgment upon the fate of those who have never heard the gospel, simply because we cannot touch this area without being irreverent to the Sovereign God. Such an attitude is never one's failure to meet their "theological duty" as Hans Küng implies in his critique of this agnostic position.[11] Indeed, a Christian theologian has a double duty, namely,

---

9. Kraemer, "Continuity or Discontinuity," 4.

10. Kraemer, 4.

11. In regard to salvation outside the church, Hans Küng launches his critique of those who hold the agnostic position. He contends that "nor can the whole problem as a whole be dismissed – as it is by other Protestant theologians [particularly mentioned here are Luther, Barth, Bonhoeffer, Gogarten, Brunner, and Kraemer] – with a supercilious 'we don't know,' as

to refrain from "the secret things [that] belong to the LORD our God," and to study and explain "the things revealed [that] belong to us" (Deut 29:29). As the apostle Peter says, we are obliged "to give an answer to everyone who asks you," but not for every question, but that pertaining to "the hope that you have" (1 Pet 3:15). Or, as Newbigin puts it, "To refuse to answer the question which our Lord himself refused to answer (Luke 13:23–30) is not 'supercilious'; it is simply honest."[12]

In conclusion, D'Costa's objection to Kraemer's *sui generis* character of the Christian revelation cannot be substantiated. This character is not inconsistent with God's general revelation. Kraemer's agnostic position is not only biblically justified but also theologically wise.

5.3 Examination of Thesis 2: Radical Discontinuity

In thesis 2 Kraemer maintains that there is a radical discontinuity between the Christian revelation and non-Christian religions. The objection raised against this thesis particularly comes from Hogg. I summarize Hogg's argument as follows. Hogg disagrees with Kraemer's radical discontinuity. He maintains that some sorts of continuity must exist between Christianity and non-Christian religions. To provide a solution, Hogg makes two types of distinctions: first, between faith and beliefs; and second, between occurrence and content of revelation. With the distinction between faith and beliefs, Hogg argues for both continuity and discontinuity. Discontinuity occurs in terms of their beliefs; whereas continuity in terms of their faith. With this Hogg argues that although non-Christian religions differ from Christianity in terms of their beliefs, they share the same faith. The Christian faith and non-Christian faith respond to the same divine revelation. Yet, this continuity will not jeopardize the uniqueness of Christianity, because what makes Christianity different from other religions is not the occurrence of revelation but its content. That unique content of revelation is the incarnation of Jesus Christ.

---

if it were no concern of theirs. If Christian theologians have no answer to the question of the salvation of the greater part of mankind, they cannot be surprised when people react again as they have done in the past." See Küng, *On Being a Christian*, 99. Cf. Newbigin, *Open Secret*, 196.

12. Newbigin, *Open Secret*, 196.

To examine Hogg's critique, I will first give attention to Kraemer's own response. In addition, I will also consider answers provided by Lesslie Newbigin, M. M. Thomas, Origen V. Jathanna, James L. Cox, and Eric Sharpe who have made contributions to the debate on this point.[13]

Kraemer's response to Hogg's position is found in his *Religion and the Christian Faith*, published in 1956, almost two decades after the Tambaram Conference.[14] This gives Kraemer a lengthy period of time to reflect on his own position and adjust it accordingly. In the first place, Kraemer appreciates Hogg's contribution to this discussion. To Kraemer, Hogg's thought is "of rare religious sensitivity." Hogg also shows that he understands "the bewildering complexity of the problem."[15] Next, Kraemer made concessions in regard to Hogg's critique of his position. Kraemer humbly acknowledges the imperfectness of his position. The factual reality that governs the relationship between the divine revelation and non-Christian religions is much more complex than this continuity or discontinuity position could capture. In the end, he accepts that there has to be some sort of continuity. Indeed, he resorts to Hogg's paradoxical position. There is both continuity and discontinuity. I quote here Kraemer's explanation of his amended position.

> We have said that when examined from our standpoint the whole controversy of "continuity-discontinuity" becomes superfluous. In fact, therefore, the only reason we have to side so resolutely with "discontinuity" and argue for it, is that the "continuity" standpoint has so many able advocates, and that it is evidently so seductive!
>
> In the last resort, if we really take our direction from revelation, in the dynamic and concrete sense we have tried to explain, all these controversies about "*praeparatio evangelica*" or not, "fulfillment" or not, "continuity" or "discontinuity," appear as secondary, so that one finds oneself often in the factual situation of discovering (to take only one example) "continuity" and

---

13. Newbigin, "Christ and the World," 16–30; *Finality of Christ*, 35–40, 49–56; *Gospel*, 171–183; Thomas, "Review of *Karma*," 92–94; Jathanna, *Decisiveness of the Christ-Event*, 260–275; Cox, "Faith and Faiths," 241–256; "Development," 356–408; Sharpe, "Legacy of A. G. Hogg," 65–69.

14. Kraemer, *Religion and the Christian Faith*, 225–228.

15. Kraemer, 226.

> "discontinuity" at the same time in regard to the same complex of spiritual reality. This is paradoxical, but true! However, this can never be made into a theory or into a system, because everything depends on the amount of obedient openness to the revelation, without which this liberty in Christ can neither grow nor exist. We are, and remain always, people who belong to the category of the *theologia viatorum* (theology of pilgrims) and to that of the stumbling learners.[16]

Having said that, he disagrees with Hogg's solution. That is to say, Kraemer does not agree with Hogg that continuity is found in the non-Christian faith. He points out Hogg's problems as follows.

First, Kraemer contends that Hogg's approach is insufficient to deal with the question of truth. To illustrate this problem, Kraemer quotes Hogg's statement: "In India, for example, what of divine truth, and reality has, owing to the initiative of the self-revealing God, succeeded in shining through to Man is all inevitably stained by the medium of monistic tendency through which it has to break."[17] Kraemer contends that even though the observation given is correct, the question posed is "serious" and "thought-provoking," and the answers provided contain "partial truth," but as such the statement underlies the weaknesses of Hogg's overall approach. In the first place, the approach comes from "a too individualistic and purely psychological angle." It is basically a phenomenological approach which is based on "comparing God-experience with God-experience." Although this approach has a place in this study, it has its limit, for it cannot answer the question of truth.[18]

Next, Hogg's approach fails to consider the gravity of human sins. Kraemer maintains that even though Hogg is right about the monistic tendency in India, he "does not dig deep enough." What Hogg has missed is that he does not see what lies behind this tendency. Hogg does not consider human sins in it. Kraemer says this tendency is "not a regrettable side issue but the pride . . . of India."[19] For Kraemer, the monistic tendency is never neutral, but negative. It is indeed a sinful tendency, an aspect which Hogg has overlooked.

---

16. Kraemer, 352.
17. Kraemer, 226. The quotation is taken from Hogg, "Christian Attitude," 100.
18. Kraemer, 226–227.
19. Kraemer, 227.

Furthermore, Hogg's approach also fails to consider "the mystery of iniquity." That is to say, Hogg's approach is too simplistic to be able to consider the complexity of spiritual reality. Here, Kraemer questions Hogg's aim to propose the notion of continuity. Hogg hopes that by establishing a continuity there is a possibility of salvation outside the sphere of the Christian revelation. But Kraemer sees the futility of this scenario. To argue his case, Kraemer gives an example of the Jewish people. They have received the divine preparation more than any nation in the world. Yet, somehow, they still failed to recognize God in Christ.[20] Here lies the epitome of the mystery of human iniquity. Kraemer says,

> He does not raise the question of how to explain that the Jewish people, prepared as no other people to understand what is meant by the Messiah, the Kingdom of God, the Suffering Servant, etc., yet did not recognize God in Him, and rejected God's self-disclosure in Christ with as great a determination as Indians, who are (according to Hogg) unable to understand, by their training in Indian thinking, the Biblical account of God's eternal activity of redemption. In the light of such questions the mystery of iniquity, precisely in the "highest" expressions of the human mind, looms up.[21]

Newbigin notes the importance of Kraemer's point here. This example of the Jewish people shows that there is continuity, but salvation cannot be guaranteed simply by having the divine revelation. In other words, there is no direct link between revelation and salvation. Newbigin says,

> Whatever may be the relation between non-Christian and Christian experience of God, it cannot be described in terms of continuity alone. There certainly is continuity; but somewhere in the argument we have to find place for the tragic fact that it is precisely those who are nearest to God who may also be those who most bitterly reject God's revelation of himself in Jesus. This is not only a matter of the Jews; essentially the same thing

---

20. Kraemer, 227.
21. Kraemer, 227.

is often seen in the contact of the Gospel with the so-called higher religions.[22]

For Kraemer, Hogg's approach to continuity is too simplistic and fails to capture the mystery of God's grace. Hogg is mistaken to assume that revelation and salvation are always concomitant. Yet, God's saving grace does not work in this way. Indeed, it is only given solely by God through his sovereign election. Newbigin explains this principle. He says, "The unexamined assumption here is that God's efforts at self-disclosure must be directed to each person individually. But the Bible seems to teach consistently that God's gift of salvation . . . works by the principle of election, one being chosen to be the means of God's saving grace to others."[23]

Hence, the question of salvation cannot be answered simply by the affirmation of the divine revelation, but, as the Bible testifies, it is a matter of the divine election. Hogg's aim – to open up the possibility of salvation by affirming the existence of God's revelation in non-Christian faith – does not work.

Finally, Kraemer deals with Hogg's two distinctions. Hogg has argued that Kraemer fails to make the distinction between faith and beliefs and between the occurrence and the content of revelation. Kraemer answers this charge as follows. First, Kraemer points out that Hogg's distinction of faith and beliefs is not analogous to his own distinction of the Christian revelation and empirical Christianity. Second, Kraemer could accept Hogg's distinction of faith and beliefs, with faith here understood as "a specific religion according to its highest and deepest motives and intentions."[24] With this understanding of faith, Kraemer has no problem distinguishing faith and beliefs, between Christianity in its purest form with empirical Christianities; or between Hinduism in its purest form with empirical Hinduisms. Still, the point Kraemer makes here is that this distinction is not parallel with the distinction between the Christian revelation and empirical Christianity. The Christian revelation is not Christianity in its purest form, but the gospel, or "the symposium of the divine acts from the Creation till the consummation

---

22. Newbigin, *Finality of Christ*, 39.
23. Newbigin, "Christ and the World," 23.
24. Kraemer, *Religion and the Christian Faith*, 227.

of man and the world."[25] For Kraemer, the Christian revelation has to be sharply differentiated from Christianity as a religion.

Furthermore, in regard to the distinction between the occurrence and the content of the revelation, Kraemer's answer is rather short. He puts it in a rhetorical question: "Why is it that you do not see that not only occurrence, but also the content of the revelation is abundantly treated?" Certainly, Kramer does not mean that he had already dealt with this matter explicitly. What he says is that the distinction between the occurrence and the content of the revelation is much more subtle than one may have thought. We get the hint of his intention from the following sentence: "The occurrence of revelation is a deeper mystery and miracle than one seems to think."[26] From this Kraemer seems to indicate that the occurrence of the revelation could not be taken as mere occurrence void of its content. Yet, it is also clear that Kraemer does not make a clear distinction between occurrence and content. This failure affects Kraemer's theology. I will return to this point later.

Kraemer's answers to Hogg's objection are summarized as follows.

1. Kraemer concedes to Hogg and amends his radical discontinuity position. There must be some sort of continuity. Indeed, there are both continuity and discontinuity.
2. Kraemer does not agree with Hogg as to where this continuity is found. For Kraemer, this continuity is not found in non-Christian faith. Kraemer, however, does not say where this continuity can be located.
3. Kraemer criticizes Hogg's continuity position as it fails to take into account the depth of human sins. Hogg is mistaken by arguing the continuity in revelation with the aim for salvation. Salvation and revelation are not identical and not linked together. Kraemer gives an example of the Jewish people to illustrate the case.
4. Kraemer can accept Hogg's distinction of faith and beliefs, with faith understood as a religion in its purest form. But this distinction is not parallel with Kraemer's distinction of the Christian revelation and empirical Christianity. However,

---

25. Kraemer, 227.
26. Kraemer, 230.

the occurrence and content of revelation are too elusive. This distinction is therefore unhelpful for this case.

On this point, we will see answers from James Cox who has defended Hogg's position in response to Kraemer. According to Cox, there are two important aspects of this debate. The first aspect is Hogg's distinction of faith and faiths. Cox says, "The central point both of Hogg's contribution to the Tambaram debate and of his critique of Kraemer was his distinction between faith and faiths."[27] The second aspect is the different anthropologies. Hogg and Kraemer have different views on the nature of human beings. For Kraemer human's biggest problem is sin, and for Hogg it is distrust. This difference affects their views on the purpose of revelation. Cox explains as follows. For Hogg, revelation is intended "to restore man to a relationship of trustful obedience." But for Kraemer, it is to produce "a fundamental reorientation of the human will."[28]

Cox argues that Kraemer has failed in the first aspect. Kraemer not only does not make the distinction of faith and faiths, but he also misunderstands it. Kraemer has identified Hogg's non-Christian faith with religion in its purest form. But this is not what Hogg means by it. According to Cox, faith in Hogg's view is "the living communion between God and man, a communion based on trust in the Personality of God and obedience to His will."[29] Thus, faith entails God's revelation. Faith "always results from God's self-disclosure."[30] To acknowledge the existence of non-Christian faith is therefore to acknowledge the existence of the divine revelation in non-Christian religions. Kraemer's problem is that he misunderstands this distinction and consequently he can quickly dismiss Hogg's criticism. Cox says, "The crux of the Hogg-Kraemer debate, therefore, centers on the right interpretation of Hogg's distinction between faith and faiths. In our judgment, Kraemer did not understand this distinction, and, thus, dismissed it too easily."[31]

Still, for Cox, the deepest divide between Kraemer and Hogg is their different views of revelation and because of this, Kraemer could never accept Hogg's

---

27. Cox, "Development," 398.
28. Cox, 399.
29. Cox, 400.
30. Cox, 401.
31. Cox, 402.

position.³² Cox says, "But in another sense, even if [Kraemer] had understood [the distinction of faith and faiths], he could never have accepted Hogg's point of view. For him, Hogg had made man and his experience the criterion for determining what is or is not a divine revelation."³³ In other words, according to Cox, Kraemer has charged that Hogg has identified religious experience with the divine revelation. For Cox, however, the reverse is true. Cox argues that Kraemer has identified revelation with the Scriptures. Therefore, there is no divine revelation in other religions. Cox says, "Kraemer effectually had restricted God's revelatory activity to the biblical record, and thus had denied the possibility of a living faith outside of empirical Christianity."³⁴ With this, Cox argues that "Kraemer's definition of revelation really refers to beliefs which men have created in response to God's revelation of Himself in Christ."³⁵

To sum, Cox sides with Hogg's position. For Cox, the crucial point of the debate is Hogg's distinction of faith and faiths, which Kraemer has misunderstood. Still, the blame is on Kraemer's concept of revelation. Because he identifies revelation with the Scriptures, Kraemer cannot allow God's revelation outside Christianity.

So far in regard to Hogg's critiques, I have examined answers from Kraemer and Cox's defense of Hogg's position. I will now proceed to give my judgment on this matter. In the first place, I acknowledge that Hogg's objection to Kraemer's radical discontinuity is a valid point. Could it be that there is no continuity at all between Christianity and non-Christian religions? Or, could we really say that only Christianity is a product of revelation, and other religions are merely a cultural, social, or psychological product? Here, I agree with Hogg that there must be some sort of continuity.

My conclusion, however, is not based on human experience but the testimony of the Scriptures. As the Scriptures testify, there is none seeking God in the first place (Rom 3:11). It is always first God who draws them to seek him (Acts 17:27). Therefore, human religious endeavors, however corrupted and twisted they are, could not grow out of themselves. They must be grounded

---

32. Cox, 402.
33. Cox, 402.
34. Cox, 399.
35. Cox, 403.

on some sort of divine activity. The radical discontinuity position cannot be substantiated biblically.

Having said that, there must be discontinuity as well. Otherwise, we will place Christianity and non-Christian religions on the same plane. Christianity is unique not only in the sense that each religion is unique in itself. Christianity is unique because the message it bears is unique. It is only in Christianity that we find the special grace available in Jesus Christ. Therefore, we admit that there have to be both continuity and discontinuity. This standpoint is in line with Kraemer's dialectical view. The relationship between Christianity and non-Christian religions is also dialectical. There are both yes and no; continuity and discontinuity. In this case, Kraemer's concession to Hogg's point fits well with his intention to stress a more dialectic position in his *Religion and the Christian Faith*.[36] This is also in line with Kraemer's idea of subversive fulfillment. Christ comes not only to fulfill the longings and anticipations in non-Christian religions but at the time he comes to judge them.[37]

In regard to where the continuity and discontinuity could be found, I side with Kraemer. I cannot concur with Hogg and Cox that Christianity and non-Christian religions differ only in their beliefs and that they share the same faith. I will explain my position as follows. I will first deal with Hogg's distinction of faith and beliefs. Cox has argued that Kraemer has misunderstood this crucial point and as a result, he was able to dismiss Hogg's criticism too easily. I recognize that Kraemer's understanding of non-Christian faith differs from that of Cox. For Kraemer, in Hogg's distinction of faith and faiths, faith has to be understood as a religion in its best form. For Cox, however, faith here is understood as communion between man and God. These two understandings are obviously different. But this does not mean that Kraemer is totally mistaken, and Cox is right. Kraemer has several valid points. First, Kraemer is right that Hogg's distinction of faith and faiths is not parallel with Kraemer's own distinction of the biblical revelation and empirical Christianity. Even if we grant that Cox's interpretation is applied to Hogg's distinction of faith and faiths, Kraemer's point is validly argued. With Cox's interpretation, faith

---

36. Kraemer, *Religion and the Christian Faith*, 6

37. For Kraemer's subversive fulfillment, see Kraemer, "Continuity or Discontinuity," 4. Goheen points out that "most commentators label Kraemer with the term 'discontinuity.' A careful reading of Kraemer, however, shows a fine integration of continuity and discontinuity within the concept of 'subversive fulfillment.'" See Goheen, "As the Father," 351.

is a human act; whereas for Kraemer, the Christian revelation is a divine act. The distinction between the Christian revelation and empirical Christianity is therefore not the distinction between "the ideal and the actual" religion, as Eric Sharpe has mistakenly stated.[38]

Second, Kraemer is right to reject Hogg's idea that non-Christian faith is the same as Christian faith. Certainly, I cannot agree with Kraemer that non-Christian faith is purely psychological. So, non-Christian faith, as with Christian faith, is a response to the divine revelation. Yet, this does not mean that the two are identical, or of the same nature. The two are different due to their relation to human sins. Johan H. Bavinck correctly points out the difference between the two types of faith. He contends that even though the two are similar, as they respond to the divine revelation, they differ in regard to the working of the Spirit. Christian faith is born out of hearts which have been renewed by the Spirit; whereas non-Christian faith, or religious consciousness, is of unregenerate hearts.[39]

Here we arrive at the core problem of Hogg's argument. As Kraemer has rightly identified, Hogg does not take into account the gravity of human sins. As we have seen above, Cox acknowledges that for Hogg humans' biggest problem is distrust, not sins. Hogg takes for granted the effects of sins in human nature. Hogg's doctrine of anthropology deeply affects his view of the nature of non-Christian faith. For Hogg, non-Christian faith is therefore as pure as Christian faith. With this faith, non-Christians are able to meet God. The only "cloud" that hinders them to come to him is "insincerity." Sins are certainly out of Hogg's consideration. Hogg writes as follows:

> By those Hindu saints who have testified that their seeking has become a finding, the realisation of God which has come to them has been felt as self-authenticating. They *know* that they have met God, and the vision prostrates them in adoration and fills them with rapture. It is no part of our Christian duty to deny the actuality of that meeting, for the only cloud that is quite impervious to the radiance of the Divine Presence is insincerity, not doctrinal error.[40]

---

38. Sharpe, "Legacy of A. G. Hogg," 67.
39. Bolt, Pratt, and, Visser, *Bavinck Reader*, 298.
40. Hogg, *Christian Message to the Hindu*, 32.

Accordingly, the errors in religions are attributed not to the faith, but to the beliefs. However, beliefs and faith are not totally separated. Beliefs are supposed to be instruments for faith to function properly. Yet, they become hindrances when they are erroneous. That the problem is due to external factors is apparent in Hogg's analogy. He explains that gazing at moonlight is easy when the sky is clear, but it is not so when the sky is cloudy. With this analogy, Hogg argues that the problem is not so much with "the soul's direct vision of God's shining," but on the external factors, that is "the enigmas of life." As such they can be cleared away by changing one's doctrinal concepts.[41] Still, as much as erroneous beliefs may hinder faith from functioning properly, it cannot block "the radiance of the Divine Presence." Hence, so long as non-Christians are sincere, they will meet God in their faith.

Is non-Christian faith as pure as Christian faith? Are their errors merely external? Here I cannot agree with Hogg. Hogg's problem is that he makes too sharp the distinction between faith and beliefs. He argues that erroneous beliefs may hinder faith to function properly, but he does not see that could happen vice versa. Newbigin correctly explains this mistake. What is the cause of the errors? If the errors are merely external, in this case, the cause is merely a misunderstanding, then it will be easier to correct. But, if the errors result from an internal problem (i.e. a misdirected faith), then it cannot be corrected simply by clarifications. He believes that the latter is true. Newbigin says,

> Is this a case of misunderstanding, or of misdirected faith? Would one say of a devout Moslem that his faith-response to God was distorted by the fact that it had to pass through the teaching and personality of the Prophet? And if we were dealing only with understanding, would not the devout Hindus and Moslems be the most eager to welcome the gospel as clarifying what they had understood in a distorted way? The experience of missionaries and evangelists does not support this view.[42]

I concur with Newbigin's conclusion that the errors result from a misdirected faith. Thomas also correctly points out Hogg's mistake in this point. He cannot accept that the errors are merely due to the beliefs. But they come

---

41. Hogg, "Christian Attitude," 113.
42. Newbigin, "Christ and the World," 21.

from a twisted response to God's revelation. The erroneous beliefs are expressions of this internal problem. Thomas says,

> It is impossible for [me] to accept that Faith, understood as the self's total response to God, is the same in all religions and that religions differ only in the intellectual expressions, and that all corruptions of faith are due to wrong beliefs. This is almost equating sin with doctrinal errors. Sin however, is the false existence of the self in its *spiritual* apprehension of and answer to God, leading to idolatry. The *intellectual* apprehension and answer may only be expressing this idolatry of the original faith-response.[43]

Thomas is right about the relationship of faith and beliefs. The two cannot be distinguished too sharply. They are closely connected. Here Hogg is simply not consistent in his argument. He happily accepts Kraemer's holistic view of religions. A religion has to be treated in its totality. The whole system is tied together. In regard to religions in India, he contends that the dye of the monistic tendency has penetrated into all elements of a religious system so that all similarities are unsafe for points of contact. But, how could Hogg not see that errors in non-Christian religions spring out of their faith?

I have shown how Hogg's anthropology affects his view on the nature of non-Christian faith. Here, I also argue that Hogg's anthropology is related to his Christology. When sins are not taken seriously in human nature, Jesus Christ is not a savior either. Here, we are reminded again of Hogg's sleepwalker analogy. For Hogg, Christ is simply an "awakener," who awakens non-Christians from their "spiritual sleep," and reveals them the universal will of God. But Hogg cannot be right. The New Testament testifies that in Christ, we are not awakened from our sleep, but made alive from our death in sin (Col 2:13). Christ is not "an awakener," but the savior of the world and the redeemer of human sins.

For Hogg, non-Christian religions share the same faith as that of Christianity, but they are inferior to Christianity. On this point Hogg's distinction of occurrence and content of revelation is crucial. So, even though both Christian faith and non-Christian faith respond to the divine revelation,

---

43. Thomas, "Review of *Karma*," 93.

they do not get the same content from it. Non-Christians cannot meet Christ Jesus through their non-Christian faith. Hogg states:

> But we do know that in that real meeting they have missed something, something which we have found to be so vital and so precious that our hearts cannot rest until they share it with us. Whatever of the Divine Reality they may have beheld more overwhelmingly than many of us have done, it has not been granted them to recognise in Jesus "The Word made flesh," and through His crucifixion to feel the utter devastatingness of God's judgment upon guilt and sin, and in His resurrection to know themselves claimed for a Cause in the following of an invincible Leader.[44]

I agree with Hogg on these two points: first, it is important to make a distinction between the occurrence and the content of revelation; second, what makes Christianity different from other religions is not the occurrence of revelation, but its content. I contend that all religions are grounded on the divine revelation. However, I disagree with Hogg about the content of revelation. For Hogg, revelation in other religions is devoid of Jesus Christ. There is no Word made flesh in their revelation. Even though they can behold the Almighty, they cannot meet Jesus Christ. Theologically this cannot be true. To say that one can behold the divine reality without meeting Christ is to put him apart from the Trinity. One cannot put asunder the eternal Logos with the Logos made flesh. Hence, all revelations contain the Logos. Jathanna is right that the content of revelation is always the word in whatever forms it appears. He says, "For the content [of revelation] cannot be really different. The Word of God constitutes the common content, whether it be the Word Made Nature, Word Made Speech or the Word Made Flesh."[45]

Revelation is God's self-disclosure. The content of revelation cannot be other than God himself. Still, some distinctions are certainly necessary. As noted, we distinguish between the word in nature and the word in flesh. As with the word, revelations also come with God's grace. Revelation always comes with divine grace. Yet, we also need to distinguish between special and

---

44. Hogg, *Christian Message to the Hindu*, 32–33.
45. Jathanna, *Decisiveness of the Christ-Event*, 264–265.

common grace. I argue that it is this special grace that makes Christianity different from other religions. In the next chapter, I will describe in detail this important distinction.

5.4 Examination of Thesis 3: Holistic Approach of Religions

In thesis 3, Kramer argues that religious consciousness is universal, but religion is particular, dialectical, and holistic. The objection is centered on the holistic character of religions. Both D'Costa and Thomas contend that Kraemer's holistic approach to religions fails to consider the dynamicity of religions. To examine this charge I will explore answers given by Tim Perry.

According to Perry, D'Costa's critiques on this point are justified, but Kraemer's view can still be salvaged as one pays attention to Kraemer's own work.[46] Perry basically acknowledges that there is a deficiency in Kraemer's holistic approach. Perry agrees with D'Costa that Kraemer has made "interpretative errors" in regard to Buddhism and Hinduism.[47] But as such, this mistake does not deserve our total rejection of this approach. He seeks to maintain its strengths and overcome its weaknesses.

Perry defends Kraemer's holistic view as follows. First, he points out the strength of this approach. Perry maintains that the approach is intended to preserve the "particularities of religious belief and practice." By this, he means that each religion is unique in itself, and each religious belief or practice needs to be interpreted within its cultural and religious contexts.[48] Next, Perry maintains that by the holistic approach, Kraemer does not mean that religions are unchangeable. Perry reminds us that Kraemer has a "penchant to overstate his case" and this is certainly true in this instance. Yet, despite Kraemer's "rhetorical emphasis," Perry states that for Kraemer religions "can and do change," and "they are dynamic and not static entities." Furthermore, Kraemer's chief concern is to emphasize that similar terms or concepts found

---

46. Perry, *Radical Difference*, 112.
47. Perry, 116.
48. Perry, 117.

in the writings of other religions (e.g. faith and grace), cannot be immediately understood in terms of Christian meanings.[49]

That said, Perry argues that despite this deficiency, one does not need to abandon Kraemer's holistic approach. Instead, it will be sufficient to modify the approach to overcome its deficiency. This modification aims to "avoid treating other religions as static entities," and to maintain its "particularity without denying the possibility of change over time." It is the later element which, according to Perry, Kraemer has overlooked due to his "highly theoretical division" of religions. Kraemer has divided religions into two categories: prophetic religions and naturalist religions. Christianity, Judaism, and Islam belong to the first category, and the remaining religions belong to the second. Perry contends that such an approach has clouded Kraemer's judgment of other religions. All religions in that second category are "ultimately monistic." Therefore, all innovations found in those religions (e.g. Ramanuja Hinduism, Amida Buddhism) are "purely cosmetic."[50]

Perry contends that such deficiency could be overcome with what he calls "a more pragmatic, local approach." With this, he argues that one should avoid treating a religion from an *a priori* standpoint. Instead, it should "begin with actual encounters with religious totalities in concrete situations." In other words, one gives priority to phenomenological accounts of a religion. The approach, Perry admits, is adopted from Wilfred C. Smith, who has taken "the diversity of religious belief seriously," doing so "by separating belief from faith." With this approach, Perry states that to maintain "religious particularity as seriously as Kraemer desires, one must begin at the level of the local religious community." Yet, this approach does not violate Kraemer's holistic approach, because "there are elements within the local communities that tender them recognizably Christian, Islamic, or Buddhist." In other words, even though each particular type of religious community may display its particularity, it is still recognized as under a wider category of religion.[51]

I, however, find Perry's defense of Kraemer's holistic approach unsatisfactory. Perry is certainly correct to point out that Kraemer's holistic approach is intended as a rebuttal of fulfillment theory and with this, he also rejects

---

49. Perry, 117–118.
50. Perry, 120.
51. Perry, 120–121.

an atomistic approach to points of contact.⁵² Perry is also correct that by this holistic approach Kraemer does not mean that religions are unchangeable. Yet, he seems to be inconsistent when he agrees with D'Costa that Kraemer has made interpretive errors in regard to Buddhism and Hinduism.

On this point, I argue, in disagreement with Perry and D'Costa, that Kraemer does not make interpretive errors in regard to Buddhism or Hinduism. When Kraemer pronounces that Buddhism and Hinduism are "naturalistic monism," he does not deny that one can find a general idea of grace and faith in them. However, he maintains that their ideas of grace and faith are fundamentally different from that of the Bible. For him, biblical ideas of faith and grace are purely divine initiative; whereas for Buddhism and Hinduism, they are "exclusively anthropocentric."⁵³ In this sense, the two ideas are incompatible.

Next, I also argue that both Perry and D'Costa have misunderstood Kraemer's holistic approach. D'Costa gives an example of Theravada Buddhism in the village of Migala, Sri Lanka, where its classical form has experienced a radical change in regard to its notion of *karunavanta* or kindness/compassion.⁵⁴ D'Costa uses this example to counter Kraemer's holistic approach. From this, it is apparent that D'Costa takes this approach from the external structure, beliefs, or practices, of non-Christian religions. With this understanding, D'Costa assumes that the holistic view of religions would make non-Christian religions or cultures rigid and unchangeable. Or, to use M. M. Thomas's term, holistic is therefore identical with "monolithic."⁵⁵ Hence, D'Costa contends that Kraemer neglects the dynamic nature of religions.

However, this is not what Kraemer means by a holistic approach. This approach does not simply relate to particular religious beliefs or practices. Nor does it postulate that they cannot change. With this approach, Kraemer means that all elements of a religion are interconnected and mutually influenced. To understand correctly Kraemer's point, a helpful insight, surprisingly, comes from Hogg. In several instances, Hogg has stated his agreement

---

52. Hallencreutz, *Kraemer Towards Tambaram*, 104; Cox, "Development," 377. Hogg's acceptance of Kraemer's holistic view of religion is also partly motivated by his rejection of fulfillment theology. See Hogg, *Towards Clarifying*, 1.

53. Kraemer, *Christian Message*, 181.

54. D'Costa, *Theology and Religious Pluralism*, 63.

55. Thomas, "Absoluteness of Jesus Christ," 137.

with Kraemer's holistic approach.⁵⁶ Yet, he does not agree with Kraemer that it should be taken as an organic unity, but an imperfect one. I quote here his clarification. Hogg says, "But my agreement as regards the necessity of such a [holistic] view is based not on K.'s contention that the non-Christian religions are organic wholes but on a recognition that, although they may be a mechanical mixture of imperfectly unified elements, this diversity is disguised by the uniformity of dye."⁵⁷

In this clarification, Hogg touches the center of Kraemer's holistic approach, namely, the relation between the core and the peripheries of a religion. Even though the practices, traditions, or rituals of non-Christian religions may look heterogeneous, like a combination of various elements, they indeed share the same core. Furthermore, this core plays an important role in characterizing its external elements. It functions like dye, tainting all elements. According to Hogg, this dye has become so fixed that all elements of non-Christian religions are no longer safe for points of contact.⁵⁸ The very reason to reject them is that they cannot be neutral as they have been tainted by monistic tendency. Here, Hogg agrees with Kraemer in regard to the danger of syncretism.

Even though Hogg disagrees with approaching non-Christian religions as an organic unity, he has nailed down what Kraemer means by the holistic character of non-Christian religions. The chief concern of this view lies in the relationship between the kernel and the shell of a religion. Hallencreutz describes this relationship as "indivisible but not unalterable."⁵⁹ The emphasis is on its indivisibility, and the indivisibility does not mean unchangeable. In the first place, there is internal religious unity. Hence, Kraemer maintains that "every religion is a living, indivisible unity."⁶⁰ Every part of it cannot be understood apart from the whole system. In the second place, Kraemer also maintains that there is "the symbiosis of culture and religion."⁶¹ Cultures and religions are "indissoluble unity." Cultures are affected or characterized by the same naturalist apprehension of life that has also affected the practices

---

56. See for example, Hogg, *Towards Clarifying*, 1; "Christian Attitude," 100.
57. Hogg, *Towards Clarifying*, 11.
58. Hogg, "Christian Attitude," 101.
59. Hallencreutz, *Kraemer Towards Tambaram*, 104.
60. Kraemer, *Christian Message*, 135.
61. Kraemer, *World Cultures*, 20.

or traditions of non-Christian religions. However, this holistic character of a religion does not postulate that cultures, practices, or traditions could not change or be changed. It is on this point where critics have strayed.

Furthermore, I also argue that Perry is mistaken when he, in agreement with D'Costa, takes Kraemer's approach as severely "dogmatic." Or, to say it in Masatoshi Doi's terms, Kraemer has emphasized "the factuality of revelation" at the expense of "the factuality of religious phenomena."[62] In other words, he charges that Kraemer has utilized a top-down approach. To illustrate this charge, D'Costa, for instance, cites Kraemer's treatment of *bhakti* traditions of Ramanuja and Kabir. According to D'Costa, Kraemer regards those traditions to be anthropocentric and monistic in their cores, because they are part of Hinduism. Hence, D'Costa charges Kraemer's procedure as being "historically and phenomenologically reductive and limiting."[63] Yet, in what follows I will show that this charge cannot be justified.

First, the holistic approach to non-Christian religions is the fruit of Kraemer's phenomenological study of religions, not the result of his dogmatic study. As noted, Kraemer maintains the primacy of a theological approach over a phenomenological study of religions. Yet, he does not discard this phenomenological approach, nor does he see it as less beneficial. Indeed, Kraemer's holistic approach is the fruit of this scientific study. As Hallencreutz points out, Kraemer was aware of this holistic approach when he was a student at the University of Leiden. Yet, he did not adopt this approach, nor did he write about it. In his dissertation, this subject was "only hinted at."[64] Rather, he adopted this approach later during his tenure as a missionary in the Dutch East Indies. This is apparent in Kraemer's treatment of the Javanese traditional shadow puppet show or *wayang*.[65] Here, Kraemer emphasizes the holistic character of the Javanese religion and *wayang* as an instrument to express Javanese apprehension of reality.[66] Hence, unlike what the critics have said, Kraemer's conviction of the holistic character of religions comes from his missionary experience, not merely from a dogmatic study.

---

62. Doi, "From Tambaram," 142–143.
63. D'Costa, *Theology and Religious Pluralism*, 62.
64. Hallencreutz, *Kraemer Towards Tambaram*, 104, 119.
65. Kraemer's treatment of *wayang* can be seen in Kraemer, "Christendom en wajang," 225–234. See also, Kraemer "De Wajang als Uiting," 33–48.
66. Hallencreutz, *Kraemer Towards Tambaram*, 150.

In addition, when I scrutinize Kraemer's writings about other religions, I find that his descriptions are not based on dogmatic study but on a phenomenological study of religions. I contend that Kraemer was not only a careful scholar of religions, but also, he spent years to observe, collect data, and get in touch with adherents of non-Christian religions. Such an experienced scholar of religions could not have lumped together a particular religious tradition, say the *bhakti* tradition of Ramapuja, into a larger group, such as Hinduism, and with that consider it monistic simply because it is part of Hinduism. An excellent example of Kraemer's careful treatment of religions could be seen in his description of Balinese religion. Bali is a small, beautiful island east of the Java Island, Indonesia. Besides being well known as a center of Indonesian tourism, Bali is also an enclave of "Hinduism" in the Indonesian archipelago. Contrary to common belief, Kraemer does not simply accept the designation of Balinese religion as Hinduism. He points out that both Buddhism and Hinduism, especially of *Ciwaism*, had deep influences in Bali centuries ago. Yet, having acknowledged such influences, he concludes that Balinese are not Hindu. Kraemer explains:

> I believe a judgment on the religious situation in Bali should be summarized as follows: there is a pluriformity of Hindu influence, but the Balinese are not Hindus. Their true religion is the ancient Balinese popular religion which is concentrated around the house temple, the *desa* temple, the temple for the dead, and the *subak* temple, and around the worship of mostly ancient Indigenous gods and the fear of evil spirits. The core of Balinese religious feeling is to be found in this socio-religious unity which is rooted in the Indigenous Balinese soil.[67]

Two things are apparent from this quotation. First, even though the Balinese religion is heavily influenced by Hinduism, Kraemer, carefully applying a phenomenological study of religions, contends that it is not Hinduism.[68] Second,

---

67. Kraemer, *From Missionfield to Independent*, 170.
68. I. Wayan Mastra, a scholar and chairman of the *Gereja Kristen Protestan di Bali* is still ambiguous pertaining the nature of Balinese religion. He maintains that it should be called "Bali-Hindu," recognizing that it is not Hinduism as such, but "a mixture of Hinduism and the native Bali religion." Paul Hiebert, however, tries to make things straight. He says, "one suspects that for many leaders in the orthodox schools of Hindu thought, Balinese Hinduism has gone too far and ended in a Hindu pagan syncretism . . . One must ask, is Bali Hinduism truly

the Balinese religion displays its holistic character. There is unity between religious and social life. Yet, this unity does not stem from Hinduism but its indigenous belief.

In sum, the charge that Kraemer's holistic character of religions is too rigid as it neglects the dynamicity of religions cannot be substantiated. The charge is essentially based on a misunderstanding of what Kraemer means by this concept. By this he does not mean that religions cannot change or be changed, but rather he emphasizes the interconnectedness and mutual influence of all elements of a religion. With this, I have shown that the objection to Kraemer's view on the holistic nature of non-Christian religions is sufficiently answered.

5.5 Examination of Thesis 4: Warning of Syncretism

I will now examine Kraemer's fourth thesis. On this point, Kraemer argues that the Christian attitude toward non-Christian religions should be evangelistic but tolerant, and adaptive but not syncretistic. Christians should not be timid in spreading the gospel. They are obliged to do evangelism, and yet practice genuine tolerance toward adherents of other religions. The church should practice adaptation. In other words, she must take a form of Christianity that fits the soil in which she has been planted. However, she must avoid syncretism. That is to say, she cannot sacrifice the core of the Christian faith.

Thomas accepts all the above points except for Kraemer's warning of the danger of syncretism. He argues that this warning has created fear of syncretism. As a result, it freezes adaptation and hinders the process of the indigenization of Christianity. Thomas agrees with Kraemer that the core of traditional Asian religions is fundamentally monistic and different from that of Christianity. Yet, he does not see that this poses a threat to Christianity. Instead, he proposes that the churches should not emphasize the danger of syncretism, but focus on "the positive potentialities of the inter-religious [relationship]."[69] His aim is to establish a "Christ-centered Syncretism." That is to say, Christians should have "a Christ-centered fellowship" with other

---

Hindu?" Here, Hiebert is certainly in line with Kraemer's analysis. See Mastra, "Christianity and Culture," 387. Cf. Hiebert, "Dialogue," 23.

69. Thomas, "Absoluteness of Jesus Christ," 135.

religions with the acknowledgment that Christ has already worked and transformed non-Christian religions.[70] This last aspect is of utmost importance to Thomas. He argues that Kraemer's theological tools fail to detect Christ's transformational work in other religions.

In his review of Kraemer's book *World Cultures and World Religions*,[71] Thomas points out that the inadequacy of Kraemer's theology is due to its one-sided emphasis on the ultimate matter and therefore neglects the penultimate matter. He says:

> The inadequacy of the theology from which Dr. Kraemer derives his criterion of cultural discrimination, and judgment is precisely its one-sided emphasis on the religious ultimates, which leaves what may be called the human ultimates without any Christian significance. Dr. Kraemer's theology can discriminate easily between God and idol in the cultural renascence, but it provides no criterion to distinguish between the human and the inhuman in it.[72]

Thomas provides three supports for the charge: first, Kraemer's theology fails to detect Christ in the lives of non-Christians; second, it does not take into account the renascence of non-Christian religions; and third, it is hostile to non-Christian cultures. Due to this inadequacy, Kraemer's theological tools hinder Christians, especially of the younger churches, from carrying out adaptation. Consequently, it hinders, rather than advances, Christian relationship with non-Christian religions, ideologies, and cultures. In sum, Thomas perceives Kraemer's theology to be deficient in affirming non-Christian cultures.

Let us now proceed to examine Thomas's critique. The first support he gives is that Kraemer's theology fails to detect the presence of Christ in non-Christian lives. In other words, it does not differentiate between "the human and inhuman" in non-Christian religions. He cites an example of Kraemer's treatment of Tilak and Gandhi.[73] Both persons were influential

---

70. Thomas, *Salvation and Humanization*, 19, 40.

71. For Thomas's review of Kramer's *World Cultures and World Religions*, see Thomas, "Rewarding Correspondence," 6–11. This review is originally published in *International Review of Missions* 50, no. 198 (April 1961): 204–209.

72. Thomas, "Rewarding Correspondence," 9.

73. Thomas, 9.

national leaders of modern India who had taken apparently contrasting paths to achieve their goal for an independent India. Bal Gangadhar Tilak was, Kraemer says, infamous for his violent action towards British authority in India; while Mahatma Gandhi fought with his ahimsa (non-violent) principle. Yet, Kraemer contends that politically Gandhi was indeed a student of Tilak. He writes, "It seems a rather fantastic stride from the violent Tilak to the frail apostle of non-violence. Yet in my opinion Sarma is right in saying that although Gandhi himself always called Gokhale his political *guru*, it was Tilak's mantle and not Gokhale's that fell on Gandhi."[74] Thomas is very unhappy with what he sees as Kraemer's "lack of discrimination" between the two figures. It is in this context, as quoted above, that he charges Kraemer of failing to differentiate between "human" and "inhuman." Kraemer treats the two as "essentially one."[75]

Kraemer had the chance to reply to Thomas's critique but did so briefly in hope that he could discuss the matter in person with Thomas and other Indian scholars. In his answer to Thomas, he responds particularly to Thomas's critical review of the book *World Cultures and World Religions*. Kraemer complains that Thomas is unfair toward his position, especially in regard to his treatment of Tilak and Gandhi, and the relation between Christianity, religions, and cultures.[76] In other words, for Kraemer, Thomas has misunderstood his thoughts.

Kraemer's assessment of Thomas's critiques is partly justified. It seems that Thomas may have missed the point. In regard to the comparison between Tilak and Gandhi, for example, Kraemer was certainly aware of the "greatest imaginable contrast" between them. He describes their contrast as follows:

> [Gandhi's] paramount feeling for justice; his astounding fairness; his fearless independence towards British and Indians alike; his unique type of Hindu spirituality, rooted in Visnuite piety of great sublimity; obedience to an elevated moral ideal of non-violence and sincere love of Truth as he saw it; his ascetic

---

74. Kraemer, *World Cultures*, 139. Also quoted in Thomas, "Rewarding Correspondence," 9. Kraemer refers to the opinion of D. S. Sarma, who contends that Gandhi took over Tilak's noncooperation strategy but abandoned the use of violence. See Sarma, *Renascent Hinduism*, 188.

75. Thomas, "Rewarding Correspondence," 9; cf. Kraemer, *World Cultures*, 317.

76. For Kraemer's reply to Thomas, see Thomas, "Rewarding Correspondence," 11.

conception of life; his fearless advocacy of the abolition of that blot on Hinduism, the pariahs . . .; in these and many other assets of his personality he is worlds asunder from Tilak's fierce, bigoted, mystical obsession with absolutist loyalty to the medieval social-religion entity of Hinduism.[77]

Surely, Kraemer was able to distinguish between "human" and "inhuman" characteristics of the two. Kraemer's point is that despite such contrast in the display, they share a similar religious ideology and philosophical thought, rooted in Indian "nationalism." Nationalism, Kraemer argues, should not be viewed as an exclusively political movement. Instead, it is a cultural and religious movement, the fruit of Western penetration. Nationalism in this sense is defined as "new visions of true nationhood, of self-respect, of acute realization of one's own spiritual and cultural authenticity and value, and not only a marriage of Western and Eastern values."[78] It is in this context that Kraemer refers to both Gandhi and Tilak as essentially one.

However, I argue that Thomas's indignation was not merely caused by his misreading of Kraemer. Here, the example of Gandhi is crucial for our case. Scholars, both Western and Indian, have taken Gandhi as a prime example of God, or rather Christ, at work in the lives of non-Christians. John Hick, for example, maintains that Gandhi is "a paradigm of the immense impact which Jesus and his teaching can have upon the adherents of another faith."[79] Earl Stanley Jones, a Methodist missionary to India and a personal friend of Gandhi, writes of his admiration of Gandhi: "I am still an evangelist. I bow to Mahatma Gandhi, but I kneel at the feet of Christ and give him my full and final allegiance. And yet a little man, who fought a system in the framework of which I stand, has taught me more of the spirit of Christ than perhaps any other man in East or West."[80] With this background, one would understand that for Thomas, Kraemer's failure to take into account Gandhi's distinctiveness is tantamount to a rejection of the presence of Christ in non-Christian lives. Elsewhere Thomas has argued that Christ has made an impact in the

---

77. Kraemer, *World Cultures*, 139–140.
78. Kraemer, 136.
79. Hick, "Jesus and the World," 183.
80. Jones, *Mahatma Gandhi*, 8.

lives of non-Christians and surely Gandhi is the epitome of such impact.[81] One could then empathize with his feeling when Kramer hits hard at the center of his argument. It is clear in this point that for Thomas, Kraemer's theological tools are inadequate because they fail to detect Christ's presence in the lives of non-Christians.

Thomas's approach, however, is not free from criticism. Two things can be said of it. First, methodologically it is questionable, for it lacks a clear criterion of judgment. Jan P. Schouten rightly says:

> But there is a question to be posed concerning Thomas' work. It is undeniably correct to look for the ways in which the Gospel inspires people to renewal, also outside the Christian church. But pointing to the intention of God in historical movements here and there is also not without risk. What is the criterion for doing so? Here Thomas remains vague.[82]

Thomas does not give us reason(s) why he thinks that God has worked in the life of Gandhi and not in that of Tilak. But, if we are allowed to make a conjecture, he seems to rest on the assumption that the divine work in human lives must produce goodness in them. This is not wrong, for the Bible indeed testifies that "every good and perfect gift is from above, coming down from the Father of the heavenly lights" (Jas 1:17). That said, this is certainly not the whole picture given in the Holy Scriptures. The Scriptures testify that God raised up Cyrus to allow the Israelites to return to their homeland; but in the same book, we also find that God also raised up Nebuchadnezzar to bring them into exile (Isa 45:1–13; Jer 43:1–13). Hence, he is the God who is sovereign over all historical events.

Second, as seen in the above quotation of Schouten, there is risk and danger in trying to pin down where in particular God works in human history. Hence, against Thomas's view, the New Delhi Report[83] states, "We must resist the temptation to see the hand of God in the particular movements

---

81. In his book *The Acknowledged Christ of the Indian Renaissance* Thomas traced the presence of Christ in the Indian reformers from Rammohan Roy that culminated in Mahatma Gandhi. See Thomas, *Acknowledged Christ*. Cf. Schouten, *Jesus as Guru*, 212–217.

82. Schouten, *Jesus as Guru*, 217.

83. The New Delhi Report captures the activities and reports of the Third Assembly of the World Council of Churches, held from 19 November to 5 December 1961 in New Delhi, India.

of history of which we personally approve, or to claim his blessing for every cause which seems righteous at the moment."[84] The statement is not to deny the divine work in human history, but rather to warn against human ability to detect particular moments of history and consider such as divinely guided movements. Thomas certainly has this propensity to see the modern history of India, especially the renascence of Hinduism, as "the design of Providence."[85]

Unhappy with the warning, Thomas retorts, "But without discernment of what is of God in the changing situation and what is not, how do Christians participate in historical action?"[86] Again, one could see the underlying assumption of Thomas's approach in this sentence – that the relevance of the gospel and Christian's participation in it depend on one's ability to discern the divine work in human history. But the report seems to point to a different direction from that of Thomas. Instead, it correctly says that "we may nevertheless proclaim in such situations the Lordship of Christ over the whole process which is changing the aspect of our world."[87] That is to say, regardless of the circumstances we face, we are called to proclaim the gospel (2 Tim 4:2). As Newbigin rightly points out,

> It is not for the evangelist to determine in advance the way in which the Gospel will "come alive." That will become clear in the experience of the hearer. When the evangelist decides in advance exactly what is the "relevance" of the Gospel, one ends with the law instead of the Gospel . . . The proclamation of the Gospel creates its own relevance and raises its own questions in every human situation.[88]

Next, Thomas takes up the support of the charge from the renascence of non-Christian religions. He contends that Kraemer has neglected the dynamicity of non-Christian religions. Kraemer's holistic character of non-Christian religions is no longer valid because religions are dynamic

---

84. Visser 't Hooft, ed., *New Delhi Report*, 85.

85. Thomas, *Acknowledged Christ*, 240.

86. Thomas contends that the report was altered in accordance to "the perspective of European Neo-orthodoxy." Therefore, it was designed to criticize the theology of Devandan, upon which Thomas's thought rests. See Thomas, *Risking Christ*, 110–111.

87. Visser 't Hooft, *New Delhi Report*, 85.

88. Newbigin, "Review of *Salvation*," 77.

and changing. The changes, Thomas explains, occur due to the impact of Christianity and Western secular cultures. Undoubtedly Thomas has a positive view of the penetration of the West into the East. As mentioned above, he reckons the British rule over India as divine providence and goes even further to suggest that Indian cultures and religions in their renascent form could serve as *praeparatio evangelica*.[89] Paul Devanandan explains this point as follow:

> In India there have been prophets and teachers who have prepared the way for Christ . . . in the sense that they have trained the people in noble ways of living and taught them by word and example receptiveness to the ministry of Jesus . . . They point out that real progress in religion is possible only with the help of a spiritual teacher which is far more effective than reading. Though these utterances refer only to human teachers, their insistence on the necessity of personal guidance finds its fulfillment in the supreme religious teacher, Jesus Christ. . .[90]

Devanandan suggests that not only the Indian spiritual teachers prepare the way for Christ, but that they also occupy the same status as the Old Testament prophets did for the Jews. He continues to say, "If Jesus blamed His contemporaries for not listening to the voice of Moses, with equal power and vehemence will He condemn us for not listening to Ramanuja, Manikkavacakar, Tukaram, Kabir and Chaitanya who have left behind them teaching of such undying value, pointing the way to Christ."[91]

As I have shown above, Kraemer's holistic view of religions does not imply that there would be no changes in religions. To be sure, Kraemer would also certainly agree with Thomas in regard to the great impact Western civilization made in all aspects of life, including religions, in the East. This is especially

---

89. On this point Thomas modifies the view of those who argue that Western culture could serve for the preparation of the gospel. Instead, he argues that "not Western culture as such, but the national cultural awakening which its impact has produced is the preparation for the Gospel." Here he points to Christ as the factor of such awakening. For that matter, "the radical break with Indian traditional culture and religions is not necessary because Christ the Eternal Word has been at work preparing for his coming in India." See, Thomas, *Acknowledged Christ*, 247–249.

90. Devanandan, "Christian and Non-Christian," 79.

91. Devanandan, 79.

true with Christian or Western education and to a certain extent it paves the way for the Gospel by loosening "the bonds of the world from which the pupils originate." Then, it also "arouses a critical attitude towards their own environment." Finally, "education awakens a desire to reflect seriously on other creeds, in our case Christianity, even a desire to talk about it and to draw comparison with their own religious traditions."[92] Hence, for Kraemer, Christian or Western education indeed has a great positive impact on the proclamation of the gospel. Yet, their agreement seems to stop at this point.

As Thomas proceeds further, his position, however, moves further away from that of Kraemer. When he suggests that the teachings of Hinduism in their renascent form could serve as *praeparatio evangelica*, one could see that his position looks similar to that of Farquhar. Thomas starts with the aim to establish a post-Kraemer theology, a position which, he says, seeks to maintain the substance of Kraemer's position but goes beyond it. But when his position turns out to be the very position which Kraemer opposed one would wonder whether he could still secure his own thesis.

Thomas's last support is that Kraemer's theological framework is hostile to non-Christian cultures due to its overemphasis on the danger of syncretism. S. Wesley Ariarajah echoes the same sentiment as that of Thomas. He says, "The relationship between the majority culture and the Christian minority" is characterized by the term "alienation" and "the Christian attitude towards the majority is 'fear.'"[93] So, we have alienation which is caused by fear, including here fear of syncretism. Julius Lipner agrees with Thomas and Ariarajah but gives a different reason. He contends that in Kraemer's position, the gospel is inimical toward culture, and the blame lies on his dialectical theology. He explains as follows:

> According to the *dialectic* tendency, the gospel is other than and inimical to culture. The gospel and culture are in perpetual conflict, and their struggle and irreconcilability are expressed in polarity terms – the gospel being one pole, culture the other – usually, but not always, in the language of contrasting spatial and temporal metaphor. It is said that the gospel is from "above," culture from "below"; the gospel is "of God," culture "from man";

---

92. Kraemer, *From Missionfield to Independent*, 138.
93. Ariarajah, "Christian Minorities," 21.

the gospel is "light," culture "darkness"; and so on. This tendency, with its characteristic mode of discourse, has always had an important place in Christian theology, from the "Jerusalem-Athens" dichotomy of a Tertullian to the modern polarities of a Barth and Kraemer.[94]

I will give responses in the following sequence. I will deal first with Lipner's point, followed by that of Thomas and Ariarajah. In regard to the former, I maintain that Lipner's accusation is not accurate. That is to say, in Kraemer's position, the gospel is not inimical toward culture but stands in paradox toward it. Hence, speaking in H. Richard Niebuhr's paradigm,[95] Kraemer's position is not "Christ against culture," but "Christ and culture in Paradox."[96] Kraemer's position in this regard is evident from his own words.

> The great merit of Richard Niebuhr's book is that it makes abundantly clear that, looking at the Christianity-culture problem in the light of the significance of Jesus Christ, one is squarely faced with paradox, in which the "in" and the "against" are in an antagonistic, polar unity. It demonstrates the peculiar tension inherent in Christianity in regard to culture.[97]

Such a position needs to be understood in light of the special status held by Christianity as a religion. Kraemer maintains that Christianity is not like other religions. In other religions, the holistic character of religions is in full display. In other words, "the symbiosis of culture and religion belongs to their essence." This, however, cannot be said of Christianity, even though to a certain extent it is also ceded to this holistic character. Still, this character does not belong to its essence. In other words, it is only accidental that it succumbs to this characterization. This is especially true when it is polluted by pagan thoughts. Instead, one will find in Christianity "a fundamental stubbornness and aloofness." That is to say, Christianity stands above or is distinct from cultures. As such, this aloof character creates "an avoidable tension; a detached 'distance' in regard to culture as the field of human creativity." Admittedly,

---

94. Lipner, "'Being One,'" 159.
95. See Niebuhr, *Christ and Culture*.
96. Kraemer, *World Cultures*, 95.
97. Kraemer, 95.

the tension has been "the cause of the many conflicts between Christianity and culture in the course of history."[98]

Having said this, Kraemer maintains that "[Christianity] certainly has a very positive relation to culture, as innate as the detachment referred to, and for the same reasons." What he means by this is that the conflicts are "the result of a misunderstanding of itself by a concrete form of Christianity, or of a right self-understanding."[99] Consequently, if the misunderstanding could be avoided or corrected, then Christianity will bring positive effects to human cultures. Kraemer uses the imagery of "salt of the world" to explain this positive relation. When it is true to its nature, its salt will create a healthy tension, and thus will bring "at the same time creative judgment and creative invigoration." On the other hand, if "Christianity is half or wholly insipid, the tension between Christianity and culture is a false, unfruitful tension, harmful both to Christianity in its essence and historical manifestation and to culture."[100] Kraemer thus contends that Christianity has inherent tension with cultures, but still has a positive relation to it when it is true to its nature.

In terms of missionary practice, Kraemer's dialectical theology does not hinder him from appreciating non-Christian spiritual lives and cultures. W. A. Visser 't Hooft writes in the introductory note of Kraemer's *From Missionfield to Independent Church*, saying:

> Through this book [*The Christian Message*] and the more recent "Religion and the Christian Faith" Kraemer has become known as the consistent opponent of syncretism or relativism in all their various forms. It was not sufficiently realized that he is at the same time a pioneer in understanding of and penetration into the world of the non-Christian religions. The real originality of his missionary attitude lies precisely in the dialectical combination of an uncompromising christocentric theology with patient, loving attention for the spiritual life of the people to whom the Gospel is to be brought.[101]

---

98. Kraemer, 20; cf. *Religion and the Christian Faith*, 26–27.
99. Kraemer, *World Cultures*, 21.
100. Kraemer, 21.
101. Visser 't Hooft, "Introductory Note," 7.

Visser 't Hooft, thus, has an opinion contrary to that of Lipner. Dialectic does not mean that there is an opposition between the gospel and cultures. But it means that there are negative and positive aspects of the gospel. Negatively, the gospel is against syncretism; and positively it reaches out toward non-Christians. Such a positive attitude toward cultures is carried out not despite, but because of his dialectic theology. This is made clear in Kraemer's own assertion in the preface of the above-mentioned book. He says,

> They [the reports] had at the same time a theoretical and practical purpose. They are based on intensive preparatory study and on a not less intensive endeavor of field-research. It led me to fundamental theological thinking into the meaning of the church and of missions, and also into launching out in many attempts at what in the present time bears the name of Cultural Anthropology. I did not intend, nor pretend to be a cultural anthropologist, but in fact I pioneered in it in my own way, simply because one cannot consider the meaning of the Church and Missions in the world without penetrating into the fundamental assumptions of Culture and Cultures.[102]

One can then see that Kraemer's interest in studying non-Christian cultures flows out of his theological framework; at the same time, he was convinced that the meaning of the church and mission could not be understood without a deep understanding of local cultures.

Next, I will deal with the charge that Kraemer's theology is hostile to culture due to its overemphasis on the danger of syncretism. I argue that Kraemer's emphasis on syncretism does not hinder Christians, especially those of the younger churches, to engage with non-Christian lives and cultures because of his simultaneous emphasis on adaptation (i.e. a proper expression of the Christian faith in and with local cultural and spiritual lives). I have dealt with Kraemer's view of both syncretism and adaptation in chapter 3 of this book. It then suffices to say that emphasis on the danger of syncretism does not deter Christians from valuing other religions and cultures, for at the same time they are also required to practice adaptation, a practice which compels them to treasure their native forms of cultural and spiritual

---

102. Kraemer, *From Missionfield to Independent*, 9.

lives. Hence, in Kraemer's theology, adaptation is never an option, but it is necessary to have a true expression of Christianity because in reality there is no Christianity but all kinds of adapted Christianities.

Thomas was certainly aware of Kraemer's double emphases on syncretism and adaptation. Still, he contends that in the end, the fear of syncretism has overcome the courage to apply adaptation. What factors could have contributed to this drawback? Thomas does not say directly but seems to indicate that the culprit lies in the misperception of Kraemer's message. Talking about the impact of the Tambaram Conference on the Indian church leaders, Thomas asserts that "the danger of syncretism was the only note they heard and heeded."[103] If it is true that the impediment is caused by this misperception, the blame could not be placed solely on the messenger. One would not do justice by judging his position simply through the impression he made in a conference. In addition to this, Kraemer's position is laid bare in his various books and essays. This is precisely what Kraemer might have thought in his reply to Thomas. He complained that Thomas had not acted fairly by not carefully reading his views on cultures and human matters scattered in many books, essays, and addresses.[104] Hence, the charge that Kraemer overemphasizes the danger of syncretism cannot be substantiated from Kraemer's own works. In other words, we argue that Kraemer's emphasis on the danger of syncretism does not lead to anti-adaptation. Being aware of the danger of syncretism is not inherently anti-culture. The following two examples will illustrate this point.

First, I will consider his advocacy of the indigenization of the younger churches. Indeed, Libertus Hoedemaker asserts that "the indigenization of the church became the major focus of [Kraemer's] work."[105] Again, Walter Horton also attests to Kraemer's tremendous passion for the spiritual lives and cultures of the local people in which he had served. Horton, while acknowledging that Kraemer's position is in opposition to that of Hocking's *Laymen's Report*, contends that "as an actual missionary in Indonesia, he was quite willing to indigenize the Christian message in non-Christian environments by borrowing from the local culture. He was not trying to 'Westernize'

---

103. Thomas, "Absoluteness of Jesus Christ," 135.
104. Thomas, "Rewarding Correspondence," 11.
105. Hoedemaker, "Hendrik Kraemer," 509.

the culture and was quite willing in this sense to 'learn as well as teach,' as the Laymen's Commission recommended."[106] Finally, Visser 't Hooft summarizes as follows: "Thus, Kraemer is always fighting on two fronts: against a watering down of the missionary motive and against lack for indigenous culture and religion."[107]

Yet, there are two ways of being appreciative for indigenous culture and religion (i.e. syncretism and adaptation). The two are not identical, but closely related. This is especially true with the indigenization of the churches in Asia and Africa, where the cultural and spiritual heritage of the younger churches in these regions are of pagan background. True indigenization of the churches, however, is not only possible but also necessary for the sake of the proclamation of the gospel. Kraemer explains:

> The smell of the earth, the brightness of the sky, the natural and spiritual atmosphere which, in the course of ages, wrought the soul of a people, have to manifest themselves in the kind of Christianity that grows there. This is far from being syncretism in the technical sense in which it is currently used, but it is a certain kind of coalescence, of symbiosis without losing identity.[108]

Hence, true indigenization is achieved when the symbiosis of a foreign religion with a local spirituality and culture does not cause that religion to lose its identity.

Kraemer's analysis of the Sundanese of West-Java, Indonesia, will illuminate my case here. The indigenization of Islam into the Sundanese society has taken root so deeply that it has been totally assimilated. In doing so, the Islamic faith has lost its identity in being totally absorbed by its pre-Islamic worldview. Kraemer explains as follows:

> Speaking about the Sundanese in general terms, we may make two statements which are both equally true. A Sundanese is not at all a Mohammedan, and yet he is a convinced Mohammedan devoted to Islam. The explanation of this contradictory statement is to be found in one thing. All things considered, the

---

106. Horton, "Tambaram," 229.
107. Visser 't Hooft, "Introductory Note," 8.
108. Kraemer, *Religion and the Christian Faith*, 390–391.

Sundanese people have almost completely assimilated Islam, fitting it into their ancient conception of the world and life. Seen from this angle, the Sundanese have preserved their identity of pre-Islamic times. Yet, precisely because they have assimilated Islam to such an extent within their own ancient way of life, Islam has grown into their life and is readily accorded its actual place of authority in the people's soul.[109]

Kraemer maintains that Christianity cannot apply the way of indigenization adopted by Islam as shown above. The reason is obvious. For Kraemer, this is an epitome of syncretistic indigenization. He, however, does not reject indigenization categorically, for it is possible to have an indigenized form of Christianity without ceding to syncretism. Hence, he explains what Christianity ought to do as follows:

> Christianity must be rooted in the soul of Sundanese, it must learn to express itself in Sundanese terms and forms, but it must also conquer the ancient view of the world and of life and transform it into spiritual life of an essentially different, Christian nature, instead of being submerged by or amalgamated with the old notions, as has been the case with Islam.[110]

Up to this point, it will be sufficient for us to see that neither dialectic theology nor the emphasis on the danger of syncretism would lead to a hostile attitude toward cultures. Still, to strengthen my point, I will also present his treatment on *wayang*, a traditional Javanese shadow puppet.[111] Kraemer's advocacy of *wayang* as a means of spreading the gospel is worth mentioning

---

109. Kraemer, *From Missionfield to Independent*, 129–130.
110. Kraemer, 130.
111. There are types of *wayang* – *wayang kulit*, *wayang golek*, *wayang wong*, etc. When our writers (i.e. Kraemer and J. H. Bavinck) speak of *wayang*, with exception in places where they specify, they generally refer to *wayang kulit*. *Wayang kulit* is the most widespread *wayang* theatre, established mostly in Java and Bali, but also enjoyed in other parts of the Indonesian archipelago and in the Malayan peninsula. It uses flat shadow puppets, usually made of water buffalo hide, and beautifully crafted and painted. The *dalang*, or the performer, directs the movements of the *wayang* puppets as he/she narrates the story, which is typically taken from *Mahabharata* and *Ramayana*. The show is always accompanied by the traditional music of *gamelan*. The audiences enjoy the show following the shadows of the puppets reflected on the screen. Hence, it is a shadow puppet show. For more information about *wayang*, see Geertz, *Religion of Java*, 261–278; Mrázek, *Phenomenology*.

because this form of local culture is loaded with philosophical and religious meaning. Kraemer's stand on this point shows that he is unhesitant to engage with an aspect of the cultural and spiritual lives of non-Christians, even with that which is on the verge of syncretism. He dares to take a risk lest he should lose the opportunity to get into the heart of people's spiritual lives and therefore be deprived of having an advantage in the proclamation of the gospel.

In his essay *De Wajang als Uiting van Javaansche Cultuur*, Kraemer maintains that "*wayang* is unquestionably the most important . . . expression of Javanese culture."[112] It is so important that anyone who wants to understand the Javanese way of life needs to turn to *wayang* as their teacher. This form of culture is so closely related to the Javanese people that its history could not be conceivable without relating it to the literature of *wayang*. It has been so deeply rooted in the lives of the people that not even the acceptance of Islam as their religion could uproot this form of culture. Even though *wayang* is obviously of Hindu tradition, the Islamic teachers, the *wali*, were unhesitant to adopt it to spread the Islamic faith. Kraemer refers to such practice as "the marriage of Islam and Hindu Javanese syncretism."[113] More important than a cultural expression, *wayang* is indeed "one of the elementary forming forces for the Javanese spirit."[114] By this, he means that *wayang* is "the ideal instrument for the Javanese to continue to hold on to the old world of mythical and naturalistic thoughts and feelings as the 'Home of the Soul.'"[115] In other words, *wayang* is the embodiment of the Javanese "mythical-naturalistic worldview." It is a form of culture that is loaded with "magic-religious meaning."[116]

Johan H. Bavinck, Kraemer's fellow missionary in Indonesia, not only agrees with his assessment of the magic-religious aspect of *wayang*, but he also points out the danger of this form of art. He describes it as follows:

---

112. "De wajang is onwedersprekelijk één der gewichtigste . . . uiting van de Javaansche cultuur . . ." Kraemer, "De Wajang als Uiting," 33.

113. "Dit huwelijk van Islam en Hindoe-Javaansch syncretism . . ." Kraemer, "De Wajang als Uiting," 35–36.

114. "de wajang een der elementaire vormende krachten is voor den Javaanschen geest" Kraemer, "De Wajang als Uiting," 36–37.

115. "Zij is het middel bij uitstek waardoor de Javaan de oude wereld van het mythische en naturalistiche denken en voelen als de 'Heimat der Seele' blijft vashouden." Kraemer, "De Wajang als Uiting," 37.

116. Yet, not all types of *wayang* have this magic-religious function. *Wayang wong* (i.e. that which is performed by real persons), "can be considered entirely as arts." See Kraemer, "De Wajang als Uiting," 40–41.

Certainly [*wayang's*] greatest danger is that it hypnotizes the soul with that amazing view of the world that involves everything.

But all of this merely is an indication of something much deeper, something that penetrates to the foundation. The whole atmosphere of the *wayang* is one that turns everything about life into a dream, and in that dream the stability of life's basic reality is lost and is immersed in one big cosmic game. And if that is where you find yourself, it seems like you are no longer yourself and that your live in a world that is not real, swept along in that huge shadow game of existence.[117]

For sure, Kraemer is cognizant of this danger. This is apparent in his report on the churches in East Java,[118] in which one can see his cautious and nuanced approach to *wayang*. In this report, Kraemer noticed that there were two groups of Christians with opposing strategies for their mission. On the one side there was the "Surabaja group" with its "excessive Europeanization" and on the other side the "Coolen group" with its "javanization of Christianity."[119] In contrast to the Coolen group, which used *wayang*, *gamelan*, and other forms of local culture and religious traditions, the Surabaja group adopted European ways of life and styles and prohibited the use of *wayang* and *gamelan*.[120] Kraemer, however, does not side with one or the other. He sees that both sides have positive aspects in their approaches and yet at the same time have practices that deserve censure. He criticized the "excessive Europeanization" of the Surabaja group and regarded it a hindrance for mission, because with this approach the gospel is presented to the people of Java in its foreign and "undiluted" form. Yet, he also saw the problem of Coolen's Javanization of Christianity as it "kept the Gospel too exclusively enclosed within Javanese forms instead of making it stand out more clearly

---

117. Bolt, Pratt, and Visser, *Bavinck Reader*, 384.

118. See Kraemer, *From Missionfield to Independent*, 73–95.

119. The Coolen group refers to a group of Christians started by Coenraad Laurens Coolen (1775–1873), born of a Russian father and a Javanese mother. Coolen's mission was started in 1827, when he settled in a newly opened area called Ngoro, about sixty miles Southwest of Surabaya. The Surabaja group was started in 1851 by Johannes Emde (1774–1859), a German-born watchmaker. Kraemer, *From Missionfield to Independent*, 73–75; see also van den End, *Ragi Carita*, 199–201.

120. *Gamelan* is a traditional Javanese musical instrument. It is always used to accompany a *wayang* show. For further information about *gamelan*, see Geertz, *Religion of Java*, 278–280.

in its essential characteristics against this Javanese background." As a result, "Christianity was veiled rather than unveiled."[121] Conversely, Kraemer also noticed positive aspects of their approaches. In regard to the prohibition of *wayang* by the Surabaja group, for example, he deemed it necessary for newly converted Christians, "because they could be dragged down by the associations evoked by *wajang* and *gamelan*."[122] Hence, one can see that Kraemer was fully aware of the danger of this type of culture.

Yet, despite the caveat, Kraemer still insists that *wayang* and other similar forms of local culture have a role to play in the proclamation of the gospel. Kraemer explains his advocacy of using *wayang* for evangelism in his essay "Wajang en Christendom."[123] In the first place, he clarifies that such advocacy involves neither syncretism nor laxism. In addition to these, he also adds that he does not advocate the usage for those who no longer use or entertain it. With this, Kraemer indicates that he does not fight merely for the sake of preserving culture. Nor does he necessitate the Christianization of *wayang*.[124] Instead, he argues that Western missionaries should "give freedom to the Javanese Christians" to utilize *wayang*.[125] Such an attitude, however, cannot be carried out with an indifference to the *wayang*. Two reasons are given here. First, indifference would be interpreted as "unconditional disapproval" by the Javanese Christians. Second, "indifference to the *wayang* is a disadvantage for the work of the proclamation of the Gospel and for the building up of the Christian consciousness of the Christian Javanese."[126] Hence, Kraemer's attitude toward culture is fundamentally driven by the motive for Christian mission. It is his conviction that "for a proper implantation of Christianity in the hearts of a people of another culture, the knowledge of the soil, in which

---

121. Kraemer, *From Missionfield to Independent*, 77–78.
122. Kraemer, 78.
123. Kraemer, "Christendom," 373–391.
124. Kraemer, 373–374.
125. "Wat invoering of verchristenlijking van de wajang als spel betreft, is mijn meening, dat wij de Christen-Javanen daarin vrij moeten laten, tenzij actueele verhoudingen ons gebieden onze meening ondubbelzinnig te doen blijken." Kraemer, "Christendom," 374.
126. "onverschilligheid voor de wajang een nadeel is voor het werk der Evangelieverkondiging en voor den opbouw van het christelijk bewustzijn der Christen-Javanen." Kraemer, "Christendom," 374.

one plants, namely, the knowledge of and understanding of the history and nature of that soil, is necessary."[127]

5.6 Internal Tensions in Kraemer's Thought

Theology of religions, Bert Hoedemaker argues, deals with three necessities: "it will never eliminate the question 'Who do you say that I am?'; it will never diminish the necessity to name the name of Jesus Christ and to explicate it in contemporary contexts."[128] Kraemer's critics – Hogg, D'Costa, and Thomas – agree with Kraemer in regard to the first two necessities; but they find Kraemer's thought to be deficient in dealing with the third. Still, I have shown that those objections to Kraemer's theses can be sufficiently answered.

That said, I argue here that some internal tensions remain in Kraemer's thought. There are three areas in which those tensions are apparent. First, Kraemer does not seem to be able to confirm fully the reality of general revelation. Previously I have shown that Kraemer admitted that the revelatory act of God in other religions and cultures was not dealt with sufficiently in his *The Christian Message*, and therefore sets to amend this deficiency in his *Religion and the Christian Faith*.[129] Yet, one will soon find vagueness in his attempt. As Gerald H. Anderson carefully observes, what Kraemer attempts to do in the first place, namely, to affirm various modes of revelation, he cancelled out in the end.[130] In the final analysis those modes of revelation are unbiblical and have no ontological status. Kraemer puts it as follows:

> We should, in our speaking about modes (in the plural) of revelation, never forget that it is, Biblically speaking, already somehow inadequate to say that God reveals Himself in nature and in history. Such abstract *Allegemeinsäze* . . . are unbiblical and, moreover, not true to fact. They are figments of thought at times useful as instruments but they do not represent anything real.[131]

---

127. "voor een goed inplanten van het Christendom in de harten van en ander volk kennis van den bodem noodig is, in welken men plant, kennis van en begrip voor de geschiedenis en den aard van dien bodem." Kraemer, "Christendom," 374.

128. Hoedemaker, "Kraemer Reassessed," 49.

129. Kraemer, *Religion and the Christian Faith*, 231–233.

130. Anderson, "Kraemer and After," 355.

131. Kraemer, *Religion and the Christian Faith*, 354.

Second, Kraemer is rather inconsistent in his affirmation of the dialectical nature of religions. Again, Kraemer was aware of the criticism of his view of non-Christian religions in *The Christian Message*. In his *Religion and the Christian Faith*, he acknowledges this deficiency, saying, "We have far too one-sidedly characterized the religions as human performances and achievements, good or bad, and dealt with them too unilaterally as purely human products. Only in short parentheses have we expressed the opinion that God is somehow active in these religions too."[132] Having acknowledged this deficiency, he attempts to amend it by stressing its dialectical nature, namely, that religions are both of humans and of God. Yet, in the same book, he again contradicts his own intention. Summarizing the trend of religions in the Old Testament, he contends that

> the world of religion and religions (of culture as a whole) belongs to the realm of the "old man," the unredeemed man, not yet re-created into the Image of God in whose likeness man was originally created, and therefore, with all its marvelous achievements and Satanic deviations, under divine judgment, dimly or unwittingly awaiting its redemption.[133]

The divine aspect in religions is totally left out and religions turn to be human and demonic products. Such a totally negative assessment of religions is rather confusing and apparently contradictory to the overall emphasis of the dialectical nature of religions.

Third, Kraemer's holistic character of religions seems to be incongruent with his positive appreciation of non-Christian cultures. I have dealt with the criticism in regard to this aspect. It has been shown that by holistic Kraemer does not intend to mean that religions are rigid and unchangeable. Instead, the emphasis lies on the interrelation between religions and cultures with their apprehension of reality. Again, it has been shown, too, that even though he was wholeheartedly against syncretism in any form, Kraemer argued for a positive relation between Christianity and non-Christian cultures. Syncretism does not mean opposition to adaptation. This positive appreciation of non-Christian cultures is, for example, apparent in his advocacy for using *wayang*

---

132. Kraemer, 316.
133. Kraemer, 257.

for evangelism, even though he is aware that *wayang* is not philosophically and religiously neutral. Now, the tension of Kraemer's thought is apparent in this point. How could Kraemer justify the usage a form of culture, tradition, and art, which is apparently tainted by naturalistic and monistic apprehensions of life, and still consider it not a form of syncretism? On this point, we feel that both Hogg and Bavinck are more consistent in the application of a holistic view of religions. As I have shown above, Hogg agreed with Kraemer that "non-Christian religions are organic wholes," but with the clarification that this is not "an achieved unity," but "an inevitable and persistent process of unification." Still, with this rather "imperfect" unity, "the dye [of 'monistic mysticism'] has become so 'fixed'" as to render it "not only little helpful, but dangerous, to borrow strands of Hindu thought for the weaving of an 'adapted' form of Christian theology."[134] J. H. Bavinck's view is similar to that of Hogg. Voicing his skepticism of adapting *wayang* into Christianity, Bavinck says:

> When a strong Christian church emerges on Java, I do not know whether that church will seize on the *wayang* as a means for leading people into the mysteries of its worship. But I certainly do know that if the *wayang* drama ever becomes a bearer of Christian ideas, it will have to be changed fundamentally. It is not about whether various characters will have to be eliminated from the *wayang* or whether various impure elements will have to be banned from it, but it is all about what makes the *wayang* drama a *wayang* – its alien vision of life and the world; this will have to be transformed.[135]

Yet, Bavinck does not totally close a possibility of transforming human culture. On this point he differs from Hogg. A possibility of transforming culture is due to common grace. I will return to this point in next chapter.

That said, I argue that those tensions could be properly addressed if the Christian doctrine of grace and of revelation are treated properly. This will be dealt with in the next chapter.

---

134. Hogg, *Towards Clarifying*, 11; cf. "Christian Attitude," 100–101.
135. Bolt, Pratt, and Visser, *Bavinck Reader*, 387.

Summary

In this chapter I have first analyzed the critiques of Kraemer's theology of religions. The critics argue against Kraemer on the following points. First, the *sui generis* character of the Christian revelation is contradictory to the attempted openness to non-Christian religions. Second, a radical discontinuity between the Christian revelation and non-Christian religions cannot be maintained. Third, the holistic character of non-Christian religions fails to account for the dynamicity of religions. Finally, the danger of syncretism is overemphasized in that it hinders the practices of adaptation.

In my evaluation of those critiques, I found that the objections to Kraemer's theses can be answered sufficiently. First, Kraemer's *sui generis* character of the Christian revelation is not in conflict with his openness to other religions. For D'Costa, the two statements are mutually exclusive; Kraemer maintains that they are not. Hence, Kraemer could maintain that the Christian revelation is absolutely *sui generis*, and at the same time he accepts other forms of revelation. He maintains that Jesus Christ is the only way of salvation, and accepts the existence of general revelation. In this case, I agree with Kraemer that the two statements are not mutually exclusive. D'Costa's charge could only be true if revelation is concomitant with salvation, but it is not. I will return to this topic later.

Second, Kraemer concedes with Hogg that a radical discontinuity position is untenable. Some sort of continuity must exist between the Christian revelation and non-Christian religions. Indeed, there must be both continuity and discontinuity. Such a position is in line with Kraemer's dialectical emphasis. Yet, Kraemer cannot agree with Hogg that this continuity occurs in the non-Christian faith. Kraemer also rejects Hogg's aim to postulate a possibility of salvation via this continuity. At this point, I agree with Kraemer. There is no direct link between revelation and salvation.

Third, in regard to the charge that Kraemer's holistic character of non-Christian religions is rigid, I disagree with Kraemer's critics. By holistic, Kraemer does not mean that non-Christian religions cannot change or be changed. Instead, he emphasizes the interconnectedness and mutual influence of all elements in a religion. The charge is therefore based on a misunderstanding of Kraemer's concept.

Fourth, Thomas's charge concerning Kraemer's fourth thesis cannot be substantiated. Kraemer's emphasis on the danger of syncretism does not hinder his appreciation of other religions and cultures. Kraemer's active advocacy for the indigenization of the churches demonstrates that the two emphases – avoiding syncretism and practicing adaptation – are not mutually exclusive.

Yet, we find that some internal tensions remain in Kraemer's thought. First, Kraemer finds difficulty in affirming the reality of general revelation. This is due to his Christocentric concept of revelation. Second, the dialectical character of religions looks imbalanced. He attempts to maintain that religions are both positive and negative. However, in the end, his model tilts toward the negative side. Third, the holistic character of non-Christian religions does not fit well with his appreciation of non-Christian religions and cultures. If non-Christian religions and cultures are thought to be organic, it will be impossible to appreciate non-Christian cultures without falling into the trap of syncretism. Here, a proper model is needed.

In conclusion, I argue that those internal tensions could be overcome if the doctrines of revelation and grace are treated properly. We will deal with this in the next chapter.

CHAPTER 6

Revelation and Grace

Before proceeding further, I would like to recapture what I have done so far. In chapters 2 and 3, I described Kraemer's theology of religions and showed that his theology of religions set out to be an alternative to that of Farquhar and Hocking. Kraemer maintains the uniqueness of Christianity and the necessity of Christian mission. He does so by emphasizing the following points: the *sui generis* character of the Christian revelation, the radical discontinuity of the Christian revelation and non-Christian religions, the holistic character of non-Christian religions, and the dangers of syncretism.

In chapter 4, I dealt with critiques of Kraemer's position given by Hogg, D'Costa, and Thomas. The critics agree with Kraemer pertaining to the uniqueness of Christianity and the necessity of Christian mission in its traditional sense. Yet, they raised objections to Kraemer's theological framework, which they saw as inadequate to deal with the relationship of Christianity with other religions and cultures. Each of them objected to one or more elements of Kraemer's theses. In chapter 5, I showed that their objections can be answered sufficiently.

I also pointed out that some internal tensions remain in Kraemer's theology. I find issues in the following points: (1) general revelation, (2) the dialectical nature of religions, and (3) the holistic character of religions. I will deal with those issues in this chapter. I argue that those internal tensions can be overcome through properly navigating two cardinal doctrines of Christianity, that is revelation and grace. Here, I will utilize thoughts of Reformed theologians (e.g. Herman Bavinck, Abraham Kuyper, and Johan H. Bavinck).

6.1 Revelation, Grace, and Salvation

Scholars have discussed impasses in the theology of religions.[1] This is also true concerning the debate over Kraemer's theology of religions. By this I mean that the debate has come to a stalemate.[2] As I have shown in previous chapters, although objections to Kraemer's theses can be sufficiently answered, the inadequacies of Kraemer's thought were exposed and left unamended. To go beyond this stalemate, I contend that it is necessary to look into factors that have contributed to it, namely, the confusion of the ideas of revelation, grace, and salvation in recent religious thought. Such confusion is the consequence when the distinction of special and general revelation is denied, and the distinction of particular and common grace is absent in a theological system. We will see briefly how this issue developed historically.

Unquestionably the idea of revelation plays a central role in various fields of study, such as philosophy, nature, history, culture, and religion.[3] Scholars have given much attention and emphasis to the idea of revelation in dealing with religions.[4] Such treatment could be seen as a reaction against the marginalization, and eventually the banishment, of the idea of revelation, which has taken place since the eighteenth century with the rise of rationalism and deism.[5] In line with this thought, revelation is regarded as unnecessary or at best something that belongs to the past. For some deists or rationalists, it is possible then to establish a "natural theology" or "natural religion" that is

---

1. See for example, Fredericks, *Faith Among Faiths*, 8–9; Hedges, *Controversies in Interreligious Dialogue*; Rose, *Pluralism*, 25–43; Yong, *Discerning the Spirit(s)*, 33–58. Fredericks provided a helpful definition of impasse in this context quoted as follows: "The proponents of the pluralistic approach have been very successful in exposing the inadequacies of more traditional views of Christianity in relation to other religions, but, at the same time, their critics have also been successful in exposing the inadequacies of the pluralists." Fredericks, *Faith Among Faiths*, 8.

2. See Anderson, "Kraemer and After," 356.

3. The significance of revelation in various fields of study can be seen in Bavinck, *Philosophy of Revelation*.

4. For discussions about revelation and religion, see for example, Bavinck, *Philosophy of Revelation*, 142–169; Dulles, *Models of Revelation*, 174–192; D'Costa, "Revelation and Revelations," 165–183; Farmer, *Revelation and Religion*; Mavrodes, *Revelation*; McDermott and Netland, *Trinitarian Theology*, 86–121; Wach, "General Revelation," 83–93; Ward, *Religion and Revelation*.

5. For the marginalization of the idea of revelation, see for example, Bavinck, *Reformed Dogmatics*, 288; Baillie, *Idea of Revelation*, 6; McDermott and Netland, *Trinitarian Theology*, 86–87. All references to Bavinck's *Reformed Dogmatics* hereafter *RD* followed by Roman numeral to indicate the volume of the series, and Arabic numeral for the page(s).

independent from divine revelation.⁶ But, the endeavor to find a "religion without revelation" proved to be so elusive that it soon ran out of steam.⁷ Then by the nineteenth century the idea of revelation made its comeback.⁸ Revelation was not only reemphasized but it was also expanded so much that, as Herman Bavinck points out, "Everything seemed to originate from revelation: religion, poetry, philosophy, history, and language."⁹ Unfortunately, it did not return to the biblical concept of revelation, but to pantheistic concepts of revelation. Bavinck mentions three features of this kind of revelation. First, revelation is confused with religion. The two are considered identical.¹⁰ Second, the history of religious consciousness is taken as the history of revelation. Third, the distinction between natural and supernatural, or general and special, revelation disappears.¹¹

Bavinck's analysis of the influence of pantheistic notions to the idea of revelation is noteworthy. It explains the root of the confusion that occurs with the concept of revelation in recent religious thought. The denial of the distinction between general and special revelation is crucial for our discussion. As such it exists in two types. The first type acknowledges that there is only general revelation, but marginalizes, or even rejects, special revelation.¹² This type is a direct result of the influence of pantheistic notions in revelation.¹³ The second type is opposite to and in reaction against the first type. It

---

6. Farmer mentions three ways by which the term natural theology could be used. In the first usage, it refers to the knowledge of God gained independently from revelation. This is in line with the definition I give above. In the second usage, however, it refers to "a process of reasoned argument to define His nature and to demonstrate His reality as so defined." In the second usage, however, natural theology does not necessarily exclude divine revelation. It is basically a kind of theistic argument. Lastly, it could be used to mean "natural religion," namely, "beliefs about divine reality . . . which arise out of some kind of spontaneous religious response to the world, and not . . . out of reasoned reflection and argument." Farmer, *Revelation and Religion*, 2–5. In line with Farmer's first usage, see, Gunton, *Brief Theology*, 41; Macquarrie, "Natural Theology," 402. For the second usage, see, Sudduth, *Reformed Objection*, 4–5; Plantinga, "Reformed Objection," 49.

7. Of course, this does not stop some to continue exploring this possibility. See, Huxley, *Religion Without Revelation*.

8. See, Bavinck, *RD I*, 289–295.

9. Bavinck, 289.

10. Kraemer also detects this problem. See, Kraemer, *World Cultures*, 329; *Why Christianity*, 39, 58.

11. Bavinck, *RD I*, 293.

12. For example, see Delitzsch, *Babel and Bible*, 166.

13. See Bavinck, *RD I*, 293; Berkouwer, *General Revelation*, 11–12.

acknowledges only special revelation and rejects general revelation.[14] The best example of the second type is Karl Barth's idea of revelation, which, I here contend, is linked closely to that of Kraemer. For this reason, I will briefly review Barth's concept of revelation.[15]

Barth's idea of revelation has two important features.[16] In the first place, it is thoroughly christological. Barth contends that "revelation in the Christian sense is the self-revelation of God."[17] Yet, this traditional statement of revelation is soon narrowed down to the person of Jesus Christ.[18] The Christian apprehension of revelation, Barth continues, is not only bound up with the name of Jesus Christ, but that name also determines "its content, its form and its limit."[19] This christological sense of revelation is so central that other ways of approaching revelation cannot be considered Christian.

In his *Church Dogmatics*, Barth talks about the word of God in its threefold form: preached (the proclamation), written (the Bible), and revealed (the revelation).[20] These three forms of the word of God are closely related. Both the proclamation and the Bible center on the revelation. The real proclamation happens when the word of God is preached. As such it "must be ventured in recollection of past revelation and in expectation of coming revelation."[21] The recollection of past revelation needs the Bible as its concrete means.[22] However, Barth maintains that the Bible is not by itself and as such God's past revelation and the proclamation is not by itself and as such God's future

---

14. For Herman Bavinck, either type of one-sidedness in regard to the doctrine of revelation is not right. But the worse of the two is to reject special revelation and to merge it with general revelation. Bavinck, *Our Reasonable Faith*, 44.

15. A thorough exposition of Karl Barth's idea of revelation is found in his *Church Dogmatics* especially in volume 1, part 1 and 2. See Barth, *Church Dogmatics*. In addition, I also utilize his short essays found in the following works: Barth, "Christian Understanding," 205–240; Baillie and Martin, *Revelation*, 41–81. All references to Barth's *Church Dogmatics* hereafter *CD* followed by Roman numeral to indicate the volume of the series, and Arabic numeral for the page(s).

16. For discussions of Barth's concept of revelation, see, Berkouwer, *General Revelation*, 21–31; Hart, "Revelation," 37–56; Parker, "Barth on Revelation," 366–382; Veitch, "Revelation and Religion," 1–22.

17. Barth, "Christian Understanding," 208.

18. Barth, 211.

19. Baillie and Martin, *Revelation*, 42–43.

20. Barth, *CD*, I/1, 88–120.

21. Barth, *CD*, I/1, 99.

22. Barth, *CD*, I/1, 111.

revelation. Both the Bible and the proclamation bear witness to the revelation that "has happened truly and definitely, once and once-for-all."[23] This revelation is Jesus Christ, the word became flesh. Barth says, "according to Holy Scripture God's revelation takes place in the fact that God's Word became a man and that this man has become God's Word. The incarnation of the eternal Word, Jesus Christ is God's revelation. In the reality of this event God proves that He is free to be our God."[24] To sum, even though Barth maintains the word of God in its three different forms, there is only one reality of revelation.[25] The first two forms (i.e. the proclamation and the Bible) eventually center on the final and ultimate form (i.e. the revelation in Jesus Christ). Both the proclamation and the Bible are not by itself and as such the revelation. They are only witnesses to the revelation in Jesus Christ.

I have shown that Barth maintains the exclusiveness of Jesus Christ as the divine revelation. In what follows I will deal with his view on general revelation. In the first place, as G. W. Bromiley contends, Barth "does not deny that there may be partial lights and words and truths even outside special revelation" in Jesus Christ.[26] Barth acknowledges that there is a second strand or line running "through the whole Bible in so far as the witness of the prophets and apostles to God's revelation," which seems to confirm revelation in nature and history.[27] However, the important question is whether this revelation has an independent status. In other words, does the Bible affirm the revelation in nature and history as a second revelation parallel to the revelation in Jesus Christ? Barth asks: "Does all this argue the right and necessity of a natural theology because it argues a knowability of God independent of His revelation but affirmed by the Bible itself?"[28] For Barth, the answer is negative.[29] He states: "From the main biblical assertions man in the cosmos is to be understood only as a dependent witness; not as a primary, but only as a secondary witness."[30] Hence, Barth concludes: "The revelation is but one . . .

---

23. Barth, *CD*, I/1, 115.
24. Barth, *CD*, I/2, 1.
25. Barth, *CD*, I/2, 1–25.
26. Bromiley, "Karl Barth," 55.
27. Barth, *CD*, II/1, 99.
28. Barth, *CD*, II/1, 99.
29. Barth, *CD*, II/1, 100.
30. Barth, *CD*, II/1, 105.

The revelation has imprinted itself upon the nature and the history of this world in quite definite forms, and this it does ever anew. These forms are not revelation itself. They are no multiplications of the Incarnation!"[31] What Christian theologians customarily regard as general revelation, Barth takes it only as tokens to the revelation in Jesus Christ.[32] As tokens of revelation they are "instituted and established" by Jesus Christ himself that "they may be witnesses and testimonies to Jesus Christ for the purpose of calling faith in Him."[33] Even more so, they do so not by their own power but Christ's, because they are only "instruments" in his hands.[34] For Barth, the status of general revelation is similar to that of the Bible. By itself and as such they are not revelation, but only witnesses to the revelation in Jesus Christ.

How does Barth deal with the biblical passages, for example, Romans 1 and Psalms 19, which are traditionally used to support general revelation? Barth tries to answer this challenge by using a "reading-into" strategy. In other words, Barth argues that what is customarily considered the knowledge of God in creation, is simply the knowledge of God derived from the revelation in Christ projected to or reading-into the creation. For Barth, "in itself and as such the text of the cosmos is, indeed, mute."[35] So, when the heavens are said to declare the glory of God, "it is rightly and properly read . . . into the text of the cosmos itself."[36] Berkouwer explains, "What is referred to is not some specific knowledge which the heathen have from a revelation in creation apart from the cross, but rather the revelation preached by Paul, and what is said of the heathen concerns 'the truth ascribed to, reckoned to and imputed to heathen over and above himself.'"[37] Hence, ontologically, there is no reality of God's knowledge in creation. There is no voice of God directly from his handiwork. That voice that one hears from it is simply an echo reflected to it from the voice of Jesus Christ. Barth explains:

---

31. Baillie and Martin, *Revelation*, 63.
32. Baillie and Martin, 64.
33. Baillie and Martin, 64.
34. Baillie and Martin, 64.
35. Barth, *CD*, II/1, 112.
36. Barth, *CD*, II/1, 112.
37. Berkouwer, *General Revelation*, 31.

Everything than can be said on this line mans the objective otherness of man in the cosmos, which becomes audible as the echo of the Word of God, and visible as the reflection of His light. In Holy Scripture man in the cosmos is addressed upon his echo and reflection, and starting from the revelation he is referred back all the more surely to the revelation itself.[38]

Why does Barth maintain revelation in the person of Jesus Christ? Two reasons can be mentioned here. First, revelation constitutes a thing that is completely new.[39] This point is in line with Barth's definition of revelation. Revelation, he says, is "the appearance of that which is new; the appearance, therefore, of that which is in no wise known before." And, he continues, "That which is new is primarily Jesus Christ Himself, His person in its concrete *reality*."[40] In the strictest sense, revelation is Jesus Christ. Only in Jesus Christ has revelation taken place "once for all." It is therefore "unique in kind." This complete newness is also understood in the sense that it is new in its potentiality as well as in its reality. With this Barth rejects a possibility of Christ as the fulfillment of human aspirations. Christ can only be the fulfillment of the divine prophecy. Barth leaves no room for any human aspect in revelation. It is purely a divine act.[41]

Second, Barth equates revelation with grace.[42] Barth maintains that "there is no knowability of the God who is knowable to us in His grace."[43] Revelation is, therefore, "*grace for sinners*."[44] This grace cannot be obtained outside Jesus Christ. Barth explains as follows: "Revelation means grace. Grace means condescension. Condescension means being made man. Being made man means being made flesh. Jesus Christ is all that. And that, and that alone, is revelation."[45] This concept is crucial for understanding Barth's rejection of

---

38. Barth, *CD*, II/1, 111.
39. Baillie and Martin, *Revelation*, 48; Barth, "Christian Understanding," 207.
40. Baillie and Martin, *Revelation*, 45–46.
41. Baillie and Martin, 46–49.
42. Baillie and Martin, 49–54.
43. Barth, *CD*, II/1, 129.
44. Baillie and Martin, *Revelation*, 49.
45. Baillie and Martin, 53.

natural theology and general revelation.[46] For Barth, to receive revelation is to receive God's grace and as such it can only be from Jesus Christ. To postulate the existence of other forms of revelation is to suggest the availability of divine grace apart from Jesus Christ. For Barth, this is an anathema. Therefore, revelations in nature, in history, and in human conscience must be rejected because one "never has perceived the Word in these things, and that moreover he neither can nor ever will perceive it in them."[47] For Barth, the grace of God is contradictory to the recognition of general revelation. That grace will eventually eliminate it. He puts it in this way: "The conception of an indirect revelation in nature, in history and in our self-consciousness is destroyed by the recognition of grace, by the recognition of Jesus Christ as the eternal Word who was made flesh: but nothing else destroys it."[48] Surely, Barth's theological system lacks what Reformed theologians call "common grace" – grace that is available to all human beings outside Jesus Christ and distinct from "particular grace," which is available only in Jesus Christ. This absence is due to his contention that grace is necessarily salvific. This brings us to the second feature of Barth's concept of revelation.

Barth's concept of revelation is not only christological, but it is also soteriological.[49] He emphatically maintains that "Jesus Christ is revelation, because in His existence He is *the reconciliation*."[50] Again, he says, "revelation in fact does not differ from the person of Jesus Christ nor from the reconciliation accomplished in Him."[51] Revelation means salvation, for the knowledge of God will bring sinners to be reconciled with their Creator. Barth, however, emphasizes the reverse. That is to say, "only as he beholds the reconciliation that has taken place between God and man, can *man* know *God*."[52] Here,

---

46. Berkouwer contends that Barth centered his attack on natural theology, but general revelation was always involved in this attack. Bromiley does not agree with Berkouwer's assessment. For Bromiley, Barth's attack applies strictly to natural theology, and not to general revelation. He, however, acknowledged that Barth does not make clear distinction between natural theology and general revelation. See, Berkouwer, *General Revelation*, 21; Bromiley, *Historical Theology*, 436; "Karl Barth," 55.

47. Baillie and Martin, *Revelation*, 50.

48. Baillie and Martin, 51.

49. Hart, "Revelation," 42.

50. Baillie and Martin, *Revelation*, 55.

51. Barth, *CD*, I/1, 119.

52. Baillie and Martin, *Revelation*, 55.

one notices that Barth's epistemology plays an important role in shaping this issue. Barth takes seriously the effect of sins on the epistemic power of the human mind. "Between God and that man stands, shrouding all things in gloom, his sin," he writes. As man's epistemic power has been destroyed by sins, he cannot come to the true knowledge of God. Whatever he imagined outside the sphere of this reconciliation is nothing but idols.[53] Yet, with reconciliation, there will be "the dissolution of darkness." What "prevents us from recognizing God, the truth (*aletheia*), and consequently the revelation" has been taken away.[54] Hence, the first and only requirement of approaching divine revelation is to know about Christ.

Here, it will be helpful to contrast Barth's position with that of John Calvin. Both Barth and Calvin give heed to the noetic effects of sin. Calvin contends that the knowledge of God as the Creator is subjectively and objectively available for human beings. Subjectively, God has implanted a "sense of divinity" or "seed of religion" in them.[55] Objectively, there is also the knowledge of God in his handiwork.[56] But they fail to apprehend God's knowledge because their minds have been blinded by sins.[57] They are in "darkness" till the light of the gospel comes on them.[58] They need the Scriptures that function like spectacles for weak eyes to see clearly what God has shown in his creation.[59] So, both Barth and Calvin agree that sins have impaired human ability to know God and that only in Christ are human beings able to come to the knowledge of God.

But they part ways in regard to the reality of God's general revelation. Calvin affirms the objective reality of revelation present in God's creation, but Barth rejects it. G. C. Berkouwer explains their difference using the distinction between noetic and ontic. He contends that "Calvin always distinguishes sharply between the *noetic* and the *ontic*, between *knowing* and *being*."[60] In other words, one needs to distinguish epistemology from ontology. Hence,

---

53. Baillie and Martin, 55.
54. Baillie and Martin, 58.
55. Calvin, *Institutes*, I.iii.1; cf. I.iv.1.
56. Calvin, I.v.1.
57. Calvin, I.iv.1.
58. Calvin, I.v.14.
59. Calvin, I.vi.1.
60. Berkouwer, *General Revelation*, 30–31.

for Calvin, ontologically there is God's revelation in his handiwork, but epistemologically humans fail to understand it due to their sins. "Therefore the *deafness* and *blindness* of which Calvin speaks in no way denies the reality of [general] revelation."[61] Barth certainly fails to make such a distinction. Or, more accurately he does not feel the need to make such a distinction, because only the revelation in Christ matters and the rest are merely tokens to it.

In sum, revelation, for Barth, is extremely narrow. It not only centers on, but also equates with, the person of Jesus Christ and his reconciliation. Or, to say more accurately, Barth equates the divine revelation with the incarnation of Jesus Christ. Barth summarizes as follows.

> If God's revelation is the way from veiling of the eternal Word to His unveiling, from crib and cross to resurrection and ascension, how can it possibly be anything else than God's becoming man, His becoming flesh? As the incarnation of the Word it can be revelation. To be revelation it had to be an incarnation. Incarnation was needed in order that God might become manifest to us, that He might be free for us.[62]

Since there is no multiplication of the incarnation, then there is only one revelation, that is Jesus Christ.[63]

This conception of revelation has consequences. First, the distinction between special and general revelation disappears. Not only revelations in nature, in history, and in human conscience are denied, but all other forms of special revelation – such as prophecy, vision, and even the Holy Scriptures – are not considered as revelation. At best they are considered as "tokens of revelation," witnesses that point to the revelation,[64] but as such they are not revelations. Second, the line between revelation, grace, and salvation also disappears. To receive revelation is to receive grace and salvation. To allow revelation apart from Jesus Christ is to allow the availability of redemptive grace outside him. The uniqueness of Jesus Christ stands and falls with the recognition of revelation in him only.

---

61. Berkouwer, 31.
62. Barth, *CD*, I/2, 43.
63. Baillie and Martin, *Revelation*, 63.
64. Baillie and Martin, 62–74; Barth, "Christian Understanding," 219.

It is not my intention to give a thorough critique of Barth's concept of revelation.[65] However, it is sufficient to point out that this concept of revelation makes it impossible to posit God's revelatory work outside the sphere of Christianity. When there is no clear line between revelation, grace, and salvation, it is inevitable that one falls into an either-or position. In other words, those who intend to maintain Christ as the only way for salvation have to affirm Christ as the only revelation. Otherwise, by affirming the existence of God's revelation in other religions and cultures, they endanger the uniqueness of Christ. A both-and position is impossible with this scheme.

Unfortunately, Barth is not alone in operating with this framework.[66] Those who oppose Barth's exclusivist position also employ a similar model in their theologies. In other words, they too do not distinguish clearly between revelation, grace, and salvation. For example, Clark Pinnock, who defends an inclusivist position, maintains that "because God is present in the whole world (premise), God's grace is also at work in some way among all people, possibly in the sphere of religious life (inference)."[67] The universal presence of God through his general revelation is concomitant with his grace. The grace that Pinnock maintains here is not a common grace. For him, there is only one type of grace. He explains as follows, "We refuse to allow the disjunction between nature and grace or between common and saving grace on the supposition that, if the triune God is present, grace must be present too."[68] Hence, Pinnock's inclusivist position would allow a "possibility that religion may play a role in the salvation of the human race, a role preparatory to the gospel of Christ, in whom alone fullness is found."[69] Certainly, Pinnock is cautious not to say that religions are the vehicles of human salvation, but he still entertains the idea that non-Christian religions may play a part in securing salvation in Christ. Such a conclusion is inevitable when one does not clearly differentiate between revelation, grace, and salvation.

---

65. Critiques of Barth's concept of revelation can be seen in the following works: Berkouwer, *General Revelation*, 87–114; Dulles, *Models of Revelation*, 94–97; Van Til, *New Modernism*, 131–159.

66. For contemporary theologians who link (general) revelation with salvation, see, Erickson, "Hope," 126; Knitter, *No Other Name*, 116; Pinnock, "Inclusivist View," 98; Sanders, *No Other Name*, 233–236. Tillich, *Systematic Theology*, 144–147.

67. Pinnock, "Inclusivist View," 98.

68. Pinnock, 98.

69. Pinnock, 98.

Still, I can give another example. Paul Knitter, a pluralist, criticizes the distinction of general and special revelation held by mainline Protestants. He agrees that some kind of distinction needs to be made between them. Yet, he does not agree that "the difference [is] to be defined as *general* revelation in other religions and *salvific* revelation in Christianity."[70] He charges that such a distinction is "arbitrary, artificial, and blind to what is evident in the lives of non-Christians."[71] Protestant theologians, he explains, talk about "God's Spirit illuminating the minds and hearts of all" but restrict salvation only to some. "But what kind of a God is this who offers a revelation that can never lead to a salvation, to an authentic experience of the divine?" he adds. Hence, according to Knitter, this distinction of revelation has turned "a God of love" into "a rather capricious, teasing God, who offers just enough knowledge of divinity to frustrate persons, or to confirm them in their sinfulness."[72] In conclusion, he states that "it seems that both human logic and Christian theology require that if one admits the fact of divine revelation apart from Christ, one must also admit at least the possibility of salvation apart from Christ."[73]

Here, again, we see that the line between revelation, grace, and salvation has disappeared. As a result, Knitter inaccurately identifies special revelation as salvific and general revelation as non-salvific. It is true that general revelation can never be salvific. However, to say that special revelation is salvific is also misleading. It is true that salvation is available within the sphere of special revelation. However, I cannot equate special revelation with salvation. Therefore, those who receive special revelation (i.e. the Jews and the church as the people of the new covenant) do not necessarily secure salvation simply by being the receivers of that special revelation. A distinction between revelation, grace, and salvation is crucial in this point. Salvation is tied up with particular grace, not with special revelation. Receiving special revelation does not mean necessarily receiving salvation, since special revelation is not always concurrent with particular grace. But, by blurring the line between revelation and grace, Knitter falls into a similar theological framework held by Barth, a position that he vehemently opposes. Only this time, Knitter chooses the

---

70. Knitter, *No Other Name*, 116.
71. Knitter, 116.
72. Knitter, 116.
73. Knitter, 116.

opposite side. By affirming the existence of God's revelation in other religions, he inevitably postulates a possibility of salvation apart from Christ.

Kraemer's critics, Hogg, D'Costa, and Thomas, also operate in a similar manner. I have dealt with their positions earlier. It will be sufficient to show from our previous discussion that they, too, operate with the axiom that revelation is eventually soteriological. The affirmation of God's presence in other religions and cultures will eventually open up a possibility of salvation apart from the Christian faith.

Kraemer's position cannot be totally excluded from this flaw, although in this case his is more nuanced than others. Contrary to some opinions, Kraemer's position is not identical with that of Barth.[74] It is true that in some aspects Kraemer closely follows Barth, but it is also equally true that he parts from him in other aspects. Kraemer's concept of revelation is surely close to that of Barth. In the first place, Kraemer follows Barth in his christological emphasis of revelation. He defines revelation as "what is by its nature inaccessible and *remains so, even when it is revealed.*"[75] As such this statement is not necessarily Barthian. Certainly, there will be no knowledge of God in his creatures except insofar as God is willing to reveal himself to them. Hence, revelation is inaccessible. It remains so even after it is revealed. This, too, can mean that the revealed knowledge of God is so broad and deep that it cannot be fully grasped by the creatures. But, when Kraemer links this statement with the incarnation of Christ, his dependence on Barth becomes apparent. The revealed and hidden revelation centers solely on the person of Christ. "God was truly revealed in Jesus Christ, but at the same time He hid and disguised Himself in the man Jesus Christ," Kraemer explains.[76] The revelation in Jesus Christ is so central in Kraemer's thought that it becomes the sole criterion in evaluating and judging all religions.

Second, Kraemer also follows Barth by emphasizing the soteriological nature of the divine revelation in Jesus Christ. Kraemer maintains that

---

74. Some have charged that Kraemer is Barthian without qualifying in what way he has followed Barth. See, Knitter, "European Protestant," 15; Aagaard, "Revelation and Religion," 149–150; Anderson, "Kraemer and After," 355; Ariarajah, "Christian Minorities," 22. Others, however, have rejected this label. See, Verkuyl, "Biblical Notion," 4; Hallencreutz, *Kraemer Towards Tambaram*, 292.

75. Kraemer, *Christian Message*, 69.

76. Kraemer, 70.

"revelation in Christ is a free divine act of redemptive irruption into the life of man and of the world."[77] Hence, revelation has a redemptive purpose. Yet, with Kraemer's obvious recognition of general revelation, this soteriological aspect takes a different turn from that of Barth. While in Barth, salvation is closely associated with revelation as such, in Kraemer, it is with the revelation in Jesus Christ. In this case, even though Kraemer is still following Barth in relating salvation with revelation, yet he takes a wider scope from that of Barth. Certainly, with this scenario Kraemer aims to affirm the divine revelation outside the sphere of Christianity without harming the uniqueness of Christ as the only way for human salvation.

Yet, as I have shown, Kraemer is only partly successful in his aim to affirm general revelation and at the same time to secure the uniqueness of Christ. As mentioned above, internal tensions remain in Kraemer's theological framework. This is partly due to the influence of Barth's concept of revelation on Kraemer's theological system. This is especially true in regard to his view of general revelation and the dialectical nature of religions. Even though Kraemer owes his Christocentric concept of revelation to Barth, he rejects Barth's view of general revelation. Unlike Barth, Kraemer acknowledges the reality of general revelation and distinguishes between general and special revelation.[78] But, it proves too difficult for Kraemer to simultaneously maintain two different systems – Barth's Christocentric revelation on the one hand, and a traditional distinction of general and special revelation on the other hand.

Soon we find that Kraemer stumbles along the way. At times, he acknowledges the reality of general revelation, but at other times he seems to move away from it. For instance, he acknowledges that there are different "modes of revelation, as found in Rom.1 and 2," and that God "discloses Himself in Christ, in nature . . . in historical human life and activity, and human consciousness (Rom.1; Rom.2)."[79] Against Barthian thought, he says, "although some schools of theology, for all kinds of reasons, raise great objections to this revelation in nature and history, it is an undeniable fact that the Bible

---

77. Kraemer, 70.
78. See, Kraemer, *Christian Message*, 125; *Religion and the Christian Faith*, 340–365.
79. Kraemer, *Religion and the Christian Faith*, 353.

says so."⁸⁰ Yet, he soon denies the reality of this revelation. He explains that in speaking of "modes" (in the plural), "it is, Biblically speaking, already somehow inadequate to say God reveals Himself in nature and in history."⁸¹ For Kraemer, Nature and History are "abstract generalizations." As such, they are "unbiblical and, moreover, not true to fact. They are figments of thought at times useful as instruments but they do not represent anything real." What he means by this is that "nature conceals God as much as it reveals Him. Nature has many riddles that embarrass us deeply. The same is true of history."⁸² In this sense, there is no real revelation, since the human mind cannot fathom those riddles. It is apparent that Kraemer cannot escape from Barth's concept of revelation. Like Barth, he fails to distinguish between noetic and ontic aspects of general revelation.

What happens to Kraemer's general revelation, to a certain extent, also occurs to his view of religions. As I have shown in previous chapters, Kraemer seeks to affirm the dialectical nature of religions, yet he looks unsettled. For Kraemer, religion is both human and divine. Human nature is both good and bad. It is good so long as it is created in the image of God. Yet, this image has been corrupted due to human sins. Religion as an expression of human nature is accordingly good and bad. Besides this internal factor, there is also an external factor, which is demonic forces, that affect human religions negatively. In this point we see that Kraemer's dialectic becomes imbalanced and the pendulum swings too far to its negative side. He rightly counts demonic powers in non-Christian religions but fails to include God's active involvement in them. In fairness to him, Kraemer indeed maintains that religions are both human achievement and God's wrestling with man. But the divine factor in religions remains undeveloped in Kraemer's thought. As the result, despite his aim to maintain a dialectical character of religions, its negative aspect still dominates the scene.

Finally, there is need to touch on Kraemer's holistic character of religions. As pointed out in the previous chapter, this view has a difficulty to accommodate appreciation for other religions and cultures. But this holistic view of religion is not so much credited to his theological framework as to his

---

80. Kraemer, 353.
81. Kraemer, 354.
82. Kraemer, 354.

phenomenological approach. Still, I argue here, the solution I am to provide for the above two tensions will also help out to mitigate the tension in this aspect. With this we need to move to working out the solution.

There are two areas that need to be addressed – soteriology and Christology. In his evaluation of recent discussions on the relation between the Christian faith and other religions, Leslie Newbigin points out that "the debate on this question has been fatally flawed by the fact that it has been conducted around the question, 'Who can be saved?'"[83] I concur with this assessment. By this I do not mean that soteriology is unimportant or irrelevant. But, is this the central question present to us in the Holy Scriptures? I believe that the answer is negative. As much as human well-being occupies an important place in God's plan, it cannot be the ultimate purpose of the divine act. That is to say, the divine act cannot end in creatures but God alone. Everything flows from him and ends with him. Here, I turn to the heart of Reformed theology (i.e. the glory of God). Hence, theology of religions as a subdiscipline of Christian theology should have its ultimate aim not on human salvation but the glory of God.

Besides soteriology, I also need to address the question of Christology. In today's theology of religions the two questions have been linked too tightly. That is to say, Christology has been dealt with solely within the question of soteriology. Christ is treated simply as the redeemer as if he cannot be anybody else but the Savior of the world. Such a narrow treatment of the Lord of the universe is not in line with the testimony of the Scriptures. Abraham Kuyper states, "The *Savior* of the world is also the *Creator* of the world, indeed that he could become its Savior only *because* he already was its *Creator*."[84] Kuyper is right. Christ is not only the Savior, but he is also the Creator, the Lord, and the judge of the living and the dead.

A solution to this flaw is not to set aside the question of Christology altogether. I do not concur, therefore, with a notion that seeks to replace a christological model with a trinitarian one. Here I agree with Newbigin that "to set a trinitarian paradigm over against a Christological one ... would surely be a disastrous mistake."[85] There are several reasons why such a project

---

83. Newbigin, *Gospel*, 176.
84. Kuyper, "Common Grace," 176.
85. See Newbigin, "Trinity as Public Truth," 7.

is incorrect. First, Christology has a legitimate place in a Christian theology of religions. All religions deal with the question of redemption.[86] In Christianity, this question is linked exclusively to Christology, because Christ is the only way for human redemption. The uniqueness of Christ as the only way for sinners to come to God is the heart of the gospel. As such, it cannot be simply set aside. A theology of religions that abandons Jesus Christ as the only way and truth is not faithful to the testimony of the Scriptures.

Second, not all trinitarian models are in line with the biblical doctrine of the Trinity. Raimundo Panikkar's trinitarian theology of religions, for example, is built on what he considered as the vestige of the Trinity found in non-Christian religions. To build a doctrine of the Trinity in this manner is not only methodologically unwarranted, but it also leads to a disastrous end. It moves away from the triune God of the Bible and ends up with a tritheism.[87]

Third, a trinitarian model will not necessarily solve the problems we face. Amos Yong, for example, sees that current discussions in the theology of religions have reached the stage of impasse due to the christological approach.[88] In response, he proposes "a pneumatological approach to Christian theology of religions," which he claims to be "robustly Trinitarian."[89] Yong is surely commended for his effort to introduce the doctrine of the Holy Spirit into the theology of religions. The Spirit's works undoubtedly have been overlooked in this field of study. However, he is mistaken when he charges that the impasse in current theology of religions is due to its christological starting point. As I point out above, I find that the problem does not lie in Christology as such, but in linking Christology too tightly with soteriology. Yong's own words seem to point to this direction. He states that "all of the christological questions posed with such force by Russell Aldwinckle (1982) almost two decades ago remain today. Who is Christ? Exclusive mediator? Constitutive mediator? Normative or perhaps even non-normative mediator . . . ? Is an

---

86. See Bavinck, *Philosophy of Revelation*, 163; Bavinvk, *RD I*, 286.

87. For Raimundo Panikkar's trinitarian model of theology of religions, see Panikkar, *Trinity*. For a critical assessment on Panikkar's theology of religions, see Johnson, *Rethinking the Trinity*, 141–184.

88. Amos Yong's thought can be found in the following works: Yong, *Discerning the Spirit(s)*; *Beyond the Impasse*. In *Discerning the Spirit(s)*, Yong discusses the christological impasse in chapter 2 followed by a pneumatological proposal in chapter 3.

89. Yong, *Beyond the Impasse*, 20.

absolute-relative Christology possible . . .?"[90] But, one should notice that the above questions are not christological as such, but Christology tied with soteriology. Christ is seen solely in regard to his role as the mediator of human salvation. Hence, the threefold typology – exclusivism, inclusivism, and pluralism – is built upon different responses to Christ as the mediator of human salvation. Shifting from a christological starting point to a pneumatological one, Yong does not move beyond this dilemma.

Having indicated the flaws in recent views on the theology of religions, I thus propose that Christian theology of religions takes the following direction. First, it must secure the uniqueness of Christ as the only way and truth and at the same time have a positive appreciation of other religions and cultures. Second, the above twofold aim can be achieved with a theological framework that places human salvation under the glory of God and Christology within the sphere of the works of the triune God.

At this point I will turn to the thoughts of Herman Bavinck, Abraham Kuyper, and Johan Herman Bavinck. In the following sections I will present their thoughts on revelation and grace and get some helpful insights to solve the dilemma I have described above.

6.2 General and Special Revelation

In this section I will present a Reformed understanding of revelation derived primarily from Herman Bavinck and Johan H. Bavinck.[91] The elder Bavinck (Herman) provides us with a solid theological framework for this subject and the younger supplies us with deep and rich reflections as this subject is applied in mission fields. I begin with the thought of Herman Bavinck.

There are four important features in Herman Bavinck's concept of revelation. First, Bavinck maintains multiplicity of the divine revelation. He defines revelation as "self-disclosure of God" which "comes in various forms."[92] By this, he means that revelation is not limited to *Deus dixit* but covers all *opera*

---

90. Yong, *Discerning the Spirit(s)*, 57.

91. Our exposition of Herman Bavinck's concept of revelation is based mostly on the following works: Bavinck, *Our Reasonable Faith*; *Philosophy of Revelation*; *Reformed Dogmatics*, vol. 1 and 2. As for the thought of Johan H. Bavinck, it is from the following works: Bavinck, *Church Between Temple*; *Introduction to the Science*; Bolt, Pratt, and Visser, *Bavinck Reader*.

92. Bavinck, *Our Reasonable Faith*, 34.

Dei ad extra. It includes not only what God says, but also all forms of God's works, in words and deeds, to and in his creation. From God's creating and sustaining the creation to the sending of his Son and the outpouring of the Spirit, each of them is a form of revelation, for "each of them tells us something of God."[93] From this point we can see that Bavinck's concept of revelation is not only broad, but more importantly it is also trinitarian. According to this model, each person of the Trinity is involved in this act of revealing. It is not to say that each person of the Trinity reveals God in a particular way. Rather, in every work of God *ad extra* the three persons of the Trinity work inseparably (*Opera Trinitatis ad extra sunt indivisa*). Hence, in the work of creation, for example, one can find the imprint of the Trinity. Bavinck writes, "God [the Father] calls all things into being by his word [the Son] as mediating agent, it is through his Spirit that he is immanent in the creation and vivifies and beautifies it all."[94] God's work *ad extra* follows this principle: it is of the Father, through the Son, and completed in the Spirit. Hence, each of God's work that "tells us something of God" is the work of the persons of the Trinity in unity. The revelatory act of God is therefore trinitarian in its nature.

Second, revelation "comes from *God Himself* acting in His freedom."[95] Revelation is thus contingent upon the willingness of God to disclose himself to his creatures. He is *Deus absconditus* – the hidden God. Without revelation there is no possibility of the knowledge of God in his creation. Yet, revelation cannot be understood as "an involuntary manifestation" of an impersonal higher being. Instead, revelation requires that "God exists personally, that He is conscious of Himself, and that He can make Himself known to creatures."[96] Revelation requires not only the distinction of the Creator and the creatures, but it also requires the self-knowledge of God. A pantheistic notion of revelation is thus rejected.[97]

Third, Bavinck continues saying that "every revelation that proceeds from God is *self*-revelation."[98] God's self-revelation means that "God is the origin

---

93. Bavinck, 34.
94. Bavinck, *RD II*, 262.
95. Bavinck, *Our Reasonable Faith*, 34.
96. Bavinck, 34.
97. Bavinck, *RD I*, 212.
98. Bavinck, *Our Reasonable Faith*, 35.

and He is also the content of His revelation."[99] This contention applies to the highest revelation, Jesus Christ, as well as to other forms of revelation. It is not only the Son who reveals the Father to us, but "all the works of God in nature and grace, in creation and in regeneration, in the world and in history teach us something of the incomprehensible and worshipful being of God."[100] Certainly there are differences between the revelation in Jesus Christ and other forms of revelation. But the differences are only in degree, not in kind. I will return to this point when I deal with the distinction of special and general revelation.

God's self-revelation is the origin as well as the content of revelation. With this statement, Bavinck distinguishes three kinds of knowledge of God. The origin of revelation (i.e. God's self-knowledge) is distinguished from the content of revelation (i.e. the knowledge of God shared with the creatures). Then, the knowledge of God in the creatures is further distinguished between that which is objectively present in the works of his hands, and that which is subjectively gained in the consciousness of rational creatures.[101] This threefold knowledge of God – God's self-knowledge, objective and subjective knowledge of God in the creatures – corresponds with Bavinck's three foundations of theology or *principia*. Bavinck explains as follows:

> Thus we have discovered three foundations (*principia*): First, God as the essential foundation (*principium essendi*), the source, of theology; next, the external cognitive foundation (*principium cognoscendi externum*), viz., the self-revelation of God . . . and finally, the internal principle of knowing (*principium cognoscendi internum*), the illumination of human beings by God's Spirit.[102]

There are three *principia* of knowledge. God is the source (*principium essendi*). All knowledge of God flows from God alone. The knowledge of God is only available to creatures so long as it is revealed by God to them. Revelation is therefore the external means (*principium cognoscendi externum*) by which creatures have the knowledge of God. Yet, having the external means alone is not enough. As light requires eyes, the external means (i.e. revelation) requires

---

99. Bavinck, 35.
100. Bavinck, 35.
101. Bavinck, 35.
102. Bavinck, *RD I*, 213–214.

the internal means, *principium cognoscendi internum*, (i.e. the illumination of the Spirit) *as* its counterpart.[103]

Bavinck then relates these three *principia* with the threefold of knowledge of God. He continues to explain:

> These three are one in the respect that they have God as the author and have as their content one identical knowledge of God. The archetypal knowledge of God in the divine consciousness; the ectypal knowledge of God granted in revelation and recorded in Holy Scripture; and the knowledge of God in the subject, insofar as it proceeds from revelation and enters into the human consciousness, are all three of them from God.[104]

The threefold knowledge is one in unity, because they have God as their author and content. But they need to be distinguished because they differ significantly. God's self-knowledge is eternal, absolute, and infinite. The knowledge of God in his creatures is, however, "only a weak likeness, a finite, limited sketch of" God's self-knowledge "accommodated to the capacities of the human or creaturely consciousness."[105] This knowledge of God shared in his creatures is "nevertheless so rich, so broad and so deep that it can never be wholly absorbed in the consciousness of any rational creature."[106] In other words, the knowledge of God subjectively present in the consciousness of a rational creature is comparably less than that objectively available in the works of his hand. Still, however "limited and finite it is and will in all eternity remain," the subjective knowledge of God "is nevertheless a real and sound knowledge."[107] The distinction of the Creator and the creatures and the pursuit of knowing God by his rational creatures are to continue eternally. This leads to the fourth point, which stresses the purpose of God's revelation.

Fourth, Bavinck maintains that not only is the revelation from God and has God as its content, but also it has purpose in God alone. As mentioned above, God's revelation shared with the creatures is so rich and abundant that no rational creatures, nor even the angels, could ever wholly grasp it.

---

103. Bavinck, *RD I*, 233.
104. Bavinck, *RD I*, 213–214.
105. Bavinck, *RD I*, 212.
106. Bavinck, *Our Reasonable Faith*, 36.
107. Bavinck, 35.

Therefore, the purpose of revelation cannot end with his creation, because it goes beyond them.[108] Hence, the purpose of God's revelation cannot be anthropological, nor soteriological, but theological. That is to say, the end of God's revelation is not primarily man's salvation, but the glory of God. This is in line with the heart of Reformed theology. When comparing Reformed theology with that of Lutheran, Bavinck maintains that the difference between them is that "the Reformed Christian thinks theologically, the Lutheran anthropologically." The primary question asked by the former is "How is the glory of God advanced?" but for the latter is "How does a human get saved?"[109] On this point I concur with Bavinck that the primary concern which the Scriptures present to us is the glory of God. The redemption of the fallen creation is secondary to the exaltation of the Creator. There is no absolute necessity for God to manifest his love and mercy upon his creatures. If he is willing to do so, it is "in accordance with his pleasure and will – to the praise of his glorious grace" (Eph 1:5–6). Therefore, the greatest failure creatures ever committed is that "although they knew God, they neither glorified him as God nor gave thanks to him" (Rom 1:21).

Here I move on to the distinction of special and general revelation. Bavinck maintains that this distinction is in line with the recognition that Jesus Christ is the highest revelation of God. The revelation in Jesus that is special and unique is at the same time the light that enlightens Christians to discover the revelation of God in nature and history. Faith in Jesus Christ is special, but not narrow. This faith enables Christians to see more clearly and broadly. In Christ, they have come to the high vantage point from which they are able to see around. In doing so, Bavinck explains, they discover "traces everywhere of that same God whom [they have] learned to know and to worship in Christ as [their] Father."[110] Hence, the highest revelation of Christ is consistent with other forms of revelation but it is also the light by which other revelations are discovered.

That said, special revelation and general revelation differ in their means, content, scope, and purpose. Bavinck explains as follows:

---

108. Bavinck, 36.
109. Bavinck, *RD I*, 177.
110. Bavinck, *Our Reasonable Faith*, 37.

> In the general revelation God makes use of the usual run of phenomena and the usual course of events; in the special revelation He often employs unusual means, appearances, prophecy, and miracle to make Himself known to man. The contents of the first kind are especially the attributes of power, wisdom, and goodness; those of the second kind are especially God's holiness and righteousness, compassion and grace. The first is directed to all men and, by means of common grace, serves to restrain the eruption of sin; the second comes to all those who live under the Gospel and has as its glory, by special grace, the forgiveness of sins and the renewal of life.[111]

For sure, their contents differ only in the aspects of God that each revelation reveals. Ultimately, both types of revelation disclose God himself. In a similar manner we can also speak about their different purposes. They differ only in their proximate purposes, but in regard to the ultimate purpose both revelations are to serve the glory of God.

Still, the two revelations cannot be treated separately. While they need to be distinguished, they are "intimately connected with each other." They share the same origin, word, and grace. Bavinck continues to explain:

> Both [revelations] have their origin in God, in His sovereign goodness and favor. The general revelation is owing to the Word which was with God in the beginning, which made all things, which shone as a light in the darkness and lighteth every man that cometh into the world (John 1:1–9). The special revelation is owing to that same Word, as it was made flesh in Christ, and now is full of grace and truth (John 1:14). Grace is the content of both revelations, common in the first, special in the second, but in such a way that the one is indispensable from the other.[112]

The Word – the Logos – is distinguished but not separated. Maintaining the distinction of general and special revelation does not jeopardize the centrality of the word in God's revelation. Instead, this position connects the Logos made flesh with the eternal Logos. This position also maintains grace

---

111. Bavinck, 37.
112. Bavinck, 37–38.

as the ultimate content of the divine revelation. On this point, Bavinck agrees with Barth. Revelation means grace. Bavinck, however, goes further to differentiate between common and special grace, a distinction that Barth fails to make. This distinction is crucial when we deal with redemption of sinners. I will return to this point later.

Bavinck brings out two dialectical facts about general revelation. On the one hand, he explains, general revelation "has been of great value" and "has borne rich fruits." Yet, on the other hand, "mankind has not found God by its light."[113] In other words, general revelation is valuable but insufficient to bring human beings to the true knowledge of God. I will deal with these two aspects of general revelation accordingly – first the value and then its insufficiency.

Bavinck maintains that general revelation has generated various positive effects on human life. Human beings have a religious and moral sense which enables them to have an orderly life. All these owe to God's general revelation. In other words, the origin of religion is traced back to divine revelation. That religion is closely related to and its essence is inseparable from revelation is an important contribution of Bavinck on this subject. At this point I will briefly explain Bavinck's view on religion.

The religious propensity in human beings is universally found. Like Calvin, Bavinck contends that this *sensus divinitatis* is an essential part of being human, not an addendum to human makeup.[114] He explains this notion further and links it with general revelation. For Bavinck, God's general revelation would be unknowable "if God had not planted in his soul an indelible sense of His existence and being." Hence, in addition to "the external revelation in nature," there is also "an internal revelation to man."[115] Bavinck clarifies that the two revelations – external and internal – cannot be treated independently. The internal revelation is not "a second, entirely new revelation, supplementing" the external revelation. Instead, "it is rather a capacity, a susceptibility, a drive to find out God in His works and to understand His revelation."[116] With this clarification, I can say that for Bavinck, *sensus divinitatis* is not implanted knowledge of God, but an internal organ of perception

---

113. Bavinck, 59.
114. See Bavinck, *RD I*, 278.
115. Bavinck, *Our Reasonable Faith*, 42.
116. Bavinck, 42.

for God's external revelation. As eyes are for light so is *sensus divinitatis* for the knowledge of God.[117] The objective knowledge of God requires its subjective counterpart. *Principium cognoscendi externum* requires the existence of *principium cognoscendi internum*.

This *sensus divinitatis* is also at the same time *semen religionis* (seed of religion). That is to say, this sense of divinity is also at the same time "a sense of absolute dependency" – a dependency in a very special sense. It is not a dependency on an impersonal supreme power, but on "a supreme power which is also perfectly righteous, wise, and good."[118] Bavinck's thought on this point is close to that of Friedrich Schleiermacher. But their agreement ends at this point as well. For Schleiermacher, religion is primarily human. The essence of religion is human "feeling of absolute dependence" and God is simply a "co-determinant" of this feeling.[119] Bavinck certainly maintains that religion is essentially part of being human. Religion is not "a super-added gift." Man is a religious being by virtue of being created in the image of God. Still, Bavinck maintains that "religion is not 'the essence' of a human" because "religion is not a substance but a disposition or virtue."[120] In other words, religion does not originate from humans. It is a human disposition or response to what has come to him from without. To put it more directly, religion is the human response to God's revelation. "Religion is a product of revelation," Bavinck succinctly states.[121] There is "no religion without revelation."[122] All religions rest on the divine revelation. By this he means not only general revelation but also special revelation. Here, Bavinck introduces the idea of "remnantal revelation"[123] – an original revelation given to human beings in ancient times and passed down through traditions.[124] Remnantal revelation is not part of general revelation but of special revelation. Religion therefore rests not only

---

117. For discussions on Bavinck's theory of knowledge, see, Sytsma, "Herman Bavinck's Thomistic Epistemology," 1–56; Vos, "Knowledge according to Bavinck," 9–36.
118. Bavinck, *Our Reasonable Faith*, 43.
119. Schleiermacher, *Christian* Faith, 17.
120. Bavinck, *RD I*, 277–278.
121. Bavinck, *RD I*, 277.
122. Bavinck, *RD I*, 284.
123. See also Bavinck, *Philosophy of Revelation*, 165.
124. Cf. Bolt, Pratt, and Visser, *Bavinck Reader*, 205; Strange, *Their Rock*, 106.

on general revelation but also on special revelation via remnantal revelation. Bavinck explains as follows:

> Pagan religions, accordingly, do rest only on the acknowledgement of God's revelation in nature but most certainly also on elements that from the most ancient times were preserved from supernatural revelation by tradition even though that tradition was frequently no longer pure. And even an operation of supernatural forces in the pagan world is not *a priori* impossible or even improbable. There may be truth in the appeal to revelations, an appeal that is common to all religions.[125]

With this emphasis, religion, for Bavinck, is primarily divine. Surely, he does not disregard human and demonic factors in it. As I have shown above, religion is an essential part of human makeup. There is also demonic influence in pagan religions. However, he takes into account "an operation of God's Spirit and of his common grace" in all aspects of human life – science, art, morality, law, and religions. Standing on this foundation, religions are fundamentally positive. "Founders of religion," he concludes, "were not impostors or agents of Satan but men who, being religiously inclined, had to fulfill a mission to their time and people and often exerted a beneficial influence on the life of peoples."[126] Idolatry "is born of the human need for a God who is near."[127] Theophany, mantic, and magic even in their corrupted forms "are the ways by which all revelation comes to human beings."[128] Hence, active operation of the Holy Spirit and common grace play an important role in Bavinck's thought of religions. I will return to this topic later.

Bavinck makes a distinction between objective and subjective religion. Both aspects – objective and subjective – are important because religion touches human beings as whole persons – body and soul. Religion is basically "the right manner of knowing and serving the true God." As such it is "not exhausted by external observance but consists above all in internal devotion."[129] Both external observance and internal devotion are closely re-

---

125. Bavinck, *RD I*, 311.
126. Bavinck, *RD I*, 319.
127. Bavinck, *RD I*, 326.
128. Bavinck, *RD I*, 326.
129. Bavinck, *RD I*, 239.

lated. On the one side, objective religion is the fruit of subjective religion. External acts of worship (*cultus*) spring from internal piety (*pietas*). On the other side, however, subjective religion is also influenced by objective religion. Subjective religion or the seed of religion is "a certain predisposition" present in every human being. Yet, having been "fecundated by an untrue and impure objective religion" this seed of religion is "corrupted" and therefore "produces worship that is 'idolatry.'"[130] Hence, objective and subjective religion are intertwined and influence each other.

Herman Bavinck (hereafter in this section HB), however, falls short of describing the essence of subjective religion. This task is taken up by his nephew Johan Herman Bavinck (hereafter in this section JHB). What HB considered as "a hopeless undertaking"[131] in JHB's hands turns out to be a fruitful discussion of religious consciousness.[132] To this I now turn.

JHB points out that religion has both social and personal aspects.[133] As such these aspects are somewhat related to HB's objective and subjective religion. That is to say, objective religion (i.e. religion in its concrete forms) – practices, traditions, rituals, and doctrines – is communally and socially oriented; whereas subjective religion provides room for personal piety and devotion. With its social character, religion influences the culture of a people group where it belongs. For sure, JHB does not deny that religion is also shaped and influenced by people's culture. Yet, he denies the notion that religion as such is a product of culture. Instead, quoting Bronislaw Malinowski, he maintains that religion is "a profound moral and social force which gives the ultimate integration to human culture."[134] Culture is never religiously neutral. It is simply "a system of customs and traditions inherited from the forefathers."[135] On this point JHB is in agreement with Kraemer that religion is a determining factor in human culture.

---

130. Bavinck, *RD I*, 241.

131. Bavinck, *RD I*, 243.

132. JHB's discussions on religious consciousness are found in the following works: Bolt, Pratt, and Visser, *Bavinck Reader*, 145–299; Bavinck, *Church Between Temple*, 25–113.

133. Bavinck, *Church Between Temple*, 19.

134. Bavinck, 21; Bolt, Pratt, and Visser, *Bavinck Reader*, 234. Cf. Malinowski, *Dynamics of Culture*, 48.

135. Bavinck, *Church Between Temple*, 21.

The relationship between culture and religion is dynamic. It is possible that the culture of a society gradually loses its religious grip or influence. This process of secularization, as seen in our modern world, will not lead to a society in which people are completely irreligious. Even though people may no longer practice positive religions, JHB argues that they still retain "religious consciousness."[136]

Many religions have their holy books, which they consider revelations. But, JHB points out that as living religions they are sometimes "much richer than what is prescribed" in their scriptures. The religion of Islam, for example, is "definitely not explainable as [merely] being derived directly from the Qur'an." There must be something more than the holy books which drive these religions. Hence, he contends that there is a "mysterious," "vague and nebulous" but "persistent force" that lies behind all religions. This force does not depend on a concrete religion to which it is connected. So, it "can continue operating even after the connection with a given religion has ceased."[137] JHB designates this force as "universal religious consciousness" – a term that he adopts from Kraemer.[138]

This universal religious consciousness is not a natural religion. In the first place, in regard to cardinal religious concepts such as sin, grace, forgiveness, and redemption, religions have such different views that it is very unlikely they could come from the same source.[139] Furthermore, religious consciousness does not consist of innate ideas from which all religions were thought to spring. Instead, it consists of questions that always drive people's hearts to get the answers.[140] JHB calls these "five magnetic points" that center on the following subjects: cosmos, norm, destiny, salvation, and higher power. He summarizes as follows:

> People are simply driven to think about a higher power, about gods and ghosts, or about whatever they might call this force. They are driven to believe in some sort of moral code, however

---

136. Recently, Stefan Paas has argued against JHB's universality of religious consciousness. See Paas, "Religious Consciousness," 35–55.

137. Bolt, Pratt, and Visser, *Bavinck Reader*, 148–149; Bavinck, *Church Between Temple*, 30.

138. See Bolt, Pratt, and Visser, 150–151; Bavinck, *Church Between Temple*, 72. Cf. Kraemer, *Christian Message*, 111–112.

139. Bolt, Pratt, and Visser, *Bavinck Reader*, 226.

140. Bavinck, *Church Between Temple*, 34.

foolishly they might subsequently work that code out. They are driven to summarize all of the connections involving personal life and the world as a whole into some sort of meaningful and coherent plan. They are driven to recognize something of their own limitation, brokenness, and thirst for something like deliverance and liberation.[141]

JHB contends that what lies behind this driving force cannot be explained psychologically but theologically. On this point JHB is in full agreement with HB that "God is not only one element in religion, but he is the origin and the deepest basis for religion. Then he is the only meaning for religion."[142] Hence, what lies behind this religious consciousness is God's revelation. Still, JHB pursues this issue further and makes important contributions on the relation between religious consciousness and general revelation. JHB summarizes his points as follows.

First, he maintains that "the point of departure for all of our consideration needs to be God's self-disclosure or the general revelation that nonetheless bears the nature of a very personal engagement of God with each person separately."[143] As with his uncle HB, JHB maintains the priority of the divine revelation in religions. Still, he emphasizes the personal character of general revelation. This is probably the most important contribution of JHB on the nature of general revelation. Holding to this thought, JHB could unhesitatingly say that founders of religions, such as Siddhartha Gautama and Muhammad, have received revelation from God. He puts it this way:

> In the night of the *bodhi*, when Buddha received his great, new insight concerning the world and life, God was touching him and struggling with him. God revealed Himself in that moment. Buddha responded to this revelation, and his answer to this day reveals God's hand and the result of human repression. In the "night of power" of which the ninety-seventh sura of the Koran speaks, the night when "the angel descended" and the Koran descended from Allah's throne, God dealt with Mohammed and

---

141. Bolt, Pratt, and Visser, *Bavinck Reader*, 227.
142. Bolt, Pratt, and Visser, 235.
143. Bolt, Pratt, and Visser, 296.

touched him. God wrestled with him in that night, and God's hand is still noticeable in the answer of the prophet, but it is also the result of human repression. The great moments in the history of religion are the moments when God wrestled with man in a very particular way.[144]

Such bold statements can be understood only when one takes into account the personal nature of general revelation. Hence, what JHB means is that this encounter with the divine revelation is particular and personal in its nature. JHB does not say that God revealed himself in Buddhism or Islam, but that he did so to Gautama and Muhammad in those particular moments. Neither does he say that their holy books are God's revelation, but human answers to the divine revelations which have been tainted by human repression. This brings me to his second point.

Second, even though God's general revelation comes to every person, and they see and understand it, it "does not produce actual knowledge" in their life due to human rejection. JHB explains that "this is because along with 'understanding' and 'seeing clearly,' two other processes are at work in human hearts. These are the processes of repressing and replacing." Despite the fact that "general revelation is so real, so concrete, so inescapable, and so compelling that no person escapes it," they don't get it eventually because of their own fault. They suppress the truth of God and replace it with their own, doing so "unconsciously."[145] Here, JHB applies a psychological interpretation to this religious phenomenon. From this perspective, it is not impossible that as people understand and see, they suppress and replace the truth.[146]

Third, religious consciousness is the product of faulty human responses to God's general revelation. JHB explains as follows:

> Religious consciousness is not to be construed as an act that flows from human nature. It does not belong to the structure as such. Rather, it should only be understood as the response of reaction to the voiceless speech of God's self-revelation. However, it needs to be kept in mind that in this reaction the

---

144. Bavinck, *Church Between Temple*, 125.
145. Bolt, Pratt, and Visser, *Bavinck Reader*, 296.
146. Bolt, Pratt, and Visser, 284.

two processes of repressing and replacing are both engaged and both reworked.[147]

JHB follows HB's notion that religion is the product of God's revelation. He, however, elaborates on it and comes out with a more nuanced description than that of HB. Religion is the human response to God's revelation but that response is a faulty one, filled with suppression and replacement of God's truth. Therefore, the result is never a true religion, but idolatry. "This religious consciousness," he explains, "reveals itself in human history as the fabrication of idols (*fabrica idolorum*)."[148] Religion, therefore, bears a dialectical character. Positively, it is the product of God's revelation; but it turns out to be negative due to human sinful responses to that revelation.

Fourth, "the Christian faith is the subjective response of the reborn person to the gospel."[149] The Christian faith is similar to and yet distinct from religious consciousness. The two are similar in the sense that they are responses to God's revelation. But the Christian faith is the product of special revelation, while religious consciousness is of general revelation. Furthermore, the Christian faith is a response coming from persons whose hearts have been renewed by God's Spirit; while religious consciousness comes from unregenerate hearts. Hence, JHB concludes that "no continuity exists between the gospel and human religious consciousness, although definite continuity does exist between the gospel and what lies behind human religious consciousness, namely God's general revelation."[150] Here, JHB agrees with Kraemer that there is no continuity between the gospel and human religious consciousness, but disagrees with him in regard to the point where continuity exists in them. Kraemer does not find any continuity except in human beings themselves. Hence, for Kraemer, the only point of contact available is the messengers of the gospel (i.e. Christian missionaries). JHB, however, sees God's revelation as the continuity between them. JHB agrees with Kraemer on the negative side of religion. Human religion, which stems out of universal religious consciousness, is "in its essence . . . nothing but a substitute. Even the so-called elements of truth in it are a lie, because in the whole context of the [holistic]

---

147. Bolt, Pratt, and Visser, 297.
148. Bolt, Pratt, and Visser, 297.
149. Bolt, Pratt, and Visser, 298.
150. Bolt, Pratt, and Visser, 297.

character of heathenism these elements of truth have a different sense and point in another direction."[151] Yet, this negative aspect is overcome by his emphasis on God's active involvement in it. JHB explains, "The admission of this fact does not imply that God's Word . . . is always thwarted and frustrated, or that it never stirs his heart, or moves his mind. God can break the resistance: He is able to overcome the rebellious force. He can prepare Himself a point of contact in the sinful soul."[152]

JHB therefore disagrees with Barth's negative perspective on religions because he pays "too little attention to the greatness of God's work."[153] With the emphasis on the divine work JHB's view on religion is closer to that of HB than to that of Kraemer. As with HB, JHB could maintain a positive aspect of religion.

From the above discussion, we learn about the value of general revelation as well as its insufficiency. It is due to general revelation that religions are born in human life. Ironically, general revelation is also insufficient. The insufficiency of general revelation is understood in two ways. In the first instance, general revelation is insufficient to lead human beings to a true knowledge of God. The fault lies not in God who reveals himself in his creation, nor in that objective knowledge he reveals, but in human beings who suppress and replace the truth of God. Furthermore, it is also insufficient in the sense that it cannot lead sinners to Christ's redemption. Thus, special revelation is of necessity for human salvation. But this has to be rightly understood. As our discussion will show, salvation is not tied with special revelation, but special grace. Hence, special revelation as such is never salvific. Special revelation is necessary only in the sense that special grace is available with it. With this I now turn to the concept of divine grace.

6.3 Particular[154] and Common Grace

In this section I will deal with the distinction between particular and common grace. Divine grace always touches human sins but does so in two different

---

151. Bavinck, *Impact of Christianity*, 108.
152. Bavinck, 108.
153. Bavinck, 108.
154. In this chapter the terms particular grace and special grace are used interchangeably.

ways. Particular grace deals with human sins by abolishing them and undoing their effects. Particular grace is therefore properly called saving grace. It is particular in the sense that it is not available to all human beings but is restricted only to the elect. Common grace, however, deals with human sins only by restraining them temporarily and minimizing their effects so that human beings may develop despite their sinfulness. It is common because it is bestowed upon all human beings – elect and nonelect.

We need to recognize the existence of common grace because we are often puzzled by the fact that outside the sphere of redemption the world still displays traces of goodness and beauty. Louis Berkhof describes this as follows:

> The question arose, how can we explain the comparatively orderly life in the world, seeing that the whole world lies under the curse of sin? How is it that the earth yields precious fruit in rich abundance and does not simply bring forth thorns and thistles? How can we account for it that sinful man still "retains some knowledge of God, of natural things, and of the difference between good and evil, and shows some regard for virtue and for good outward behavior"? What explanation can be given of the special gifts and talents with which the natural man is endowed, and of the development of science and art by those who are entirely devoid of the new life that is in Christ Jesus? How can we explain the religious aspirations of men everywhere, even of those who did not come in touch with the Christian religion? How can the unregenerate still speak the truth, do good to others, and lead outwardly virtuous lives?[155]

The above questions certainly demand an explanation. Kraemer acknowledges these seemingly paradoxical facts in human lives. That is to say, despite their sinfulness human beings still retain goodness in their lives "manifested in [their] great achievement in the field of culture, art, science, political, social and economic life."[156] Kraemer explains that this goodness originates from their being created in the image of God. Unfortunately, Kraemer stops at this point. He does not ask further how human beings are able to retain this

---

155. Berkhof, *Systematic Theology*, 432.
156. Kraemer, *Christian Message*, 101.

original goodness in them even though they have been corrupted by their sins. This fact can only be explained satisfactorily if we take into account the possibility of continual divine favor showered upon sinful human beings. Surely, Kraemer does not deny divine intervention in human lives, because "the world remains the domain of God who created it." However, God's actions in human life are limited to "His new initiative of reconciliation" and done through his church as "the witness to and representative of the new order salvation and reconciliation."[157] But to limit divine favor within his redemptive purpose does not answer the fact that, as Berkhof points out above, even among the unregenerate one can still find traces of goodness, beauty, and truth. It is at this point where it is necessary to postulate divine works not only in terms of general revelation but also common grace which God displays to all human beings.

In what follows I will explicate the doctrine of common grace based on the thoughts of Abraham Kuyper and Herman Bavinck.[158] This doctrine does not originate from Kuyper and Bavinck. Both theologians credited the reformer John Calvin as its progenitor.[159] But, it is in their hands that this doctrine was developed to its full form. It is for this reason I will concentrate my presentation on their thoughts.

In the first place, we need to see the relationship between revelation and grace. As I have pointed out previously, in agreement with Barth, Bavinck also maintains that revelation means grace. That is to say, revelation is always accompanied by God's grace. The content of revelation is God's grace. However, Bavinck differs from Barth as he makes the distinction between general and special revelation and of common and special grace, while Barth doesn't.[160] This distinction is of utmost importance to my argument as I show below.

---

157. Kraemer, 104.

158. Abraham Kuyper's thought on common grace first appeared in a series of articles in *De Heraut*, which were published later as books in three volumes under the title *De Gemeene Gratie* in 1902. The English translation of the first volume of this series is now available. See Kuyper, *Common Grace*. Besides the above volume, I also use the following work: Kuyper, "Common Grace," 165–201; and for Herman Bavinck's thought on this same subject, I use the following work: Bavinck, "Common Grace," 35–65.

159. See Bavinck, "Calvin and Common Grace," 437–465. For an extensive study of Calvin's thought on this subject, see Kuiper, *Calvin on Common Grace*.

160. See Bavinck, *Our Reasonable Faith*, 38.

Bavinck traces divine grace and revelation back to the garden of Eden. Divine revelation existed before the fall. God revealed himself in his creation and he spoke to the first couple. Hence, prior to the fall we already have the distinction between special and general revelation. The human relationship with God at this point is based on *foedus operum* (the covenant of works). This original religion rests on God's revelation as well. The fall does not change this fundamental truth. That is to say, religions always rest upon God's revelation. However, after the fall, God's revelation takes a significant turn. From this time on, it becomes "a revelation of grace."[161] Yet, this does not mean that there is no grace prior to the fall. As Kuyper correctly points out, "Human life in Paradise was inconceivable without an environing and invasive grace." In the state of integrity "to every creature grace is the air he breathes." But after the fall, "this divine grace assumes its character as *saving* grace."[162] Or, to put it differently, from this time on, grace is divided into saving and common grace.[163] There is grace that touches human sin and grace that does not. Next, it is also divided in the sense that these two graces are bestowed upon human beings from two different lines. Common grace is given to people of all nations; whereas saving grace is primarily given through a special line from Seth, Noah, Abraham, to Israel. Hence, after the fall we have not only the distinction of general and special revelation but also the distinction of common and special grace.

God's general revelation and his common grace go hand by hand. That is to say, God not only reveals himself to all people in nature, history, and human conscience, but he also showers divine favor upon them. As Bavinck points out, "The revelation of God in nature and history is never a mere passive pouring forth of God's virtues but is always a positive act on the part of God."[164] Here, we see that there is a close relationship between God's general revelation and his common grace. To put it differently, general revelation is always accompanied by common grace.

Having said that, I need to make two clarifications about this relation. In the first place, general revelation is not identical with common grace. William

---

161. Bavinck, "Common Grace," 39–40.
162. Kuyper, "Common Grace," 167.
163. Bavinck, "Common Grace," 40.
164. Bavinck, 41.

Masselink points out that there are at least four differences between them. First, they differ in their origin. General revelation exists prior to the fall, but common grace after the fall. Second, they differ in regard to their purpose. General revelation is intended to reveal God himself to human beings, but common grace is to restrain the effects of sin so that human beings are able to flourish despite their sinfulness. Third, our knowledge of common grace is from special revelation, not from general revelation. Fourth, the two need to be distinguished but not separated. God uses the effects of general revelation (i.e. sense of divinity and sense of morality) coupled with his common grace to restrain sin.[165]

In the second place, this concurrent relationship between general revelation and common grace cannot be applied strictly to the relationship between special revelation and special grace. It is true that special grace is available only through special revelation. But special grace is not necessarily concurrent with special revelation. Therefore, receiving special revelation does not always mean receiving special grace. This subtle difference is of utmost importance. With this we are able to answer why Jews, or Christians, cannot be saved simply by being the recipients of God's special revelation. Salvation is therefore attached to special grace, not special revelation. This is the determinant factor which distinguishes the religion of Israel from other religions. Bavinck states that "all religions are positive: they rest upon real or supposed revelation. The true, material difference in question lies in *gratia; gratia specialis* [special grace] is something unknown to the heathen."[166] Special grace is therefore available only in the religion of Israel.

But, the division of common and special grace, however, does not last forever. First, the dividing line between the two ends with the coming of Christ. In the economy of Israel special grace is available only within the religion of Israel. But, in Christ, the two lines of grace finally become one again. Special grace now is made available to all men and women.[167] It is still divided into saving and common grace, but for now in Christ people of all nations can enjoy not only one grace but two graces together. Second, the two aspects of

---

165. Masselink, *General Revelation*, 69.
166. Bavinck, "Common Grace," 41.
167. Bavinck, 44.

grace – saving and common – will be reunited in the consummation of the kingdom of God. Bavinck explains as follows.

> If the revelation in Christ is only a modification of the original revelation, then it naturally possesses only a temporary and transitory character. It is not absolutely but only accidentally necessary. It became necessary only because of sin, which is accidental and does not pertain to the essence of things. The *foedus gratiae*, in all its divisions, is destined to pass away . . . When the kingdom has fully come, Christ will hand it over to God the Father.[168]

What is the relationship between special and common grace? Kuyper points out that the two aspects of grace are closely related. In the first place, "special grace presupposes *common grace*."[169] Special grace is made possible because of the existence of common grace. Without common grace, the elect could not have been born, life on earth would not be possible, and the church could not have been established. Hence, by his common grace God preserves his creation and provides ground to exercise his special grace to the elect.

Still, the emphasis is placed on special grace not common. Kuyper maintains that in the end "not *common grace* but the order of *special grace* prevails."[170] God will not simply maintain the world in which sins are restrained; he will eventually abolish sins completely, restore and renew the world to the point sins may not exist. Hence, as much as common grace is important, it is "only an emanation of special and all its fruit flows into special."[171] Yet, it does not mean that common grace exists only for the sake of the elect. To place human salvation as the ultimate purpose is a faulty thought. Here, Kuyper brings us back to the glory of God. "All things exist *for the sake of Christ*," he explains. The church of God shares this honor only as his body. But, he alone is "the reflection of God's glory."[172] Therefore, the ultimate end of special grace is not the salvation of the elect but "the Son's glorification of the Father's love."[173]

---

168. Bavinck, 59.
169. Kuyper, "Common Grace," 169.
170. Kuyper, 170.
171. Kuyper, 170.
172. Kuyper, 170.
173. Kuyper, 171.

With this, I will move to my next point, the relation between Christology and the two aspects of grace.

Kuyper's discussion on this point is important to counter a tendency in recent theology of religions to limit Christology to soteriology. Against this tendency, Kuyper argues that Christ's role is wider than a reconciler of human souls. Here, Kuyper widens the scope of Christology in two ways. First, Christ's redemption covers both nature and grace. Christ is the reconciler of both soul and body. Christ is not only the "Reconciler of our soul" but he is "the Savior of both soul and body and is the Re-creator not only of things in the invisible world but also of things that are visible and before our eyes."[174] Kuyper emphasizes the significance of Christ for the whole person – body and soul. He is the Lord of nature and grace.

Second, Christ is the mediator not only of redemption, but also of creation. Kuyper rejects the idea that "Christ has no significance but as the Lamb of God who died for our sin."[175] This idea is not in line with the witness of the Scriptures. According to the Scriptures, Kuyper maintains, "the *Savior* of the World is also the *Creator* of the world, indeed that he could become its Savior only *because* he already was its Creator."[176] The eternal Logos who has created the world is also the incarnate Logos who has come into the world. As the creator, he is connected to nature; and as the re-creator he is connected to grace. Here, again, Kuyper brings us back to the significance of Christ in nature and grace. But grace is not "exclusively concerned with atonement for sin and salvation for souls," because it is not "something located and operating outside nature."[177] Hence, Kuyper asserts, "*common grace* has been shown to nature and *special grace* to God's elect."[178] Here, Christ is connected to both common and special grace. He is indeed the source of both. In reference to Colossians 1:15–17, Kuyper explains,

> Does not the apostle write to the church of Colossae that the self-same Christ is simultaneously two things: the root of the life of creation as well as the root of the life of the new creation?

---

174. Kuyper, 171.
175. Kuyper, 171.
176. Kuyper, 173.
177. Kuyper, 173.
178. Kuyper, 174.

> First we read that Christ is "the first-born of all creation, for in him all things were created, in heaven and on earth," so that he is "before all things and in him all things hold together." It could hardly be stated more plainly and clearly that Christ is the root of creation and therefore of common grace, for it is common grace that prevents things from sinking into nothingness. (Does not the text say that all things *hold together* in him?) But we immediately note in the second place that the same Christ is "the *Head of the body* and the first-born from the dead," hence also the root of the life of the new creation or the special grace. The two things are even stated in parallel terms: he is the root of common grace for he is *the first-born of all creation*, and simultaneously the root of special grace, for he is the *first-born from the dead*. There is thus no doubt whatever that common grace and special grace come most intimately connected from their origin, and this connection lies in Christ.[179]

With Christology that maintains the lordship of Christ above nature and grace, one will see that there is no antithesis between nature and grace.

Another important aspect to bring out here is the relation between common grace and the image of God. As I have mentioned above, Kuyper maintains that common grace exists not for the sake of the elect. Instead, it is for the glory of God. This will be manifest in the development of human beings as the image of God. What he means is not individual beings but the whole humanity. Here, Kuyper widens the scope of the image of God to include the entire human race. Bavinck argues that "a human being does not *bear* or *have* the image of God but he or she *is* the image of God." On this point, Bavinck emphasizes that the image of God is "not *something in man* but *man himself*."[180] In other words, the whole person is the image of God. Kuyper surely agrees with Bavinck's point. He does not deny that each individual person is the image of God. But he also maintains that the entire human race is the image of God. Each individual person can only be said to be the image of God relatively. But, in its fullest sense, the image of God is found in the whole humanity. For Kuyper, "the image of God is certainly much too

---

179. Kuyper, 186–187.
180. Bavinck, *RD II*, 554.

rich a concept to be realized *in one single person*."[181] There is only one person who can be said to be the image of God in its fullest sense and this person is Jesus Christ. This cannot be applied to the rest of humanity individually. Even in the case of Adam, this can be applied only in the sense that he bears the whole human race in himself.

Furthermore, Kuyper also maintains that the image of God in its richness can be found and seen only when the entire human race has developed to its fullest sense. The development of the human race is solely from God himself. In the first place, it is God who has deposited "an infinite number of nuclei for high human development in [human] nature."[182] As such, "these nuclei cannot develop except *through the social bond between people*." Here, Kuyper maintains that this social aspect of the image of God has an independent goal apart from human salvation. God wants these nuclei in human nature to develop to their fullest "not for the sake of humanity but for God." "The brilliance of his image *has* to appear" in order to display God's glory. Thus, it is also God himself who is actively involved in the development of human nature. "He himself will bring it about and into view."[183] At this point we need to consider the works of the Spirit, for it is through the operation of the Spirit that God involves himself in the development of human nature.[184]

In the first place, Kuyper maintains that we need to deal with the work of the Spirit from a higher and correct standpoint, namely that the end of all things is not the salvation of the elect but the glory of God. From this superior standpoint, one will see that the work of the Spirit not only touches "the sanctification of the redeemed," but also includes the things in the past, such as "the Incarnation, the preparation of Scripture, the forming of man and the universe," and extends to the things to come, such as "the Lord's return, the final judgment, and that last cataclysm that shall separate heaven from hell forever."[185] Indeed, the scope of the work of the Spirit extends from eternity past to our temporal world and from this temporal world to the eternity to

---

181. Kuyper, "Common Grace," 177.
182. Kuyper, 178.
183. Kuyper, 178.
184. For Abraham Kuyper's thought on the work of the Spirit, I will use the following work: Kuyper, *Work of the Holy Spirit*.
185. Kuyper, *Work of the Holy Spirit*, 9.

come. Hence, Kuyper concludes that "the Spirit's work must touch the entire *host of heaven and earth.*"[186]

In the second place, the work of the Spirit in this world is not separated but distinguished from the works of the other persons of the Trinity (i.e. Father and Son). All things flow from the Father through the Son, and are perfected by the Spirit. The work of God in this world is therefore terminated in the work of the Spirit. With this understanding, Kuyper maintains that "to lead the creature to its destiny, to cause it to develop according to its nature, to make it perfect, is the proper work of the Holy Spirit."[187] The Spirit is to lead the creation to its destiny, namely, the glory of God. God's glory is most reflected in the lives of the elect. God is most pleased when we become "his family of sons and daughters, begotten of his own blood, trained by his wisdom, animated by his ideals, one with him in the plans, purposes, and spirit of his life."[188] However, God's glory is not confined to all these. Spiritual things are hardly separated from nonspiritual things. The lives of the elect are affected by things surrounding them. Therefore, the Spirit also works in those things "that affect man in the attaining of his destiny or in the failure to attain it."[189] Sin does not alter the purpose of the Spirit's work. His work is always to bring the creation to the glory of God. Hence, Kuyper maintains that the Spirit "undertook to bring all things to their destiny either *without* the disturbance of sin or *in spite of it*; first, by saving the elect, and then by restoring all thing in heaven and on earth at the return of the Lord Jesus Christ."[190]

In relation to our subject, the work of the Spirit touches not only aspects of special grace, but also those of common grace. In regard to the former, it is the work of re-creation, and to the latter the work of creation. The development of human nature is therefore related to the latter aspect of the Spirit's work. He does so bestowing human beings with natural "gifts, talents, and abilities."[191] With this, Kuyper positively affirms human culture. "Art is not man's invention, but God's creation," Kuyper asserts. It is God's creation in two ways. First, "God must have placed in [those materials, such as gold, silver, wood,

---

186. Kuyper, 8.
187. Kuyper, 21.
188. Kuyper, 22.
189. Kuyper, 24.
190. Kuyper, 24.
191. Kuyper, 38.

and iron] certain possibilities," and, second, "have created inventive power in man's mind, perseverance in his will, strength in his muscle, accurate vision in his eye, delicacy of touch and action in his fingers, thus qualifying him to evolve what is latent in the materials."[192] So, God not only creates materials with their possibilities to be developed, but through the Sprit he also endows human beings natural gifts, talents, and abilities to develop them.

Summary

Kraemer's theology of religions has internal tensions in the following areas: (1) general revelation, (2) dialectical nature of religions, and (3) holistic nature of religions. This chapter seeks to resolve those tensions. These shortcomings, I argue, could be overcome by having a proper doctrine of revelation and grace. I have shown that those problems are rooted in the confusion of the ideas of revelation, grace, and salvation. The confusion occurs when the distinction of general and special revelation disappears, and revelation and grace are not differentiated. These three ideas – revelation, grace, and salvation – have been linked too tightly. Revelation is thought to be concomitant with grace and salvation. Consequently, the argument for general revelation will eventually lead to a possibility of salvation outside Christ. In line with this scheme, the uniqueness of Christ as the way, truth, and life and the existence of general revelation are thought to be mutually exclusive. However, I have shown that this is not necessarily so. The distinctions of general and special revelation and of common and special grace are crucial at this point. Here, the thoughts of Herman Bavinck, Abraham Kuyper, and Johan H. Bavinck are helpful for our case.

Herman Bavinck maintains the multiplicity of divine revelation. There are many forms of revelation which culminate in the person of Jesus Christ. He is the highest form of revelation. Yet, the revelation in Jesus Christ is not contradictory with other forms of revelation. Instead, it is due to the revelation in Christ that we find God's revelation in nature and history. Those many forms of revelation are essentially one, and they differ only in their means, content, scope, and purpose. Hence, Bavinck makes a clear distinction between special and general revelation.

---

192. Kuyper, 40.

General revelation is valuable. Human religious and moral sense are owed to God's general revelation. Bavinck maintains a positive view of religion. There is no religion without revelation. All religions rest on divine revelation. J. H. Bavinck's contribution to this point is found in his notion of universal religious consciousness. It is in this religious consciousness that the drama between God and man occurs. With this, JHB brings out the personal aspect of general revelation. This point is of utmost importance to our discussion. The arena where the divine works happen is not non-Christian religions or cultures, but personal human lives. God meets humans personally not in or through their religions. Religions are the result of this divine-human encounter. Religions are the human response to God's revelation. Yet, however valuable general revelation is, it is insufficient for human salvation. This brings us to special and common grace.

In addition to special and general revelation, we need also to make a distinction between special and particular grace. This distinction is crucial for our discussion. Revelation always comes with grace. But, as with revelation, the Bible reveals two forms of grace – special and common. Both graces deal with human sins differently. Special grace touches sin by redeeming it and abolishing its penalty (i.e. death). Special grace is therefore saving grace. Human salvation is tied with this grace. Common grace, however, only restrains the effects of sin. It does not save human from their sins, but it provides an environment where human beings may thrive despite their sinfulness.

In the next chapter, I will apply these insights to address the shortcomings of Kraemer's theology of religions.

CHAPTER 7

An Amended Version of Kraemer's Theology of Religions

In chapter 6, I argued that the shortcomings of Kraemer's theology of religions can be addressed by properly navigating two Christian doctrines – revelation and grace. I described and drew insights from those doctrines which are derived primarily from Herman Bavinck, Johan H. Bavinck, and Abraham Kuyper. This chapter applies those insights to amend the deficiencies of Kraemer's theology of religions.

M. M. Thomas uses the category ultimate and penultimate matters to evaluate Kraemer's theology of religions. The ultimate matter refers to the truth in Christ and the penultimate matter the values of non-Christian religions and cultures. Thomas contends that Kraemer's theology of religions is strong in regard to the ultimate matters, but weak in regard to the penultimate matters. W. A. Visser 't Hooft disagrees with Thomas. Instead, he contends that Kraemer is strong on both matters. Kraemer's ingenuity lies in his ability to maintain both seemingly dialectical elements. Visser 't Hooft says:

> The real originality of his missionary attitude lies precisely in the dialectical combination of an uncompromising Christocentric theology with patient, loving attention for the spiritual life of the people whom the Gospel is to be brought. It is not too difficult to find men who refuse to deviate an inch from the affirmation that the revelation in Christ is unique and absolute. It is not too difficult to find others who show a profound understanding for the spiritual contents and structure of the religions of Asia and

Africa. But there have not been many of whom these two things can be said at the same and among these few Kraemer is the most lucid expositor of the dialectical tension of the genuine missionary approach.[1]

Undoubtedly, Kraemer is strong in the ultimate matters. Both Thomas and Visser 't Hooft affirm this point. Yet, in regard to the penultimate matters they disagree. I contend that there are truths in both sides. Thomas is right that Kraemer is weak in this point. But the weakness is not, as Thomas has suggested, in Kraemer's affirmation of non-Christian values. On this point, Visser 't Hooft is right. Kraemer firmly affirms non-Christian values. However, this affirmation, as discussed in chapter 6, is not theologically but practically oriented. That is to say, even though Kraemer could affirm non-Christian values, he does not have a strong theological framework to support them. Here lies his shortcoming which needs to be addressed. Yet, before I amend the weaknesses of his theology, I begin first with its strengths. Here, I contend that the strengths of Kraemer's theology of religions lie in the ultimate matters, namely, a strong affirmation of the uniqueness of Jesus Christ and the necessity of Christian mission.

7.1 The Uniqueness of Jesus Christ

The uniqueness of Jesus Christ is the foundation that cannot be taken away. No theology can survive without the name of Christ. Johannes Verkuyl rightly says, "A theocentric theology that is not simultaneously Christocentric simply cannot be termed Christian theology. Any *theologia religionum* that is ashamed of the name of Jesus ought to be deeply ashamed of *itself*. There is no Kingdom without the King: no other gods, no other name."[2] On the uniqueness of Jesus Christ, Kraemer's theology of religions stands fast.

Kraemer firmly maintains the *sui generis* character of the Christian revelation. By this he does not mean that there is no other revelation beside that in Jesus Christ. The *sui generis* character of the Christian revelation does not contradict God's general revelation. The triune God reveals himself to us in many ways and ultimately in his Son Jesus Christ. Kraemer maintains the

---

1. Visser 't Hooft, "Introductory Note," 7.
2. Verkuyl, "Biblical Notion," 77.

multiplicity of revelation – general and special revelation. Yet, by the *sui generis* character of the Christian revelation, he affirms the uniqueness of Jesus Christ. Jesus Christ is unique, not in the sense that he is different from others, nor in the sense that he is the best among others, but in the sense that he is one of a kind. He is one and the only truth, way, and life. It is only through him that man can have a true relationship with God the Father.

It is important to note here that Kraemer does not refer to Christianity, but to the Christian revelation. For Kraemer, Christianity is not absolute. It is not even the "best" religion in terms of expressing religious truth.[3] In this regard, Kraemer explains, other religions may surpass Christianity in its praxis. For example, the idea of devotion and submission to the sovereign God is profoundly expressed in Islam. Still, Christianity is the best religion by virtue of its association with the gospel. Kraemer says, "Christianity . . . and the Christian Church with all her crying sins, continue to exist and to be 'best' religion; not because everything about it is so very good but *because it is there that the Gospel is to be heard.*"[4]

Some scholars of religion have challenged the relevance of Christ's uniqueness for today's pluralistic society. Gordon D. Kaufman, for example, emphasizes the necessity for us to live peacefully amidst our diversity. He asks, "How, in all our diversity, can we humans learn to live together fruitfully, productively and in peace in today's complexly interconnected world . . . ?"[5] For Kaufman, this question is of utmost importance, because if we fail to do so, "we may well succeed only in bringing all of human life on earth to its final end."[6] Hence, our survival depends on our success to live peacefully with others. To do so, we need "to take other faiths, other life-orientations, with full seriousness."[7] Here, Kaufman argues, the claim of Christ's uniqueness will lead Christians to a sort of idolatry. In other words, it confuses a human claim of God's absolute with the reality of God's absolute. This claim becomes a stumbling block for Christians to relate with others. He explains:

---

3. Kraemer, *Why Christianity*, 115.
4. Kraemer, 117.
5. Kaufman, "Religious Diversity," 3.
6. Kaufman, 4.
7. Kaufman, 4.

> The tendencies toward absoluteness and exclusivity in traditional Christian faith easily lead to a kind of idolatry that makes it difficult to take other faiths seriously in their own terms, searching out their insights into human existence and the deepest human problems, attending carefully to their proposals regarding how those problems should be approached.[8]

In a similar vein, John Hick maintains that the uniqueness of Christ is a poison to a Christian's relationship with others. Hick says, "Christian absolutism, in collaboration with acquisitive and violent human nature, has done much to poison the relationship between the Christian minority and the non-Christian majority of the world's population by sanctifying exploitation and oppression on a gigantic scale."[9]

However, I contend here that the above charge is not warranted. Here, we need to turn to the notion of truth. As Kraemer maintains, the relation between Christianity and other religions is an issue of truth. Rejection of an absolute is possible only when one disregards the question of truth. Kraemer explains, "The only people who maintain that it all boils down to the same thing are those who have never taken the trouble to find out what 'it all' is. In any case, such a verdict entirely misses the real point of the question, which has to do with truth and the intrinsic value of truth."[10] In a similar vein, Newbigin says, "If a man says 'my religion is only one among various religions in the world,' then one can confidently say that that is not his real religion; that is not the thing to which he is really committed."[11] Here, religion involves two elements: "apprehension of truth" and "commitment to the truth." The two elements cannot exist separately. Hence, Newbigin contends: "We are not concerned with apprehension of the truth in a manner which leaves us uncommitted. It is indeed questionable whether any truth is apprehended without an eloquent commitment."[12]

But, when we consider matters of truth, the charge – that an exclusive claim of truth is morally flawed – cannot be substantiated. Here Alvin

---

8. Kaufman, 5.
9. Hick, "Non-Absoluteness of Christianity," 17.
10. Kraemer, *Why Christianity*, 13.
11. Newbigin, "Finality of Christ," 15.
12. Newbigin, 15.

Plantinga's defense is clear-cut. In the first place, he contends that to hold to an exclusive claim of truth cannot be charged as oppressive or imperialistic. Plantinga explains, "I daresay there are some among you who reject some of the things I believe; I do not believe that you are thereby oppressing me, even if you do not believe you have an argument that would convince me. It is conceivable that exclusivism might in some way *contribute to* oppression, but it isn't in itself oppressive."[13] Second, to hold to an exclusive claim of truth is logically consistent. It is a matter of simple logic. Again, Plantinga says, "If she believes [that p is true], then she must also believe that those who believe something incompatible with [p] are mistaken and believe what is false. That's no more than simple logic."[14] Christopher Wright illustrates this logic as follows:

> If I tell you that my name is Chris Wright, and that is accepted as true, then it excludes the possibility that I am Charles Wilkinson. If we agree on the truth of the statement that Paris is the capital of France, we exclude the proposition that Lyons is the capital of France. The truth that two and two make four excludes the possibility that in some circumstances they might make five.[15]

Still, Plantinga continues to point out that an exclusive claim of truth also involves a personal commitment to the value of that claim and a belief of being privileged to have it. He says:

> Furthermore, she must also believe that that those who do not believe as she does – *fail* to believe something that is true, deep, and important, and that she *does* believe. She must therefore see herself as *privileged* with respect to those others – those others of both kinds. There is something of great value, she must think, that *she* has and *they* lack. They are ignorant of something – something of great importance – of which she has knowledge.[16]

Yet, even with this belief, her stand cannot be charged as morally flawed, because there is no alternative one can do otherwise. Here, Plantinga leads

---

13. Plantinga, "Pluralism," 197.
14. Plantinga, 197.
15. Wright, *Uniqueness of Jesus*, 38.
16. Plantinga, "Pluralism," 197.

us to an inevitable exclusivist position. In other words, whatever position one takes, they end up with an exclusive position. In regard to proposition p, one could believe it, reject it, or abstain from believing and rejecting it. So, if the position of those who believe it is morally flawed, then so are the other positions. Plantinga explains:

> My claim is that if contradicting others . . . is arrogant and egostistical, so is dissenting. . . . For suppose you believe some proposition p but I don't; perhaps you believe it is wrong to discriminate against people simply on the grounds of race, but I, recognizing that there are many people who disagree with you, do not believe this proposition. I don't disbelieve it either, of course, but in the circumstances I think the right thing to do is to abstain from belief. Then am I not implicitly condemning your attitude, your *believing* the proposition, as somehow improper – naïve, perhaps, or unjustified, or in some other way less than optimal? I am implicitly saying that my attitude is the superior one; I think my course of action here is the right one and yours somehow wrong, inadequate, improper, in the circumstance at best second-rate.[17]

The charge – that an exclusive claim of the uniqueness of Christ is arrogant, egoistic, or imperialistic – is unwarranted. However, the relevance of Christ's uniqueness in today's world of religions is not dependent simply on the success to answer the objection of those who are against it. The uniqueness of Christ, I argue here, is always relevant by its own virtue. As Hans Küng correctly says, the relevance of Christianity is dependent on the uniqueness of Jesus Christ. Küng maintains that the difference between Christianity and other religions lies in their acknowledgment of the status of Jesus. It is only in Christianity that Jesus is acknowledged as Christ. Küng puts it this way: "The special feature, the most fundamental characteristic of Christianity is that it considers this Jesus as ultimately decisive, definitive, *archetypal*, for man's relations with God, with his fellow man, with society: in the curtailed biblical formula, as 'Jesus Christ.'"[18] This acknowledgment of Jesus as Christ

---

17. Plantinga, 199.
18. Küng, *On Being a Christian*, 123.

makes Christianity not only special, but also always relevant. The relevance of Christianity is therefore dependent only on its stand on the uniqueness of Christ. Küng writes:

> If Christianity seeks to become relevant, freshly relevant, to men in the world religions, to the modern humanists, it will certainly not be simply by saying later what others said first, by doing later what others did first. Such a parrot-like Christianity does not become relevant to the religions and the humanisms. In this way it becomes irrelevant, superfluous. Actualization, modernization, involvement, *alone*, will not make it relevant ... Hence Christianity can ultimately be and become relevant only by activating – as always, in theory and practice – the *memory of Jesus Christ as ultimately archetypal*: of Jesus the Christ and not only as one the "archetypal men."[19]

The drawback of Küng's idea of Christ's uniqueness is that it falls into the idea of "an inclusive Christian universalism."[20] For Küng, in the end all will be saved in Christ. Carl Braaten proposes a similar position as that of Küng. He maintains both the uniqueness and universality of Jesus Christ.[21] This occurs when Christology is taken too narrowly. It is tied up solely with soteriology. Newbigin is right on this point. He says that "the whole debate about the uniqueness of Christ has for many decades been skewed by the notion that the only question at stake is the question of the fate of the individual soul in the next world."[22] Yet, as we have shown, the Scriptures maintain Jesus Christ not only as the savior, but also the sovereign Lord, of the world. Hence, the emphasis is not on human salvation but on the glory of God. We have to tie up the uniqueness of Jesus Christ with the glory of God. With this emphasis, we will not fall into two extremes – on the one side the Scylla of particularism and on the other side the Charybdis of universalism. We will not say that only those who have an explicit faith in Jesus Christ shall be saved; and at the same time avoid saying that all things will be saved in Christ. Instead, the uniqueness of Jesus Christ means that all those saved are saved in Jesus Christ; and

---

19. Küng, 123–124.
20. Küng, 112.
21. Braaten, "Who Do We Say," 2–8.
22. Newbigin, "Religious Pluralism," 54.

yet, not all are saved but only those who have been chosen according to his sovereign will. Ultimately, it is not about salvation of all but about the glory of God. Now I turn to the second strength of Kraemer's theology of religions.

7.2 The Necessity of Christian Mission

There is a close relationship between theology of religions and missiology. The two are subdisciplines of Christian theology whose fields of study often overlap. It is not my intention here, however, to deal thoroughly with their similarities and differences.[23] Suffice it to say, the two disciplines need to complement each other. Verkuyl summarizes their interdependence as follows:

> If a theologian of religions lacks missionary motivation and perspective, he has actually traded in the real foundation of his discipline for something which provides no basis at all. On the other hand, if a missiologist both in his method and his conclusions fails to take theology of religions into account, he will be blind to what is actually transpiring among human beings and religions and thus talk on in thin air and grope about in a fog.[24]

One important commonality in both disciplines is the emphasis on the proclamation of Jesus Christ in this religiously diverse world. Yet, what must be the core of these disciplines has been gradually marginalized. In both theology of religions and missiology, Christian mission has either been reinterpreted or set aside altogether. This is not a stand-alone phenomenon, but a direct effect of the abandonment of Christ's uniqueness. Kraemer maintains that "missions inevitably must lose their vital impetus if this conviction [of the uniqueness of Jesus Christ] becomes thin or turns out to be invalid, or is held with an easy conscience and a confused intellect."[25] So, when Jesus loses his uniqueness, his mandate loses its authority. Verkuyl succinctly says: "The subversion of the missionary mandate . . . is [a] betrayal of Jesus Christ."[26] Hence, the uniqueness of Christ goes hand in hand with the necessity of Christian

---

23. For the relationship between the two disciplines, see, Netland, "Theology of Religions," 141–158; Verkuyl, *Contemporary Missiology*, 361–362.
24. Verkuyl, *Contemporary Missiology*, 361–362.
25. Kraemer, *Christian Message*, 106.
26. Verkuyl, "Biblical Notion," 77.

mission. As Kraemer's theology of religions stands fast on the uniqueness of Christ, it also fervently advocates for the necessity of Christian mission.

It seems natural for Kraemer to emphasize Christian mission. He was a missionary in the first place. Kraemer's theology of religions, found in his magnum opus *The Christian Message*, was intended for a missionary conference. As we have shown, he rejected the dilution of Christian mission in the theologies of religions prevalent in that era. Still, Kraemer's emphasis on the necessity of Christian mission stems from his conviction of obeying the divine mandate. Verkuyl points out that Kraemer was fighting to counter "the antimission tendencies of his day by claiming that if one gives up mission both at home and abroad, he is being disobedient to his Lord."[27] Kraemer never ceased stressing the necessity of Christian mission in his theology of religions. In his later work *Religion and the Christian Faith*, published in 1956 – almost two decades after *The Christian Message* – Kraemer still emphasized the necessity of Christian mission even though this work was dedicated to the subject of religion.[28]

As Tim Perry correctly observes, Kraemer's theology of religions is closely linked with his ecclesiology. For Kraemer, theology of religions is not a subdivision of theology in general, but of ecclesiology.[29] Again, ecclesiology is also inseparable from missiology. The church's essential nature is "an *apostolic body*."[30] The church has to be a missionary church. When a church fails to carry out its missionary task, it ceases to be a living church. Kraemer says, "A church without a mission is a galvanized corpse."[31] The study of religions is meant to serve the church as an apostolic body. Theology of religions is to equip the church with an understanding of religions as it carries out its missionary outreach.

For Kraemer, the greatest challenge the church faces is not secularism but relativism. As the church faces non-Christian religions and cultures, it needs to deal with the problem of syncretism. Kraemer maintained this stand in his

---

27. Verkuyl, *Contemporary Missiology*, 164.
28. Kraemer, *Religion and the Christian Faith*, 404–417.
29. Perry, *Radical Difference*, 56, 98.
30. Kraemer repeatedly maintains that the church is an apostolic body. See, Kraemer, *Christian Message*, 2, 34, 36.
31. Quoted in Verkuyl, *Contemporary Missiology*, 113.

early writings[32] and held firmly to the same conviction decades later.[33] Yet, for Kraemer, the problem of syncretism cannot stay merely as a theological discourse. Kraemer refused to deal with this topic simply as "a theological problem."[34] In other words, syncretism cannot be dealt with theoretically. It must be solved practically. That is to say, syncretism is a missionary problem. It is through its missionary outreach, that the church faces and solves this problem. The church will never understand the danger of syncretism if it does not practice missionary outreach. Kraemer says:

> A church without missionary outreach, introverted in its own life and interest (there are amongst the so-called "younger churches" those which tend in that direction) will not meet the problem and will easily conclude that there is no danger or concern whatever to it in the whole matter of syncretism. In fact this is escapist introvertism, the retribution of which inevitably is sterilization by isolation.[35]

How can the church understand and solve the problem of syncretism through its missionary outreach? Here, I turn to Kraemer's understanding of mission. For Kraemer, Christian mission's primary aim is church planting. In so doing, Christian missions cannot adopt syncretistic programs. Otherwise, Christian missions will become "a movement for cultural religious chemistry, and not the sustained, determined act of announcing the Good News."[36] Instead, evangelism, or the proclamation of the gospel, must aim at conversion. By conversion, he means that "the convert leaves his original spiritual home and enters a new, different home."[37] Conversion is opposite to syncretism. When a sinner puts his faith in Jesus Christ, they has to leave their old life, including their old spiritual life. The churches – both younger and older – can fight against syncretism as they are involved in Christian mission.

---

32. Kraemer addressed this topic in his inauguration speech at Leiden University. Again, this topic was discussed extensively in *The Christian Message*. See Kraemer, *De Wortelen*; *Christian Message*, 200–210.

33. Kraemer continued to discuss this topic in his later writings. See, Kraemer, *Religion and the Christian Faith*, 387–417; "Syncretism," 253–273.

34. Kraemer, "Syncretism as a Theological Problem," 179–182.

35. Kraemer, *Religion and the Christian Faith*, 406.

36. Kraemer, "Syncretism," 249.

37. Kraemer, 249.

In its fight against syncretism, the church, however, is not anti-culture. Instead, it seeks to establish a kind of Christianity that fits the soil in which it is planted. Christian mission aims to plant not only churches, but indigenous churches. This is what Kraemer calls adaptation. Therefore, Christian mission has a twofold aim. It seeks conversion by avoiding syncretism and establishing indigenous churches through adaptation.

I have described two strengths of Kraemer's theology religions. Kraemer strongly affirms the uniqueness of Christ and the necessity of Christian mission in its traditional sense. Next, I will deal with its weaknesses.

I contend that Kraemer's view of religions requires modifications. First, theologically Kraemer maintains a dialectical character of religions. Religion is both positive and negative. It is positive due to its divine origin and negative due to human and demonic influences. I concur with Kraemer that religion is dialectical, but, the emphasis must be placed on the divine aspect. Religion is not equally dialectical. It is primarily divine. Second, phenomenologically Kraemer takes a holistic approach to non-Christian religions. Every religion is a living and indivisible unity. Religion and culture are an inseparable unity. As such, this character is organic. In other words, the symbiosis between non-Christian religions and their cultures belong to their essence. I agree with Kraemer, but disagree with him that this holistic character is an organic unity. Instead, I take it as an abortive unity. To these two points I now turn.

7.3 Divine-Driven Character of Religions

Where do religions originate? Are they from God, humans, or demons? A correct answer to this question, I argue, is a combination of those three. Undoubtedly, religions are closely tied up with the social, cultural, and psychological makeup of human beings. Yet they cannot be a purely human phenomenon. A human's search for reality beyond themself could not come from themself. Man cannot surpass his own nature. The awareness of the reality outside him must originate from outside. An eye in total darkness could not have an awareness of light by itself. It made aware of the light, only when the light shines into it. From a theological standpoint, it is not man who searches for God, but God first searches for man (Rom 3:11). Still, another extreme needs to be avoided. I reject a sheer demarcation between Christianity and non-Christian religions in regard to divine revelation. I cannot agree with the notion that Christianity originates from divine revelation and non-Christian religions from demonic influences. Instead, in agreement with Kraemer, we need to consider these three factors – the divine, human, and demonic – in religions.

Next, we need to consider the interplay of these factors. For example, let us first consider Peter Beyerhaus's tripolar view of religions. On the origin of religions, Beyerhaus writes, "The evangelical view of non-Christian religions takes into account three constituent elements in them: the divine, because of general revelation; the human, because of human beings as (distorted) image of God; and the demonic."[38] Beyerhaus is right that religions cannot be neutral. The divine, human, and demonic factors in religions cannot be set aside. The Scriptures certainly support this notion. But Beyerhaus comes short of weighing the interplay of those factors. He does not consider how deep each factor may impact religions. One cannot assume that each of the factors has the same pull on religions. This cannot be true, because God, humans, and Satan cannot be put on the same plane. When one puts emphasis on the wrong side, religions turn out to be quite negative. This is certainly true with Daniel Strange's view on religions. Strange also maintains the divine, human, and demonic factors of non-Christian religions. Yet, he places so much stress on human and demonic factors that they overwhelm the divine. As a result, non-Christian religions are viewed negatively. They are simply "human idolatrous responses behind which stand deceiving demonic forces."[39] But, how could human and demonic powers outweigh God's powers? This is impossible.

Kraemer maintains a dialectical model of religions. As I have shown, there is significant change in regard to Kraemer's position on this point. In his early writings he maintained a radical discontinuity position. But later, in response to Hogg's critique, he softened this position. He held a position of both continuity and discontinuity. This position is in line with his dialectical stand. Kraemer also maintains these three factors – divine, human, and demonic – in religions. Yet, he differs from Beyerhaus and Strange in emphasizing on divine and human factors. The demonic factor functions only to enhance human's negative response to God's revelation. In the final analysis, we conclude that Kraemer's position on the nature of religions is

---

38. Beyerhaus, "My Pilgrimage," 174; "Authority of the Gospel," 141–143.
39. Strange, *Not Our Rock*, 42.

solidly dialectical. Religion is both divine and human. However, Kraemer fails to give priority to the divine factor. As a result, Kraemer's dialectical model loses its balance. It swings heavily to its negative. This shortcoming can be overcome when the divine factor is given its proper due.

Religion is primarily divine. The term "primarily" is intentional. I do not deny human and demonic factors in religions. Yet, the divine factor should take priority among the others. In the first place, in agreement with Herman Bavinck and Johan H. Bavinck, I contend that all religions rest on divine revelation.[40] By this, I mean that all religions come from revelation. Religion is a product of divine revelation. To put it differently, religions are human responses to divine revelation.[41] However, this does not mean that God reveals himself in or through religions. Johan H. Bavinck's personal aspect of general revelation is helpful for our case. God speaks to human beings personally. He does not speak to them in or through their religions. God might have spoken to Siddharta Gautama, but God does not speak in or through Buddhism. God might have spoken to Muhammad, but not in the religion of Islam.[42] As Newbigin rightly points out, the Scriptures do not indicate that religions are the arena in which the God-human drama happens. He says:

> The contemporary debate about Christianity and the world's religions is generally conducted with the unspoken assumption that "religion" is the primary medium of human contact with the divine. But this assumption has to be questioned. When the New Testament affirms that God has nowhere left himself without witness, there is no suggestion that this witness is necessarily to be found in the sphere of what we call religion.[43]

Instead, he continues, in the New Testament, when the gospel was preached, common people came to Jesus, but religious people rejected him. So, Newbigin rightly concludes: "It is made clear that religion is, above all, the area of darkness."[44] I concur with Newbigin's conclusion. God does not leave

---

40. Bavinck, *RD I*, 284.

41. In his later writings, Kraemer came to this point as well. See Kraemer, *Religion and the Christian Faith*, 257.

42. Bavinck, *Church Between Temple*, 125.

43. Newbigin, *Gospel*, 172.

44. Newbigin, "Christ and the World," 22.

himself without a witness. He reveals himself to human beings universally in nature, history, and human conscience. But he does not speak to them in and through their religions. Religions are human responses to God's revelation. They are the product of revelation, but not the medium through which God speaks. It is only in this sense that we can speak of God's revelation in non-Christian religions and cultures.

Religions are primarily divine. I argue that in respect to its origin, religion cannot be tripolar; nor can it be equally dialectical. I agree with Kraemer that religions must consider these three elements – divine, human, and demonic. However, the divine factor must take priority. I reject Beyerhaus's tripolar model. However powerful satanic influences on religions may be, demons are not the originator of human religious consciousness. In other words, they are not part of human religious makeup. They are like parasites in a human body. So, in agreement with Kraemer, we can say that religions are dialectical. Yet, we still find this model unsatisfying. Two reasons can be cited here. First, one cannot put God in the same position as humans. It is dialectical, but not a perfect one. The divine gravitational force is certainly stronger than the human force. Second, this model lacks God's active involvement in human religious consciousness. God is always working in the lives of humans. Therefore, in the final analysis, religions are somewhat elliptical, with two foci – divine and human – on opposite sides, pulling one another. But the divine gravitational force is certainly stronger than the human one. With this elliptical model, a positive view of religions can be established without setting aside the fact that religions are corrupted by human sins and influenced by demonic powers.

Now, I will deal with continuity and discontinuity between Christianity and non-Christian religions. In his early writing, Kraemer maintained a radical discontinuity position. According to this scheme, there is no point of contact other than an anthropological one. As Christians come into contact with non-Christians, they have no other points of contact but themselves. There are only human-to-human contacts.[45] But, later Kraemer changed his position. On this point, he affirmed a position of both continuity and discontinuity. Yet, his position on points of contact does not follow through. In other words, even though he affirms that human religious consciousness is the

---

45. Kraemer, *Christian Message*, 140–41.

sphere where the God-drama occurs, Kraemer's position on points of contact remains unchanged.[46] This is theologically inconsistent. Still, this shortcoming can be addressed by returning to God's revelation as the foundation of all religions. On this point, I concur with Johan H. Bavinck's position. If religions are primarily divine and all religions rest on God's revelation, then continuity between Christianity and non-Christian religions can be found only in God's revelation itself.[47] If both Christianity and non-Christian religions are based on the same divine revelation, then we cannot say that there are only anthropological points of contact. If we truly affirm God's general revelation that exists universally, then a theological point of contact must exist between the gospel and non-Christian religions. J. H. Bavinck pointedly says, "No continuity exists between the gospel and human religious consciousness, although definite continuity does exist between the gospel and what lies behind human religious consciousness, namely God's general revelation."[48]

The existence of a theological point of contact is necessary for Christian mission. It is not enough for Christian missionaries to have themselves as points of contact. Christian mission is not a human endeavor, but a spiritual one. Not only can we not win this spiritual warfare by human strengths, but trying to do so is tantamount to semi-pelagianism. Man cannot help God to create a point of contact for his gospel. Therefore, spiritual points of contact – a point of contact created by God himself – are indispensable for Christian mission. Fortunately, God has provided it through his general revelation. His works precede our works. He was already there long before missionaries came. Hence, Verkuyl rightly says, "We must be fully conscious of the fact that God has been there long before our arrival and that we find ourselves in the arena of divine-human encounter."[49]

This, however, cannot be the whole picture of truth, if we do not proceed with discontinuity between Christianity and non-Christian religions. If all religions – Christian and non-Christian – are responses to the same divine revelation, then what makes Christianity different from other religions? The answer must be found in the quality of those responses. Christianity differs

---

46. Kraemer, *Religion and the Christian Faith*, 6, 363–364; Cf. *Christian Message*, 130–141.
47. Bolt, Pratt, and Visser, *Bavinck Reader*, 297.
48. Bolt, Pratt, and Visser, 297.
49. Verkuyl, "Biblical Notion," 75.

from other religions because the former is the product of those whose hearts have been renewed by the Spirit; whereas the latter, is of unregenerate hearts. In addition, it is only in Christianity that God's saving grace in Jesus Christ is made available. Christianity also differs from other religions as it is tied up with the gospel of Jesus Christ.

7.4 Abortive Unity of Religions and Cultures

For Kraemer, religions are theologically dialectical and phenomenologically holistic. I have modified his theological model. Religions are not equally dialectical, but somewhat elliptical. Or, they are primarily divine. Now, I proceed to modify Kraemer's phenomenological model. I agree with Kraemer that religions are phenomenologically holistic. Religions and cultures are holistically united. But I disagree with Kraemer that this unity is organic. I contend that it is an abortive unity. That is to say, it attempts to become completely united, but fails to do so.

Kraemer's holistic approach to non-Christian religions is related closely to his stand on the danger of syncretism. For Kraemer, the danger of syncretism stems from two sources; first, the spirit of relativism inherent in many religions; and second, the holistic character of non-Christian religions. Religions and cultures are a living and indivisible unity. As a new church is planted in this environment, it faces challenges to adapt to the soil. The Christian faith demands that it must have a kind of Christianity that fits the soil. In other words, it cannot remain foreign, but must be indigenized. Kraemer is at the forefront arguing for the indigenization of younger churches. He is not hesitant to adopt local cultural and spiritual heritages for the purpose of spreading the gospel. The problem is that his holistic approach seems to contradict this practical approach. If the symbiosis of religions and cultures is organic, and all elements of cultures and religions have been tainted by a monistic tendency, then how could they be used without being trapped in syncretism? Here, the critique of Hogg and J. H. Bavinck is justified. They agree with Kraemer's holistic approach, but disagree with him about its organic unity. At best, Hogg contends, it is "a mechanical mixture" which forms "an imperfect unity."[50] Still, the dye of monistic tendency has tainted all ele-

---

50. Hogg, *Towards Clarifying*, 11; cf. "Christian Attitude," 100–101.

ments. It is so fixed that all elements of non-Christian religions are no longer safe for points of contact. For Hogg, there is no way out, but despair. However, this is not necessarily so. Hogg's problem is that he does not look deeper into the cause of this imperfect unity. He does not take into account God's active involvement in human religions. Here, JHB's contribution is very significant.

JHB agrees with Kraemer's holistic character of non-Christian religions. This character poses extreme difficulty for preaching the gospel. He says, "Here we are confronted with one of the most serious difficulties of missionary work. The heathen religions are indivisible unities which control the whole life from the cradle to the grave. This holistic characteristic of heathen religion makes it extremely difficult for the missionary to preach the gospel in the appropriate way."[51] He continues to explain that in every aspect of their life (e.g. building a house, sowing their fields, and giving a daughter for marriage) they have to do it religiously. He concludes: "It is not possible to describe the life of a tribe without at every point coming across religion as the invisible background."[52] As such, this characteristic poses extreme challenges for Christian mission to take root in this environment. JHB describes the challenges as follows:

> Can the gospel take the place of the old religion? Can it maintain the unity of life while laying new foundations? An old native once said to a missionary in one of the islands of the [Indonesian] Archipelago: "We know concerning everything exactly how we should do it, but when we follow you, we know nothing any more. If we accept your book, how shall we then build our houses? How shall we sow our fields and bury our dead?" That is the embarrassment every heathen has to face when he begins to appreciate the meaning of the gospel.[53]

Still, for the Christian church to exist, the gospel must take root in this environment without losing its identity. In other words, it cannot fall into the trap of syncretism. How could it be possible then? JHB's answer is that this unity between religions and cultures is not absolute. Somewhere in this religious

---

51. Bavinck, *Impact of Christianity*, 21.
52. Bavinck, 21.
53. Bavinck, 21.

system, there are "hidden cracks" that provide ways for Christians to engage with non-Christian values.

JHB observes two of those cracks. First, there is always a discrepancy between practice and belief. That is to say, although beneath a non-Christian custom lies its theological or metaphysical belief, the link between the practice and its belief is not always clear-cut. Bavinck points out as follows:

> It is worth noting that the culture of a nation is never an adequate expression of the religious faith that is living behind it. It may be true that the laws and customs are always rooted in metaphysical and theological doctrines, but they never reflect these dogmas in a perfect and adequate way. There will always remain a certain distance between belief and practice.[54]

JHB gives an example of the belief in the divine character behind a tribal organization. With this belief, social obligations are intertwined with religious belief. However, in practice the link is not always as clear as it is believed to be. JHB concludes: "The tribal community is indeed inclined to self-deification, but his inclination will never reach its goal completely. Every social institution has its religious background, but in none of them is the religious faith of the people expressed adequately."[55]

Second, there is also a chasm between morality and its religious foundation. JHB cites an example of the filial piety in Chinese customs. Behind this concept, there is a belief that "the ancestors were celestial beings and worthy to be venerated."[56] Therefore, the moral obligation of children to honor their parents and of citizens to submit to their rulers is based on "the deification of the community." Theologically, it is different from the fifth commandment. Yet, in its outward practice, the two are very similar. Since there is a chasm between morality and its theological foundation, it is possible to adopt Chinese filial piety and renew it according to the gospel of Christ.

More importantly, JHB points out that God's work is behind this imperfect, or abortive, unity. Those cracks are from God. He says:

---

54. Bavinck, 71–72.
55. Bavinck, 72–73.
56. Bavinck, 73.

> The culture of a nation is an indivisible unity: it is a system of tenets, principles, customs which all are interdependent. That is true, but it is not absolutely true. The culture of a nation tries to become an indivisible unity but it never succeeds. Somewhere in its structure there is a hidden crack. The culture of a nation is a product of humans, but there is untraceable influence in it that cannot be scrutinized because it has its origin in the mercy of God.[57]

Religions and cultures are in unity, but not in an absolute unity. This imperfectness is not natural but due to God's intervention. God works in human cultures and somehow creates openings for the gospel to penetrate into them. What JHB indicates without naming it is God's common grace. It is because of common grace that the symbiosis between religions and cultures can never be wholly unified. As God reveals himself universally, he also showers upon human beings his common grace. General revelation is concurrent with common grace. God will not leave us without a witness of his presence and neither will he let the creation be overcome by sins. Even though common grace does not abolish human sin, it brings two important effects. First, negatively it limits the effects of sin so that human beings may live in a relatively decent and peaceful environment. Second, positively it enables human beings to develop their technologies, arts, cultures, and social and political lives. Furthermore, JHB also indicates that it hinders the development of corrupted cultures. It creates "cracks" in this religiously holistic way of life. It hinders complete unity.

This is a very important contribution from JHB. It provides a firm theological framework to engage with non-Christian religious and cultural values. God's common grace makes it possible for the gospel to take root and even to renew non-Christian spiritual and cultural heritage without necessarily being trapped in syncretism. JHB points out:

> That is why this world still exists; that is why the gospel of Jesus Christ can assume the garment of human language; that is why Jesus Christ is not the great destroyer of all the products of human culture, but the great renewer and regenerator. This

---

57. Bavinck, 77.

mysterious influence cannot be ascribed to man's virtuousness; it is not to be credited to man's account. It is not man's aptitude or his nobility. It comes from the mercy of God.[58]

Here we see the link between common and special grace. Common grace provides the foundation for Christians to engage with non-Christian cultures. It, however, does not work evenly in human cultures. As with Kraemer, Bavinck acknowledges the dialectical character of human cultures. They are both good and bad. Yet, due to the uneven work of common grace, the degree of corruption varies. There are customs that cannot be redeemed, such as head-hunting, widow burning, sexual perversity, and manslaughter. Those customs must be totally rejected. Still, there remain customs and practices, despite being tainted by human sin, that are redeemable.

The renewal of cultures, however, is not by common grace, but special grace. So, those cultures must be taken over and renewed in Christ. In this respect, JHB prefers the term *possessio* to accommodate or adapt. He explains: "The Christian life does not accommodate or adapt itself to heathen forms of life, but it takes the latter in possession and thereby makes them new."[59] We follow Christ's example in engaging with human culture. JHB says, "It would not be irrelevant to pay attention to the fact that what Jesus Christ is doing with many customs and laws is comparable to what He is doing with languages. He takes the old words and renews them, recoins them, gives them a new meaning so that they are completely regenerated."[60]

Summary

This chapter attempts to maintain the strong points of Kraemer's theology of religions and modify its weaknesses. Kraemer is strong in his affirmation of the uniqueness of Christ and the necessity of Christian mission. His appreciation of non-Christian values, however, needs modification in terms of its theological framework. In times when the uniqueness of Christ is being put aside and seen as a hindrance to interreligious interaction, Kraemer affirms it. Kraemer maintains this position as a matter of truth. The relevance of

---

58. Bavinck, 77.
59. Bavinck, 178–179.
60. Bavinck, 75.

Christianity is not dependent on its acceptance by others, but on the uniqueness of Christ. The uniqueness of Christ is not limited to him as the savior of the world. It is necessarily tied with him as the Creator and the Lord of the universe. The uniqueness of Christ also requires the obedience of the church to carry out its missionary task. Christian mission is understood in its traditional sense. It is the proclamation of the gospel aiming for conversion. Only by involvement in mission, can the church fight against syncretism and establish an indigenous Christianity.

Kraemer's view of religions, however, needs modification. First, religions are equally dialectical, but primarily divine. Even though these three factors – divine, human, and demonic – should be considered in our view of religions, the divine factor must take priority. Humans and demons cannot be put in the same position as God. Only in this way can we establish a positive view of religions without neglecting their dialectical character. With this, we also acknowledge that there exists continuity and discontinuity between Christianity and non-Christian religions. Continuity is found in God's revelation. God alone provides points of contact for Christians to relate to non-Christians. All religions are a response to God's revelation. But they differ in terms of the quality of that response. The Christian faith is born of hearts renewed by the Spirit; non-Christian religions are of unregenerate hearts.

Second, religions and cultures are an indivisible unity. This holistic character poses an extreme difficulty for Christians to engage non-Christian spiritual and cultural heritages. Yet, this engagement is possible, because the unity of religions and cultures is not absolute. This imperfect unity is due to God's intervention through common grace. Common grace is not evenly distributed in human cultures, therefore, there are customs that cannot be redeemed, but must be totally rejected. Yet, some can be reclaimed and redeemed in Christ.

CHAPTER 8

Conclusion

This work examines Hendrik Kraemer's theology of religions. Kraemer's position is a direct response to the fulfillment theology of J. N. Farquhar and the cooperation theology of William Hocking. Fulfillment theology argues that there is continuity between Christianity and non-Christian religions. Christ is the fulfillment of non-Christian religions. Non-Christian religions are seen as *praeparatio evangelica*. Cooperation theology maintains that Christianity can no longer treat non-Christian religions as enemies to conquer. Instead, Christians and non-Christians have to work together to fight their common enemies, namely, secularism and materialism. Both theologies have similarities. They adopt a sympathetic approach toward non-Christian religions on the expense of the uniqueness of Christ and the necessity of Christian mission in its traditional sense.

In response to these theologies, Kraemer proposes a theology of religions that maintains the *sui generis* character of the Christian revelation, a radical discontinuity between the gospel and non-Christian religions, and the dialectical and holistic character of non-Christian religions. The Christian revelation, or the gospel, is unique. The gospel is not the fulfillment of non-Christian religions. There is only discontinuity between the gospel and non-Christian religions. With these theses, Kraemer aims to maintain the necessity of Christian mission and to safeguard the purity of the gospel. Kraemer does not deny the values of non-Christian religions and cultures, but stresses their dialectical character. Since religions and cultures are a living and indivisible unity, the church in this pagan environment must adapt and be indigenized. However, in so doing the church must be aware of the danger of syncretism and guard the purity of the gospel. Kraemer's critics agree with his stand on the uniqueness of Jesus Christ and the necessity of Christian mission. They, however, object to his view of non-Christian religions and cultures. They charge it is insufficient to appreciate non-Christian religions and cultures. This study shows that the critics' objections cannot be substantiated. Kraemer is indeed strong in his appreciation of non-Christian religions and cultures. However, the critics have a point as well. Kraemer's affirmation of non-Christian religions and cultures are practically oriented. He does not have a solid theological framework to undergird this notion. This study analyzes and finds Kraemer's weaknesses in three areas: general revelation, dialectical character of religions, and holistic approach to religions.

Kraemer is still vague in affirming the reality of general revelation. This study shows that this ambiguity is due to his Christocentric concept of revelation. Although Kraemer does not totally follow Karl Barth, he is very dependent on Barth pertaining to the concept of revelation. Kraemer maintains that religions are dialectical. They are divine and human. However, he does not emphasize the divine factor. As a result, his view of religions tilts to its negative side. Again, religions and cultures are a living and indivisible unity. This holistic character of non-Christian religions is organic. It belongs to the essence of non-Christian religions. Yet, this view is incoherent with Kraemer's view on adaptation. If the holistic character is organic, it will be impossible to adopt non-Christian spiritual and cultural heritages without necessarily falling into syncretism.

This study also shows that Kraemer's shortcomings can be addressed by properly navigating the doctrines of revelation and grace. The problem occurs because these three ideas – revelation, grace, and salvation – have been treated too tightly. There is no distinction between them. As a result, the existence of revelation in other religions will eventually open up a possibility of salvation outside the gospel. Barth's solution is to reject totally the idea of general revelation. There is only one revelation in Jesus Christ. Kraemer does not follow Barth. He still acknowledges both special and general revelation. Yet, his concept of revelation is still influenced by Barth. He is ambiguous concerning the reality of general revelation. The solution for this problem is straightforward. It is necessary to return to the biblical understanding of revelation and grace. For this purpose, this study utilizes the thought of Herman Bavinck, Johan H. Bavinck, and Abraham Kuyper.

Revelation, grace, and salvation must be differentiated clearly. Revelation always comes with grace. But we need to make a distinction between special and general revelation, and special and common grace. General revelation is concomitant with common grace. God not only reveals himself universally, but also showers his common grace on all human beings. Special revelation, however, does not necessarily come with special grace. Salvation is not tied up with revelation, but with special grace. Therefore, one is not saved simply by being the recipient of divine revelation. The ultimate purpose of divine revelation and grace is not human salvation, but the glory of God. Jesus Christ is not only the savior of the world, but also the Lord of the universe.

Kraemer's theology of religions is strong in its emphasis on the uniqueness of Christ and the necessity of Christian mission. At times when the uniqueness of Christ is being challenged and the necessity of Christian mission is being marginalized, Kraemer stands fast on this point. It is the testament of Kraemer's faithfulness to Jesus Christ, the way, the truth, and the life, and obedience to his mandate. Kraemer's view of religions, however, needs modifications. Instead of stressing the dialectical character of religions, this study emphasizes the primary divine involvement in religions. It does not deny that there are human and demonic factors in religions. However, it sees that religions are primarily from God and he is actively involved in them through his general revelation and common grace. In this way, religions can be viewed positively without rejecting their dialectical character. Furthermore, this study accepts Kraemer's holistic approach to non-Christian religions. However, the unity of religions and cultures is not organic. It is an imperfect unity due to God's intervention through his common grace. It is therefore possible for churches to engage with non-Christian spiritual and cultural heritages without necessarily being trapped in syncretism. In addition, there is also the possibility of renewing human sinful cultures in Christ.

Bibliography

Aagaard, Johannes. "Revelation and Religion: The Influence of Dialectical Theology on the Understanding of the Relationship between Christianity and Other Religions." *Studia Theologica - Nordic Journal of Theology* 14, no. 1 (1960): 148–185.
Anderson, Gerald. "Kraemer and After: A Survey Review." *Encounter* 27, no. 4 (1966): 355–362.
Ariarajah, S. Wesley. "Christian Minorities Amidst Other Faith Traditions: A Third-World Contribution." *Ecumenical Review* 41, no.1 (January 1989): 20–29.
Baillie, John. *The Idea of Revelation in Recent Thought*. New York: Columbia University Press, 1956.
Baillie, John, and Hugh Martin, eds. *Revelation*. New York: Macmillan, 1937.
Barth, Karl. *Church Dogmatics*. 4 vols. Edited by G. W. Bromiley and T. F. Torrance. Edinburgh: T&T Clark, 1956–1975.
———. "The Christian Understanding of Revelation." In *Against the Stream: Shorter Post-War Writings 1946–52*, edited by Ronald Gregor Smith, 205–240. London: SCM Press, 1954.
Barth, Karl, and Emil Brunner. *Natural Theology: Comprising 'Nature and Grace' by Professor Dr. Emil Brunner and Reply 'NO!' by Dr. Karl Barth*. Translated by Peter Fraenkel. Eugene: Wipf and Stock, 2002.
Bavinck, Herman. "Calvin and Common Grace." *The Princeton Theological Review* 7, no. 3 (1909): 437–465.
———. "Common Grace." *Calvin Theological Journal* 24, no. 1 (1989): 35–65.
———. *Our Reasonable Faith*. Grand Rapids: Eerdmans, 1956.
———. *Reformed Dogmatics*. Vol. 1, *Prolegomena*. Edited by John Bolt. Translated by John Vriend. Grand Rapids, MI: Baker Academic, 2003.
———. *The Philosophy of Revelation*. Grand Rapids: Eerdmans, 1953.
Bavinck, Johan H. *An Introduction to the Science of Missions*. Translated by David Hugh Freeman. Philadelphia: Presbyterian and Reformed Publishing, 1960.

———. *The Church Between Temple and Mosque: A Study of the Relationship between the Christian Faith and Other Religions*. Grand Rapids: Eerdmans, 1981.

———. *The Impact of Christianity on the Non-Christian World*. Grand Rapids: Eerdmans, 1948.

Berkouwer, G. C. *General Revelation*. Grand Rapids: Eerdmans, 1955.

Berkhof, Louis. *Systematic Theology*. Grand Rapids: Eerdmans, 1994.

Beyerhaus, Peter. "The Authority of the Gospel and Interreligious Dialogue." *Trinity Journal* 17, no. 2 (Fall 1996): 141–143.

———. "My Pilgrimage in Mission." *International Bulletin of Mission Research* 24, no. 4 (Oct 2000): 172–174.

Bishop Anastasios. "Emerging Perspective on the Relationships of Christians to People of Other Faith." *International Review of Mission* 77, no. 307 (July 1988): 332–346.

Bolt, John, James D. Pratt, and Paul J. Visser, eds. *The J. H. Bavinck Reader*. Translated by James A. De Jong. Grand Rapids: Eerdmans, 2013.

Braaten, Carl E. "Who Do We Say That He Is? On the Uniqueness and Universality of Jesus Christ." *Occasional Bulletin of Missionary Research* 4, no.1 (January 1980): 2–8.

Bromiley, Geoffrey W. *Historical Theology: An Introduction*. Grand Rapids: Eerdmans, 1978.

———. "Karl Barth." In *Creative Minds in Contemporary Theology*, edited by Philip E. Hughes, 27–62. Grand Rapids: Eerdmans, 1969.

Calvin, John. *Institutes of the Christian Religion*. Edited by John T. McNeill. Translated by Ford Lewis Battles. Louisville: Westminster John Knox, 1960.

Chao, T. C. "Revelation." In *The Authority of the Faith*, edited by William Paton, 22–57. London: International Missionary Council, 1939.

Chenchiah, P. "The Christian Message in a Non-Christian World." In *Rethinking Christianity in India*, edited by D. M. Devasahayam and A. N. Sudarisanam, 2nd ed., 143–196. Madras: A. N. Sudarisanam, 1939.

———. "Jesus and Non-Christian Faiths." In *Rethinking Christianity in India*, 2nd ed., edited by D. M. Devasahayam and A. N. Sudarisanam, 49–64. Madras: A. N. Sudarisanam, 1939.

Cox, James L. "The Development of A. G. Hogg's Theology in Relation to Non-Christian Faith: Its Significance for the Tambaram Meeting of the International Missionary Council, 1938." PhD dissertation, University of Aberdeen, 1977.

———. "Faith and Faiths: The Significance of A. G. Hogg's Missionary Thought for a Theology of Dialogue." *Scottish Journal of Theology* 32, no. 3 (1979): 241–256.

D'Costa, Gavin. "The Impossibility of a Pluralist View of Religions." *Religious Studies* 32, no. 2 (1996): 223–232.

———. *The Meeting of Religions and the Trinity*. Maryknoll, NY: Orbis Books, 2000.

———. *Theology and Religious Pluralism: The Challenge of Other Religions*. Oxford, UK: Blackwell, 1986.

———. "Revelation and Revelations: Discerning God in Other Religions. Beyond a Static Valuation." *Modern Theology* 10, no. 2 (April 1994): 165–183.

Delitzsch, Friedrich. *Babel and Bible: The Significance of Assyriological Research for Religion*. Translated by Thomas J. McCormack and W. H. Carruth. Chicago: Open Court, 1903.

Devanandan, Paul D. "Christian and Non-Christian Faith." *The Indian Journal of Theology* 6, no. 3 (1957): 74–79.

Dewey, John. *A Common Faith*. New Haven, CT: Yale University Press, 1934.

Djung, Philip. "Review of *Their Rock is Not Like Our Rock* by Daniel Strange." *Calvin Theological Journal* 52, no. 2 (2017): 419–421.

Doi, Masatoshi. "From Tambaram to Kandy." *Japan Christian Quarterly* 35, no. 3 (1969): 140–152.

Dulles, Avery. *Models of Revelation*. Maryknoll, NY: Orbis Books, 2008.

Eck, Diana. "The Religions and Tambaram: 1938 and 1988." *International Review of Mission* 77, no. 307 (July 1988): 375–389.

Erickson, Millard J. "Hope for Those Who Haven't Heard? Yes, But…" *Evangelical Missions Quarterly* 11 (1975): 122–126.

Farmer, Herbert H. "The Authority of Faith." In *The Authority of the Faith*, edited by William Paton, 22–57. London: International Missionary Council, 1939.

———. *Revelation and Religion: Studies in the Theological Interpretation of Religious Types*. London: Nisbet, 1954.

Farquhar, John Nicol. *The Crown of Hinduism*. London: Oxford University Press, 1913.

Fredericks, James. *Faith Among Faiths: Christian Theology and Non-Christian Religions*. New York: Paulist Press, 1999.

Geertz, Clifford. *The Religion of Java*. Glencoe, IL: Free Press, 1960.

Goheen, Michael. "As the Father Has Sent Me, I Am Sending You: J. E. Lesslie Newbigin's Missionary Ecclesiology." PhD dissertation, Universiteit Utrecht, 2000.

Gunton, Colin E. *A Brief Theology of Revelation*. Edinburgh: T&T Clark, 1995.

Hallencreutz, Carl F. *Kraemer towards Tambaram: A Study in Hendrik Kraemer's Missionary Approach*. Lund: Gleerup, 1966.

———. "Tambaram Revisited." *International Review of Mission* 77, no. 307 (July 1988): 347–359.

Hart, Trevor. "A Capacity for Ambiguity?: The Barth-Brunner Debate Revisited." *Tyndale Bulletin* 44, no. 2 (1993): 289–305.

———. "Revelation." In *The Cambridge Companion to Karl Barth*, edited by John Webster, 37–56. Cambridge: Cambridge University Press, 2000.

Hartenstein, K. "The Biblical View of Religion." In *The Authority of the Faith*, edited by William Paton, 117–136. London: International Missionary Council, 1939.

Hedlund, Roger E. *Roots of the Great Debate in Mission: Mission in Historical and Theological Perspective*. Madras: Evangelical Literature Society, 1981.

Hedges, Paul. *Controversies in Interreligious Dialogue and the Theology of Religions*. London: SCM Press, 2010.

———. *Preparation and Fulfilment: A History and Study of Fulfilment Theology in Modern British Thought in the Indian Context*. New York: Lang, 2001.

Hick, John. "Jesus and the World Religions." In *The Myth of God Incarnate*, edited by John Hick, 167–185. Philadelphia: Westminster, 1977.

———. "The Non-Absoluteness of Christianity." In *The Myth of Christian Uniqueness: Toward a Pluralistic Theology of Religions*, edited by John Hick and Paul F. Knitter, 16–36. Maryknoll, NY: Orbis Books, 1987.

Hiebert, Paul. "Dialogue on 'A Contextualized Church: The Bali Experience.'" *Gospel in Context* 1, no. 2 (1978): 24–29.

Hocking, William E. *Living Religions and a World Faith*. New York: Macmillan, 1940.

———. *Re-thinking Missions: A Laymen's Inquiry After One Hundred Years*. New York: Harper & Brothers, 1932.

Hoedemaker, Libertus A. "Hendrik Kraemer 1888–1965: Biblical Realism Applied in Mission." In *Mission Legacies: Biographical Studies of Leaders of the Modern Missionary Movement*, edited by Gerald H. Anderson, et al., 508–515. Maryknoll, NY: Orbis Books, 1994.

———. "Kraemer Reassessed." *Ecumenical Review* 41, no. 1 (1989): 41–49.

Hogg, Alfred G. "The Christian Attitude to Non-Christian Faith." In *The Authority of the Faith*, edited by William Paton, 94–116. London: International Missionary Council, 1939.

———. *The Christian Message to the Hindu: Being the Duff Missionary Lectures for Nineteen Forty Five on the Challenge of the Gospel in India*. London: SCM Press, 1947.

———. *Karma and Redemption: An Essay toward the Interpretation of Hinduism and the Re-statement of Christianity*. Madras: Christian Literature Society, 1970.

———. "Review: The Crown of Hinduism, and Other Volumes." *International Review of Mission* 3, no. 1 (1914): 172–173.

———. *Towards Clarifying My Reactions to Dr. Kraemer's Book*. Madras: Diocesan Press, 1938.

Horton, Walter M. "Between Hocking and Kraemer." In *The Authority of the Faith*, edited by William Paton, 137–149. London: International Missionary Council, 1939.

———. "A Tambaram Thesis Re-Stated: Religion and the Christian Faith by Hendrik Kraemer." *International Review of Mission* 46, no. 182 (1957): 205–206.

———. "Tambaram: Twenty-Five Years After." In *Philosophy, Religion, and the Coming World Civilization: Essays in Honor of William Ernest Hocking*, edited by Leroy S. Rouner, 225–234. The Hague: Martinus Nijhoff, 1966.

Huxley, Julian S. *Religion Without Revelation*. New York: Harper and Brothers, 1927.

International Missionary Council. "Findings of the Madras Meeting." In *The Authority of the Faith*, edited by William Paton, 169–199. London: International Missionary Council, 1939.

James, William. *The Varieties of Religious Experience*. London: Longmans, Green, and Co., 1905.

Jathanna, Origen V. *The Decisiveness of the Christ-Event and the Universality of Christianity in a World of Religious Plurality: With Special Reference to Hendrik Kraemer and Alfred George Hogg as Well as to William Ernest Hocking and Pandipeddi Chenchiah*. Bern: Lang, 1981.

Johnson, Keith E. *Rethinking the Trinity and Religious Pluralism: An Augustinian Assessment*. Downers Grove, IL: IVP Academic, 2011.

Jones, E. Stanley. *Mahatma Gandhi: An Interpretation*. New York: Cokesbury, 1948.

Jongeneel, Jan A. B. "Christianity and The-Isms: A Description, Analysis and Rethinking of Kraemer's Theology of Missions." *Bangalore Theological Forum* 20, no. 1–2 (1988): 19–23.

———. "Hendrik Kraemer." In *Biographical Dictionary of Christian Missions*, edited by Gerald H. Anderson, 374–375. New York: MacMillan, 1998.

Joseph, P. V. "M. M. Thomas (1916–1996)." In *Biographical Dictionary and Christian Missions*, edited by Gerald H. Anderson, 666–667. New York: Macmillan, 1998.

Kärkkäinen, Veli-Matti. *An Introduction to the Theology of Religions: Biblical, Historical and Contemporary Perspectives*. Downers Grove, IL: InterVarsity, 2003.

Kaufman, Gordon D. "Religious Diversity, Historical Consciousness, and Christian Theology." In *The Myth of Christian Uniqueness: Toward a Pluralistic Theology of Religions*, edited by John Hick and Paul F. Knitter, 3–15. Maryknoll, NY: Orbis Books, 1987.

Kraemer, Hendrik. "Christendom en Wajang." *De Opwekker* 71 (1926): 225–234.

———. *The Christian Message in a Non-Christian World*. London: Edinburgh House Press, 1938.

———. *The Communication of the Christian Faith*. Philadelphia: Westminster, 1961.

———. "Continuity or Discontinuity." In *The Authority of the Faith*, edited by William Paton, 1–21. London: International Missionary Council, 1939.

———. *From Missionfield to Independent Churches: Report on a Decisive Decade in the Growth of Indigenous Churches in Indonesia*. The Hague: Boekencentrum, 1958.

———. "Introduction." In *The Meaning of Religion* by W. Brede Kristensen. Translated by John B. Carman, xi–xxv. Dordrecht: Springer Science & Business Media, 1960.

———. *Mijn Tweede Zes-Jaar in Indië*. Amsterdam: Ned. Bijbelgenootschap, 1936.

———. *Religion and the Christian Faith*. Philadelphia: Westminster, 1956.

———. "Syncretism as a Religious and a Missionary Problem." *International Review of Missions* 43, no. 3 (1954): 249–273.

———. "Syncretism as a Theological Problem for Missions." In *The Theology of the Christian Mission*, edited by Gerald H. Anderson, 179–182. New York: McGraw-Hill, 1961.

———. *Why Christianity of All Religions?*. Translated by Hubert Hoskins. Philadelphia: Westminster, 1962.

———. "De Wajang als Uiting van Javaansche Cultuur." In *Indische Dag*, 33–48. Heemstee: Kramer, 1941.

———. *World Cultures and World Religions: The Coming Dialogue*. Philadelphia: Westminster, 1960.

———. *De Wortelen van Het Syncretisme*. 's-Gravenhage: Boekencentrum, 1937.

———. *Zes jaar padvinden: Rede uitgesproken door Dr. H. Kraemer in de Algemeene Vergadering van het Nederlandsch Bijbelgenootschap op donderdag 21 Juni 1928 in de Doopsgezinde Kerk te Amsterdam*. Amsterdam: Ned. Bijbelgenootschap, 1928.

Knitter, Paul F. "Christomonism in Karl Barth's Evaluation of the Non-Christian Religions." *Neue Zeitschrift für systematische Theologie und Religionsphilosophie* 13, no.1 (1971): 99–121.

———. "European Protestant and Catholic Approaches to the World Religions: Complements and Contrast." *Journal of Ecumenical Studies* 12, no. 1 (Winter 1975): 13–28.

———. *No Other Name? A Critical Survey of Christian Attitudes Toward the World Religions*. Maryknoll, NY: Orbis Books, 1985.

Küng, Hans. *On Being a Christian*. Translated by Edward Quinn. New York: Doubleday, 1966.

Kuiper, Herman. *Calvin on Common Grace*. Goes: Oosterbaan & Le Cointre, 1928.

Kuyper, Abraham. "Common Grace." In *Abraham Kuyper: A Centennial Reader*, edited by James D. Bratt, 165–201. Grand Rapids: Eerdmans, 1998.

———. *Common Grace: God's Gifts for a Fallen World*. Vol. 1, *The Historical Section*. Edited by Jordan J. Ballor and Stephen J. Grabil. Translated by Nelson D. Kloosterman and Ed M. van der Maas. Bellingham, WA: Lexham Press, 2016.

———. *The Work of the Holy Spirit*. Grand Rapids: Eerdmans, 1975.

Lipner, Julius. "'Being One, Let Me Be Many': Facets of the Relationship between the Gospel and Culture." *International Review of Mission* 74, no. 294 (April 1985): 158–168.

Macquarrie, John. "Natural Theology." In *The Blackwell Encyclopedia of Modern Christian Thought*, edited by Alister E. McGrath, 402. Oxford: Blackwell, 1993.

Malinowski, Banislaw. *The Dynamics of Culture Change: An Inquiry into Race Relations in Africa*. New Haven, CT: Yale University Press, 1945.

Masselink, William. *General Revelation and Common Grace*. Grand Rapids: Eerdmans, 1953.

Mastra, I. Wayan. "Christianity and Culture in Bali." *International Review of Mission* 63, no. 251 (July 1974): 386–399.

Mavrodes, George I. *Revelation in Religious Belief*. Philadelphia: Temple University Press, 1988.

McDermott, Gerald R., and Harold A. Netland. *A Trinitarian Theology of Religion: An Evangelical Proposal*. Oxford: Oxford University Press, 2014.

Moses, D. G. "The Problem of Truth in Religion." In *The Authority of the Faith*, edited by William Paton, 58–82. London: International Missionary Council, 1939.

———. *Religious Truth and the Relation between Religions*. Madras: Christian Literature Society for India, 1950.

Mrázek, Jan. *Phenomenology of A Puppet Theatre: Contemplations on the Art of Javanese Wayang Kulit*. Leiden: KITLV Press, 2005.

Muller, Richard. *Dictionary of Latin and Greek Theological Terms: Drawn Principally from Protestant Scholastic Theology*. Grand Rapids: Baker Books, 1985.

Netland, Harold. "Theology of Religions, Missiology, and Evangelicals." *Missiology* 33, no. 2 (April 2005): 141–158.

Newbigin, Lesslie. "Christ and the World Religions." *Churchman* 97, no. 1 (1983): 16–30.

———. "Christian Faith and World Religions." In *Keeping the Faith: Essays to Mark the Centenary of Lux Mundi*, edited by Geoffrey Wainwright, 310–340. Philadelphia: Fortress, 1988.

———. *The Finality of Christ*. London: SCM Press, 1969.

———. "The Finality of Christ within A Plurality of Faiths." *Dialogue* 24 (1972): 15–19.

———. *The Gospel in A Pluralist Society*. Grand Rapids: Eerdmans, 1989.

———. *The Open Secret: Sketches for a Missionary Theology*. London: SPCK, 1978.

———. "Religious Pluralism and the Uniqueness of Jesus Christ." *International Bulletin of Missionary Research* 13, no. 2 (April 1989): 50–54.

———. "Review of *Salvation and Humanization* by M. M. Thomas." *Religion and Society* 18, no.1 (1971): 71–80.

———. "A Sermon Preached at the Thanksgiving Service for the Fiftieth Anniversary of the Tambaram Conference of the International Missionary Council." *International Review of Mission* 77, no. 307 (July 1988): 325–231.

———. "The Trinity as Public Truth." In *The Trinity in a Pluralistic Age: Theological Essays on Culture and Religion*, edited by Kevin J. Vanhoozer, 1–8. Grand Rapids: Eerdmans, 1997.

Niebuhr, H. Richard. *Christ and Culture*. New York: Harper & Row, 1951.

Niles, Damayanthi. *Worshipping at the Feet of Our Ancestors: Hendrik Kraemer and the Making of Contextual Theology in South Asia*. Berlin: Lit Verlag, 2012.

Paas, Stefan. "Religious Consciousness in a Post-Christian Culture: J. H. Bavinck's *Religious Consciousness and Christian Faith* (1949), Sixty Years Later." *Journal of Reformed Theology* 6, no. 1 (2012): 35–55.

Panikkar, Raimundo. *The Trinity and the Religious Experience of Man*. Maryknoll, NY: Orbis Books, 1973.

Parker, T. H. L. "Barth on Revelation." *Scottish Journal of Theology* 13, no. 4 (1960): 366–382.

Paton, William, ed. *The Authority of the Faith*. London: International Missionary Council, 1939.

Perry, Tim S. *Radical Difference: A Defense of Hendrik Kraemer's Theology of Religions*. Toronto: Wilfred Laurier University Press, 2001.

Pinnock, Clark H. "An Inclusivist View." In *Four Views on Salvation in a Pluralistic World*, edited by Dennis L. Okholm and Timothy R. Philips, 93–148. Grand Rapids: Zondervan, 1995.

Plantinga, Alvin. "Pluralism: A Defense of Religious Exclusivism." In *The Rationality of Belief and the Plurality of Faith: Essays in Honor of William P. Alston*, edited by Thomas D. Senor, 191–215. Ithaca: Cornell University Press, 1995.

———. "The Reformed Objection to Natural Theology." *Proceedings of the American Catholic Philosophical Association* 54 (1980): 49–62.

Plantinga, Richard. "Missionary Thinking about Religious Plurality at Tambaram 1938: Hendrik Kraemer and His Critics." In *The Changing Face of Christianity: Africa, the West, and the World*, edited by Lamin Sanneh and Joel A. Carpenter, 159–190. Oxford: Oxford University Press, 2005.

Race, Alan. *Christians and Religious Pluralism: Patterns in the Christian Theology of Religions*. New York: Orbis Books, 1982.

Reichelt, Karl L. "The Johannine Approach." In *The Authority of the Faith*, edited by William Paton, 83–93. London: International Missionary Council, 1939.

Rose, Kenneth. *Pluralism: The Future of Religion*. New York: Bloomsbury, 2013.

Rouner, Leroy S. "The Making of a Philosopher: Ernest Hocking's Early Years." In *Philosophy, Religion, and The Coming World Civilization: Essays in Honor of William Ernest Hocking*, edited by Leroy S. Rouner, 5–22. The Hague: Martinus Nijhoff, 1966.

Sanders, John. *No Other Name: An Investigation into the Destiny of the Unevangelized*. Grand Rapids: Eerdmans, 1992.

Samartha, Stanley J. "Contact, Controversy and Communication: Review Article on Hallencreutz's book: Kraemer Towards Tambaram." *Indian Journal of Theology* 17, no. 1 (January-March 1968): 21–26.

———. "Mission in a Religiously Plural World Looking Beyond Tambaram 1938." *International Review of Mission* 77, no. 307 (July 1988): 311–324.

Sarma, D. S. *Renascent Hinduism*. Bombay: Bharatiya Vidya Bhavan, 1966.

Schleiermacher, Friedrich. *The Christian Faith*. Translated by H. R. Mackintosh and J. S. Stewart. Edinburgh: T&T Clark, 1928.

———. *On Religion: Speeches to Its Cultured Despisers*. Translated and edited by Richard Crouter. New York: Harper & Row, 1996.

Schmemann, Alexander. *For the Life of the World: Sacraments and Orthodoxy*. New York: St. Vladimir's Seminary Press, 2004.

Schouten, Jan Peter. *Jesus as Guru: The Image of Christ among Hindus and Christians in India*. Translated by Henry and Lucy Jansen. New York: Rodopi, 2008.

Sharpe, Eric J. *Faith Meets Faith: Some Christian Attitudes to Hinduism in the Nineteenth and Twentieth Centuries*. London: SCM Press, 1977.

———. "The Legacy of A. G. Hogg." *International Bulletin of Missionary Research* 6, no. 2 (1982): 65–69.

———. "The Legacy of J. N. Farquhar." *International Bulletin of Mission Research* 3, no. 2 (1979): 62–64.

———. *Not to Destroy but to Fulfil: The Contribution of J. N. Farquhar to Protestant Missionary Thought in India before 1914*. Lund: Gleerup, 1965.

———. *The Theology of A. G. Hogg*. Madras: Christian Literature Society, 1971.

Smith, Wilfred Cantwell. "Mission, Dialogue, and God's Will for Us." *International Review of Mission* 77, no. 307 (July 1988): 360–374.

Soper, Edmund Davison. *The Philosophy of the Christian World Mission*. New York: Abingdon-Cokesbury, 1943.

Strange, Daniel. "For Their Rock is Not as Our Rock: The Gospel as the 'Subversive Fulfillment' of the Religious Other." *Journal of the Evangelical Theological Society* 56, no. 2 (2013): 379–395.

———. *Their Rock is Not Like Our Rock: A Theology of Religions*. Grand Rapids: Zondervan, 2014.

Sudduth, Michael. *The Reformed Objection to Natural Theology*. Farnham, England: Ashgate, 2009.

Sytsma, David. "Herman Bavinck's Thomistic Epistemology: The Argument and Sources of His *Principia* of Science." In *Five Studies in the Thought of Herman Bavinck, a Creator of Modern Dutch Theology*, edited by John Bolt, 1–56. Lewiston: Edwin Mellen, 2011.

Temple, William. "Foreword." In *The Christian Message in a Non-Christian World* by Hendrik Kraemer, ix. London: International Missionary Council, 1938.

Thomas, M. M. "The Absoluteness of Jesus Christ and Christ-centered Syncretism." *The Japan Christian Quarterly* 52, no. 3 (1986): 133–142.

———. *The Acknowledged Christ of the Indian Renaissance*. London: SCM Press, 1969.

———. "An Assessment of Tambaram's Contribution to the Search of Asian Churches for an Authentic Selfhood." *International Review of Mission* 77, no. 307 (1988): 390–397.

———. "Christology and Pluralistic Consciousness." *International Bulletin of Missionary Research* 10, no. 3 (1986): 106–108.

———. *Man and the Universe of Faiths*. Madras: Christian Institute for the Study of Religion and Society, 1975.

———. "My Pilgrimage in Mission." *International Bulletin of Missionary Research* 13, no. 1 (1989): 28–31.

———. "Review of *Karma and Redemption* by A. G. Hogg." *Religion and Society* 18, no. 1 (March 1971): 92–94.

———. "A Rewarding Correspondence with the Late Dr. Hendrik Kraemer." *Religion and Society* 13, no. 2 (1966): 5–14.

———. *Risking Christ for Christ's Sake: Towards an Ecumenical Theology of Pluralism*. Geneva: World Council of Churches, 1987.

———. *Salvation and Humanization: Some Crucial Issues of the Theology of Mission in Contemporary India*. Madras: Christian Institute for the Study of Religion and Society, 1971.

———. *Some Theological Dialogues*. Madras: Christian Institute for the Study of Religion and Society, 1977.

Tillich, Paul. *Systematic Theology*. Vol. 1, *Reason and Revelation, Being and God*. Chicago: University of Chicago Press, 1951.

Troeltsch, Ernst. "Christianity among World Religions." In *Christian Thought: Its History and Application*, edited by Baron von Hügel, 35–63. New York: Meridian Books, 1957.

van den End, Th. *Ragi Carita 1: Sejarah Gereja di Indonesia th. 1500–1860-an*. Jakarta: Gunung Mulia, 1980.

van Leeuwen, Arend Theodor. *Hendrik Kraemer: Dienaar der Wereldkerk*. Amsterdam: W. Ten Have, 1959.

Van Til, Cornelius. *The New Modernism: An Appraisal of the Theology of Barth and Brunner*. Philadelphia: Presbyterian & Reformed, 1973.

Veitch, J. A. "Revelation and Religion in the Theology of Karl Barth." *Scottish Journal of Theology* 24, no. 1 (1971): 1–22.

Verkuyl, Johannes. "The Biblical Notion of Kingdom: Test of Validity for Theology of Religion." In *The Good News of the Kingdom: Mission Theology for the Third Millennium*, edited by Charles Van Engen, Dean S. Gilliland, and Paul Pierson, 71–81. Maryknoll, NY: Orbis Books, 1993.

———. *Contemporary Missiology: An Introduction*. Grand Rapids: Eerdmans, 1978.

Visser 't Hooft, W. A. "Accomodation: True and False." *The South East Asia Journal of Theology* 8, no. 3 (January 1967): 5–18.

———. "Introductory Note." In *From Missionfield to Independent Church: Report on a Decisive Decade in the Growth of Indigenous Churches in Indonesia*, by Hendrik Kraemer, 7–8. The Hague: Boekencentrum, 1958.

———, ed. *The New Delhi Report: The Third Assembly of the World Council of Churches 1961*. New York: Association Press, 1962.

Vos, Arvin. "Knowledge according to Bavinck and Aquinas." *The Bavinck Review* 6 (2015): 9–36.

Wach, Joachim. "General Revelation and the Religions of the World." *The Journal of Bible and Religion* 22, no. 2 (1954): 83–93.

Ward, Keith. *Religion and Revelation: A Theology of Revelation in the World's Religions*. Oxford: Clarendon, 1994.

Wood, Nicholas J. *Faiths and Faithfulness: Pluralism, Dialogue and Mission in the Work of Kenneth Craig and Lesslie Newbigin*. Milton Keynes: Paternoster, 2009.

World Missionary Conference. *Report of Commission IV: The Missionary Message in Relation to Non-Christian Religions*. New York: Revell, 1910.

Wright, Christopher. *The Uniqueness of Jesus*. London: Monarch, 2001.

Yoder, John H. *To Hear the Word*. Eugene, OR: Cascade, 2010.

Yong, Amos. *Beyond the Impasse: Toward a Pneumatological Theology of Religions*. Grand Rapids: Baker Academic, 2003.

———. *Discerning the Spirit(s): A Pentecostal-Charismatic Contribution to Christian Theology of Religions*. Sheffield: Sheffield Academic Press, 2000.

Langham Literature, with its publishing work, is a ministry of Langham Partnership.

Langham Partnership is a global fellowship working in pursuit of the vision God entrusted to its founder John Stott –

> *to facilitate the growth of the church in maturity and Christ-likeness through raising the standards of biblical preaching and teaching.*

Our vision is to see churches in the Majority World equipped for mission and growing to maturity in Christ through the ministry of pastors and leaders who believe, teach and live by the word of God.

Our mission is to strengthen the ministry of the word of God through:
- nurturing national movements for biblical preaching
- fostering the creation and distribution of evangelical literature
- enhancing evangelical theological education

especially in countries where churches are under-resourced.

Our ministry

Langham Preaching partners with national leaders to nurture indigenous biblical preaching movements for pastors and lay preachers all around the world. With the support of a team of trainers from many countries, a multi-level programme of seminars provides practical training, and is followed by a programme for training local facilitators. Local preachers' groups and national and regional networks ensure continuity and ongoing development, seeking to build vigorous movements committed to Bible exposition.

Langham Literature provides Majority World preachers, scholars and seminary libraries with evangelical books and electronic resources through publishing and distribution, grants and discounts. The programme also fosters the creation of indigenous evangelical books in many languages, through writer's grants, strengthening local evangelical publishing houses, and investment in major regional literature projects, such as one volume Bible commentaries like the *Africa Bible Commentary* and the *South Asia Bible Commentary*.

Langham Scholars provides financial support for evangelical doctoral students from the Majority World so that, when they return home, they may train pastors and other Christian leaders with sound, biblical and theological teaching. This programme equips those who equip others. Langham Scholars also works in partnership with Majority World seminaries in strengthening evangelical theological education. A growing number of Langham Scholars study in high quality doctoral programmes in the Majority World itself. As well as teaching the next generation of pastors, graduated Langham Scholars exercise significant influence through their writing and leadership.

To learn more about Langham Partnership and the work we do visit **langham.org**

www.ingramcontent.com/pod-product-compliance
Lightning Source LLC
Chambersburg PA
CBHW051540230426
43669CB00015B/2664